FIRE OF GENIUS

FIRE OF GENIUS

Inventors of the Past Century

BASED ON THE FILES OF *POPULAR SCIENCE*

MONTHLY SINCE ITS FOUNDING IN 1872

———————

by *Ernest V. Heyn*

in collaboration with
Alden P. Armagnac, Arthur Fisher,
Devon Francis, and C. P. Gilmore

ANCHOR PRESS/DOUBLEDAY
GARDEN CITY, NEW YORK
1976

Library of Congress Cataloging in Publication Data

Heyn, Ernest Victor, 1904–
Fire of genius.

Includes index.
1. Inventors—Biography. I. Popular science monthly.
II. Title.
T39.H49   608′.7′22
ISBN 0-385-03776-7
Library of Congress Catalog Card Number 75–21227

DEDICATION

This book about the wonder workers of science in the past century is lovingly dedicated to the wonder worker in my life, my wife Ethel.

—E.V.H.

AN ACKNOWLEDGMENT TO
POPULAR SCIENCE MONTHLY

When I retired as editor-in-chief and associate publisher of *Popular Science Monthly* at the end of 1970 the late Eugene S. Duffield, then president of the Popular Science Publishing Company, granted me the right to mine the rich lode contained in the magazine's file of issues since its founding in May 1872. Bound volumes of all past issues were placed at the unlimited disposal of myself and my collaborators. Out of this generous dispensation grew *A Century of Wonders—100 Years of Popular Science* with the same imprimatur as this book.

My collaborators and I offer *Fire of Genius* with renewed appreciation of treasures we were able to unearth from the same and more recent bound volumes of the magazine. Since the point of departure of this book is concentration on the *people* rather than the *inventions,* our research led us into many other sources. But without the understanding and generous cooperation of J. Michael Hadley, present president of the company (Times Mirror Magazines) that publishes *Popular Science Monthly,* this book could not have been written, since at its heart is the substance culled from the pages of the magazine. As with the first book, the material which originally appeared in *Popular Science Monthly* and was copyrighted at the time is reproduced here by that special permission.

ERNEST V. HEYN

ILLUSTRATIONS IN THIS BOOK

have been chosen largely from pictures in the past issues of *Popular Science Monthly*. All pictures not otherwise credited are from *Popular Science Monthly* and are reproduced here by its special permission.

In instances of illustrations obtained elsewhere, the sources are as follows:

Alcoa: pictures of aluminum buttons and pots and pans, page 222; all pictures, pages 226–227; pictures of Hunt and Davis (top), drawings (below), page 230; both pictures, page 231; charcoal grill, page 236; picture, page 237.

American Telephone and Telegraph: Boston School for the Deaf, bottom, page 49; Centennial Exposition, top, pages 58, 59; 1877 demonstration, top, page 63; Chichester A. Bell, bottom, page 70.

Atomic Energy Commission: Fermi and Szilard pictures, page 304.

A. P. Armagnac: briquettes in E. Gerstmann Collection, bottom, page 138.

Columbia Broadcasting System: Goldmark picture, at top, page 213.

Du Pont: Brandenberger picture, page 33; Nylon and Carothers picture, page 41.

Eastman Kodak: NASA camera, left, page 94; Mannes and Godowsky, page 291.

Edison National Historic Site: Edison's mother, bottom, page 110; three pictures, page 111; electric vote recorder, top, page 114; Mary Stilwell Edison, top, page 118; Menlo Park home, top, page 119; Edison and wax-cylinder model, page 125; Mackenzie picture, top, page 131; Mina Miller picture and West Orange home, page 133; pictures top of page 137; top and middle pictures, Ogdensburg, page 138; Edison as iron miner, top, page 139; cement-making machinery, bottom, page 139; Edisons in electric automobile, bottom, page 142; Edison family, bottom, page 143; Mina Miller Edison, page 154.

Electrical Engineer Magazine: X-ray fluoroscope, page 9.

Evinrude Motors: Ole Evinrude, page 284.

Firestone Tire & Rubber Company: Edison, Ford and Firestone picture, page 146.

Arthur Fisher: Museum picture, bottom, page 85.

General Electric: bulb at top, page 131.

Library of Congress: picture of Edison with children, bottom, page 146.

Helen Marcus: Dorothy Rodger's picture, page 41.

New York Times: top picture, page 144.

Norelco: bottom right, page 40.

Ronson: middle picture, at bottom, page 40.

Schick: top left, bottom left, and middle pictures, page 40.

Sears, Roebuck Catalog, 1902: top, page 136.

Sears, Roebuck Catalog, 1908: five-cent theater, page 136.

Smithsonian Institution: Graphophone pictures, top, page 70; printing telegraph, bottom, page 114; pictures, page 20.

The Bell Family® National Geographic Society: Bell's father, mother, Bell at 16, page 49; Hubbard picture, page 51; Bell at 29, page 55; model at bottom, page 63; picture at bottom, page 71; Bell family, page 73; picture at top, page 76; Baldwin, page 77; tetrahedral tower, page 78; picture at top, page 85.

United Press International: Wright brothers with sister, page 180; Daimler automobile, Roentgen picture, page 274; Rudolf Diesel, page 280.

U. S. Air Force: Orville at Fort Myer, bottom, page 215.

U. S. Patent Office: Lincoln patent and model, page 3; Clemens' scrapbooks, page 9; Glidden wire-fences, Judson and Sundback "zipper" patents, page 13; Painter bottle cap, page 32; Gillette razor, page 33; D. F. Rodgers' Jonny Mop patent, page 41; Bell "telegraphy" patents, page 62; Bell and Tainter patent, page 70; Eastman 1880 patent, page 87; Kinetographic camera patent, page 113; patent for breaking rock, page 139; Marconi patent, page 243.

Grey Villet, Time: Abplanalp with aerosol valve, page 21.

Xerox Information System: Charles Carlson and copying machine, page 32.

CONTENTS

FIRE OF GENIUS

"...Fire of Genius..."

THE only President of the United States ever granted a patent was Abraham Lincoln.

"To all whom it may concern": reads U.S. patent number 6,469, dated May 22, 1849, "Be it known that I, Abraham Lincoln, . . . have invented a new and improved manner of combining adjustable buoyant air chambers with a steamboat or other vessel for the purpose of enabling . . . them to pass over bars or through shallow water . . ."

The patent is titled "Buoying Vessels over Shoals." To obtain a patent, an applicant then had to file specifications, drawings, and a model. The forty-year-old Lincoln himself actually whittled the twenty-inch-long model, which later went on display at the Smithsonian Institution's National Museum.

On a flatboat trip down the Ohio and Mississippi rivers, young Lincoln had observed the troubles of navigators on shoals, which inspired his idea, *Popular Science* noted in January 1928. While his invention apparently was never built and used, the future President maintained an interest in the welfare of inventors. Ten years after his patent, he gave a lecture titled "Discoveries, Inventions, and Improvements" at Springfield, Illinois, on February 22, 1859.

He spoke about the patent laws. They began, he said, in England in 1624, and in this country with the adoption of our Constitution. "Before then," he told his listeners, "any man might instantly use what another man had invented, so that the inventor had no special advantage from his invention." The patent system, he went on, "changed this, secured to the inventor for a limited time exclusive use of his invention and added the fuel of interest to the fire of genius in the discovery and production of new and useful things."

If you go to the Department of Commerce building in Washington, D.C., over Entrance 12 on the Fifteenth Street side between E and Constitution Avenue you can see the inscription engraved in stone over the lintel:

THE PATENT
SYSTEM ADDED THE FUEL
OF INTEREST TO THE FIRE
OF GENIUS—LINCOLN

How is that fire of genius lit? Why do inventors invent? For profit ("the fuel of interest")? Necessity, the mother? Inspiration, the father?

Lincoln's motive was simple: to fill a need—to prevent boats from running aground on river shoals. Two other Presidents were also inventors—George Washington and Thomas Jefferson—but neither ever applied for a patent. Their motive was personal—to solve their own domestic and farming problems. Neither man profited from his inventions. No gentleman, wrote Jefferson, could take money for the product of his brain and hands. (With changing times, people thought differently.)

George Washington wrote in his diary on March 26, 1760: "Spent the day in making a new plow of my own invention." A later entry recorded that "she answered very well in the lower pasture." Even later: "Made another plow, the same as my former, except that it has two eyes and the other, one." He also created and used a "barrel plow" for sowing grain.

His diary reveals the invention of a "wine coaster" which could be passed at table from one guest to another. The name "coaster" came from the fact that the basket had a roller by which the wine could easily be moved along the surface of the table.

It was an inventor, then, named George Washington who on January 8, 1790, addressed the second session of the First Congress meeting in New York City. He begged the assembled representatives to give "effectual encouragement . . . to the exertion of skill and *genius* at home" (Italics added).

On April 10 of that year he signed the bill which created the patent system. Before, patents were issued only by special acts of a legislature of a state or colony. But now a Board consisting of the Secretary of State, the Secretary of War, and the Attorney General had the responsibility for granting patents. (Not for years was a separate Patent Office established, first under the jurisdiction of the Department of State, and eventually, in April 1925, under the Department of Commerce.)

When the Patent Office was established by Congress, Thomas Jefferson was Secretary of State and thus became the first administrator of the new law. He said later: "The issue of patents for new discoveries has given a spring to invention beyond my conception."

It was Jefferson the inventor who originated the swivel chair, the

Abraham Lincoln, first and only President of the United States to patent an invention, whittled out a model in his spare hours.

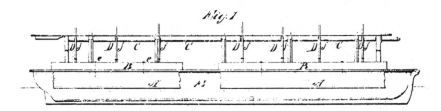

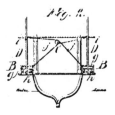

Patent of May 22, 1849, "Buoying Vessels over Shoals," was never put to use but the model (left) is housed at the National Museum (Smithsonian Institution) in Washington, D.C. Three figures from Lincoln's patent are shown above. During his trips on the Mississippi young Abe saw the troubles of navigators on shoals.

folding buggy top, a three-legged folding camp stool, and a "modern" type of plowshare. A writing desk with an adjustable top, which could be folded for traveling, designed by Jefferson and possibly made by his own hands (though more probably by one of the carpenters among his slaves), became an exhibit in the Smithsonian Institution at Washington.

Although neither Washington nor Jefferson made money from his inventions, other early American celebrities had no such scruples. Benjamin Franklin made money on his stove, which is still to be seen today in many houses. He also invented a copperplate press for printing paper money, a mangle for pressing linen, and a clock that showed hours, minutes, and seconds on three revolving wheels. He also conceived of a mechanical arm for taking books down from high shelves, and the first bifocal spectacles with double lenses for reading and distance. And Samuel L. Clemens (Mark Twain) received patents for an adjustable and detachable strap for the backs of waistcoats and trousers, and for a self-pasting scrapbook in which the pages were gummed and needed only to be moistened to make clippings adhere to them.

(For many of these footnotes to the history of invention, we are indebted to "Invention—Hobby of Great Men" from the January 1928 issue of *Popular Science Monthly*.)

A landmark decision in a patent suit contained a phrase by which Supreme Court Justice William O. Douglas defined the necessary ingredient of a patentable invention, as distinguished from an improvement that might naturally occur to anyone skilled in the field concerned. While inventors' techniques could be as infinitely varied as their personalities, what their creations all had in common, as Douglas saw it, was a "flash of genius," a corollary to Lincoln's concept of the inventor's "fire of genius."

Granting the mutual experience of the "flash of genius" in the process of invention, an outstanding contrast in approach and methods is to be found in two great inventors, each of whom has a separate chapter in this book: Thomas A. Edison and Nikola Tesla.

Edison was the celebrated example of a "try-anything" inventor. In the case of his carbon-button telephone transmitter, his "flash of genius" might be considered his recognition that what was needed was a substance whose electrical resistance varied with pressure from a diaphragm. He vainly tried every one of the hundreds of chemicals on his laboratory shelves, but finally found the right one in lampblack sooting a lamp chimney that an assistant brought him. In an earlier book, *A Century of Wonders*, we cited a "try-anything" example when an old friend named J. V. Mackenzie visited his laboratory while Edison was seeking a material for his electric lamp's filament. Mackenzie wore a luxuriant red beard, which the young inventor eyed eagerly, exclaiming: *"There's* something we haven't tried yet!" Thereupon he plucked a hair from his friend's whiskers and put it into the carbonizing furnace and then into a lamp bulb. We concluded: "To Edison's merriment the lamp burned with 'a peculiar reddish glow,' one of his assistants later insisted. With mock solemnity, the Wizard of Menlo Park named it the 'Edison-Mackenzie lamp.'"

In contrast to Edison's pragmatic style Tesla's famous induction motor was a purely mental feat of invention. The November 1928 issue of *Popular Science Monthly* records this extraordinary incident:

> Unlike inventors who work with the tedious process of trial and error, Tesla visualizes his inventions, full-fledged, even to the smallest detail. One evening he was walking with a friend through the City Park of Budapest, quoting from a book of poems he had learned by heart. In the middle of a line he broke off, seized a small stick, and scratched a rough picture on the sand. It was his induction motor, revealed to him in its entirety! And the plan he drew was the same that, seven years later, he presented to the American Institute of Electrical Engineers.

Tesla hadn't the slightest need to build his induction motor to see if it would work—he knew that it would. He concluded his demonstration on the sand in the Budapest park by exclaiming to his friend, "Look, watch me reverse my motor!" and then showed how it would be done.

A report of an early interview with Edison in which a reporter asked him his motives for inventing, offers this quotation: "All I want now is to have a big laboratory, and just as long as I can to keep on experimenting and making useful inventions, and having them successful. But there isn't a bit of philanthropy in it. Anything that won't sell I don't want to invent, because anything that won't sell hasn't reached the acme of success. Its sale is proof of its utility, and utility is success" (*Edison and His Phonograph,* by J. Lewis Young, 1890).

Although money-making was a motive frankly acknowledged by Edison, his claim that "there isn't a bit of philanthropy in it" is belied in at least one instance by the story of his invention of the X-ray fluoroscope.

Professor W. K. Roentgen announced his discovery of the X-ray late in 1895. Edison got busy (as did other scientists) to find chemicals that would fluoresce under the rays. Out of 8,000 or so that he tested he found hundreds that would. Edison discovered that calcium tungstate, if fused to the inside of a glass vacuum tube containing an X-ray electrode, would glow visibly when exposed to the invisible

Earlier Presidents were inventors too. George Washington used successful new plows of his invention on his estate. Records of these inventions are to be found in his diary. Among others, he created and used a "barrel plow" for sowing grain and covering it with earth at one time. In January 1790, he spoke to the second session of the first Congress, begged for "effectual encouragement . . . of skill and genius at home."

Besides being an inventor, like Washington, Thomas Jefferson also drew plans for the University of Virginia. Left, a portable writing desk he invented. It could be folded for traveling and is preserved at the Smithsonian Institution. No gentleman, he wrote, could take money for his inventions.

The First Bifocals "Helped His French"

ABOVE is Franklin's own design for the first double spectacles or bifocals, made in Paris under his personal direction. Requiring two sets of lenses, one for reading, another for distingushing distant objects, he hit upon the idea of the split lens. "By this means," he wrote, "as I wear my spectacles constantly, I have only to move my eyes up and down, as I want to see distinctly far or near, the proper glasses being always ready. This I find more particularly convenient since my being in France. . . . When one's ears are not well accustomed to the sound of a language, a sight of the movements in the features of him that speaks, helps to explain; so that I understand French better by the help of my spectacles."

Above, an item from the November 1926 issue of *Popular Science* explains Benjamin Franklin's invention of bifocal spectacles for reading and distance. His most famous invention, still in common use, is the stove named after him. At right are three versions of Franklin's time. It is actually a fireplace which heats a room and also carries the smoke away.

PROFILE of the Chimney and FIRE-PLACE.

M The Mantle-piece or Breast of the Chimney.
C The Funnel.
B The false Back & Closing.
E True Back of the Chimney.
T Top of the Fire-place.
F The Front of it.
A The Place where the Fire is made.
D The Air-Box.
K The Hole in the Side-plate, thro' which the warm'd Air is discharg'd out of the Air-Box into the Room.
H The Hollow fill'd with fresh Air, entring at the Passage I, and ascending into the Air-Box thro' the Air-hole in the Bottom-plate neat
G The Partition in the Hollow to keep the Air and Smoke apart.
P The Passage under the false Back and Part of the Hearth for the Smoke.
ʃ ʃ ʃ ʃ ʃ ʃ The Course of the Smoke.

Left, a modern version of a Franklin stove, made by King, a practical heater as well as a cozy fireplace. Right, Franklin's own sketch of his stove. A false back was the feature of Franklin's fireplace. The warmed air rose but, prevented from going up the chimney by this back, passed into the room, being replaced by fresh air. Smoke passed unhindered up the chimney.

X-rays. Thus he was led to the fluoroscope—an instrument for viewing, on a fluorescent screen, the picture made by X-rays passing through an object such as the human body.

Edison sent one of his fluoroscopes to Michael Pupin, a professor at Columbia University, who himself was the inventor of the loading coil that first made transcontinental telephony possible. The professor used Edison's fluoroscope to show his students shotgun pellets lodged in a man's hand; plainly, X-rays and the new fluoroscope could guide surgery to remove them, giving an instant view without need to wait for X-ray films to be made and developed. Subsequently Edison's fluoroscope became an invaluable medical aid.

Edison did not patent his invention of the fluoroscope. Instead, he donated this great medical advance to humanity. However, out of his research in the 1890s for the fluoroscope grew the fluorescent lamp, a new concept of artificial lighting which he did patent, but put aside for other projects. The first fluorescent lamp was not seen publicly until 1938, at expositions in New York and San Francisco!

The "why" of Nikola Tesla's inventing emerged in an interview in 1928 with Alden P. Armagnac, a co-author of this book. Armagnac asked Tesla what part of his lifework lay closest to his heart. Tesla's answer surprised the interviewer. It was not his induction motor, which is the basis of industries in which billions of dollars are invested all over the world. Instead, it was the discovery of the *principle* that made the motor possible—the "rotating magnetic field."

"When I made the discovery of the rotating magnetic field," Dr. Tesla said, "I was a very young man. The revelation came after years of concentrated thought and it was my first great thrill. It was not only a valuable discovery, capable of extensive practical applications. It was a revelation of new forces and new phenomena unknown to science before.

"I would not give my rotating-field discovery for a thousand inventions, however valuable, designed merely as mechanical contraptions to deceive the eye and the ear. A thousand years hence, the telephone and the motion picture camera may be obsolete, but the principle of the rotating magnetic field will remain a vital, living thing for all time to come."

Tesla was pre-eminently the scientist. Probably his tremendously valuable practical inventions like the induction motor were important to him mainly because they helped finance his lifelong quest for other great scientific discoveries, described later in this book.

So Edison and Tesla may have shared the profit motive, perhaps for different reasons. Certainly Edison's more than 1,000 patents (1,093 to be exact) look like a prime example of an inventor being spurred by the "fuel of interest," as Abraham Lincoln called it.

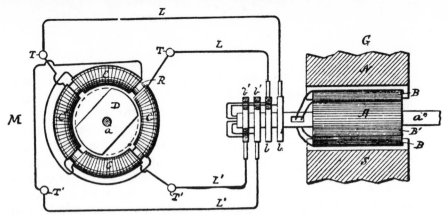

Nikola Tesla, the "mind's-eye" inventor, visualized his revolutionary induction motor full-fledged. He drew a diagram of it in the sand in a Budapest park. Above, *Popular Science's* version, printed in 1893.

Thomas Edison, the "trial and error" inventor, tested every chemical in his lab before he hit on lampblack from a lamp chimney to make the carbon button (arrow) for his improved telephone transmitter.

Rare photo of Thomas Edison's X-ray fluoroscope, left, is from *The Electrical Engineer* magazine. Edison claimed that his motive for inventing was strictly business but he never patented his fluoroscope; instead, it was his gift to humanity.

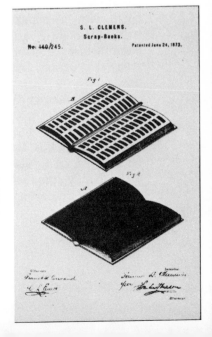

The great American humorist Samuel Clemens (Mark Twain) received several patents, including his "self-pasting" scrapbook with gummed pages or inserts. Two versions are shown at right, the upper with gummed inserts, the lower with gummed pages. The patent application, granted June 24, 1873, was titled "Improvements in Scrap-books" and was signed Saml. L. Clemens.

In its September 1973 issue *Popular Science* magazine spoke to today's inventors with a report from the U. S. Patent Office in an article called, "A New Program to Protect Your Invention." For profit? Of course.

The article explains that on April 17, 1969, the U. S. Patent Office inaugurated a new program. "Unknown to most inventors," says the writer, "the Patent Office now offers a service that provides ironclad proof of a 'date of conception' [of the invention]. It's known as the 'Disclosure Document Program' . . . an inventor need only send his disclosure to the Patent Office with a request that it be accepted under the program, and they will retain it in strict confidence for two years or until a patent application is filed. After the two years, the disclosure will automatically be destroyed."

During the two years that the Patent Office retains the disclosure, the inventor has the time to perfect and improve his invention before he applies for his patent.

Under the patent system, in the view of the Department of Commerce, "American industry has flourished. New products have been invented, new uses for old ones discovered, and employment given to millions. Under the patent system a small struggling nation has grown into the greatest industrial power on earth."

As seen by an encyclopedia (American People's), the patent system "implies the right of the inventor to keep his discovery secret and offers to reward him for disclosing it . . . The patent is a reward for the creation of something new, for an addition to and not a subtraction from the public wealth."

If his invention proves marketable, the inventor has an opportunity for financial rewards for seventeen years, the life of a patent. The term seems equitable but is still limited. The high point of profit could begin with the eighteenth year and doubtless many an inventor has ruefully watched vast profits from his innovation pouring in to the manufacturer after his own royalties have expired. Perhaps a patent renewal program, like that for a copyright, will someday be developed.

But Lincoln rightly recognized the great improvement which the American patent system offered the inventor. Whatever its limitations, the system has encouraged the scientific wonder workers to whom this book is devoted. Whether their motives were to fill a need (necessity), or to develop an inspiration (the flash of genius) or to make money (the fuel of interest), these inventors have changed their physical world beyond recognition.

CHAPTER 2

They Invented
Tremendous Trifles

THOUSANDS of inventions, the great bulk of them un-
described publicly except in patent papers, affect the daily lives of
hundreds of millions of people throughout the world. Who thought up
the kitchen friction match? (John Walker in 1827.) Foam rubber?
(A research team led by E. A. Murphy of the Dunlop Rubber Co.,
1928.) The safety pin? (Walter Hunt, 1849.) The modern adding
machine? (William Burroughs, 1885.) The gas burner? (Robert
Bunsen, 1855.) The thermometer? (Galileo, 1593.)

This chapter makes no pretense of doing anything except telling the
stories of the people behind just a few of the tremendous trifles,
selected at random (not including those listed above), that the
civilized world today accepts for what they are—commonplaces.

It answers some provocative questions:

How did a typewriter get to bear the name of an arms manufacturer?

What inventor was so poor that he carried his lunch to work in a
paper bag—and grew so rich that he gave away money in bulk?

What inventor famous the world over died in disgrace?

Who amassed a fortune of $100 million by perfecting an item you
could hide behind a dime?

Who was responsible for fines levied on motorists in the tens of
thousands daily?

What writing instrument sold in the millions despite the fact that, at
first, it was a colossal failure?

Who thought up the bottle cap?

BARBED WIRE

Two pieces of wire, twisted together, with a short third piece inserted
at a right angle, precipitated bloody "wars" on the American Great

Plains just before the nation's first Centennial. The product made men rich, caused years of lawsuits, and—much later—provided scenarios for some of Hollywood's most profitable movies. It was barbed wire and was covered by patents that had few parallels in simplicity. The text of the bellwether patent, first of several, covers exactly one page in the U. S. Patent Office files.

The wars erupted because cattle growers gradually were fenced out of open grasslands on the plains that for decades they had considered their domain for fattening their beef. Their antagonists were men they sneeringly called "sodbusters," and these worthies, homesteading farmers, fenced their acreages so that the rich loam furrowed by their plows could produce crops free from trampling hooves. They used barbed wire for three reasons: it was easier to put up than wood fences, it was cheaper, and it was far more effective against cattle. Both sides used firearms with a viciousness that is legend to this day.

The story of the first really successful barbed wire involves three men, and it opens on a day in 1873 when, together, they examined an exhibit of the wire at a county fair in De Kalb, Illinois. They were friends and neighbors. Their names: Joseph Farwell Glidden, Jacob Haish, and Issac L. Ellwood. All, subsequently, according to the Dictionary of American Biography, made fortunes out of barbed wire. Barbed wire already was in being, having been invented by one Henry M. Rose. Rose's product left something to be desired. Both Glidden and Haish came away from the exhibit with secret thoughts on improvement.

Glidden is the key man in the story. A New Hampshireman by birth, he grew up on a farm in New York State and in his maturity bought land in Illinois. He was sixty before he began thinking about improving barbed wire. He applied for a patent in October of the year of the county fair. Two months later Haish also applied for a patent improving barbed wire. In the clash of priority claims Glidden won. He had devised a novel method of holding the spur wires, the barbs, in place, so good that to this day it has survived hundreds of other ideas. Glidden approached Ellwood, the other friend he had gone to the fair with, and coaxed him into investing $265 in a partnership. His invention was a smashing success from the start. Glidden sold his half interest for $60,000 plus a hefty royalty to the Washburn & Moen Manufacturing Company of Worcester, Massachusetts, and proceeded to amass a fortune. At his death he owned farms and ranches in Illinois and Texas—growing the cattle he had fenced out —plus a gristmill and a hotel, and was vice-president of a bank.

Glidden's legal victory on his barbed-wire patent didn't deter Jacob Haish. He designed a competitor, an S-shaped barbed wire, patented it, and proceeded to manufacture it. A year later Washburn & Moen

The first typewriter, the Remington, was demonstrated by the inventor's daughter, Lillian Sholes, in this photo published in 1919, more than a half century after the fact, by *Popular Science*. The lid swung down over the keyboard and locked. Christopher Sholes (right) sold his invention to the Remington Arms Co. for only $12,000.

The slide fastener, marketed under several names commercially, including "Zipper," was not a success until it was re-invented twenty years after being first patented. In the files of the U. S. Patent Office is this entry in the application: "I, Gideon Sundback, a subject of the King of Sweden . . . have invented certain new and useful improvements in Separable Fasteners . . ."

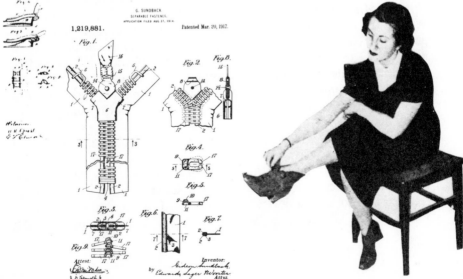

bought up Haish's patents and cornered the market. Haish fought them. All the lawsuits were not settled until 1892. A building contractor and lumber dealer, Haish made a lot of money not only from his own production of barbed wire but from machines to manufacture it as well. These he leased to other manufacturers, including Washburn & Moen, whom he had challenged in the courts.

It took the majesty of the U. S. Supreme Court to settle patent-infringement suits over the design of a piece of pronged wire.

TYPEWRITER

The invention of the typewriter occurred almost by chance. Its beginnings were rooted in a machine for numbering pages. It was regarded not as an indispensable piece of office equipment but as an aid to the blind. An armament company, in financial straits, proved to be the fulcrum for its success—and it sold out too soon. And the man chiefly responsible for the typewriter engaged in all sorts of wholly unrelated business and political activities before, well past middle age, he turned his attention to perfecting it.

Christopher Latham Sholes, the father of the typewriter, was not the first person by any means to think of a mechanical means of replacing pen and ink. That idea went back to the seventeenth century. Writing machines of sorts preceded Sholes's work in the nineteenth century. But Sholes and two companions supplied two missing pieces of the puzzle of how to put a letter of the alphabet on paper by striking a key.

Sholes is listed in the Dictionary of American Biography as a printer, journalist, inventor, and a public office holder. A farm boy from Pennsylvania, he is said to have been a lineal descendant of John and Priscilla Alden, immortalized in Longfellow's *The Courtship of Miles Standish*. Sholes got around. A successful printer in Wisconsin, to which his parents had moved, he became a newspaper editor, clerk of the territorial legislature, a postmaster under President Polk, a member of the legislature, and collector of the port of Milwaukee under Lincoln. He had an inventive turn of mind. In 1864 he and a machinist friend, Samuel W. Soulé, obtained a patent on a paging machine and in 1866 one for serially numbering the pages of blank books.

In the small machine shop where Soulé and Sholes tinkered was a third inventor, Carlos Glidden (no relation to the barbed wire fellow). Glidden suggested to Sholes that his success with the numbering machine qualified him to invent a letter-printing machine, and referred him to such a device newly invented in London by one John Pratt. Sholes, Glidden, and Soulé patented a typewriter on June 23,

1868, and an improvement on it a month later. It was rough going to gain acceptance. For five years Sholes fruitlessly tried to make and market the machine. He was granted an improvement patent in 1871. Glidden and Soulé gave up. For a time Sholes worked with Thomas A. Edison on the invention. Edison missed a bet. He was interested only in a printing device for a telegraph system. Sholes sold out in 1873, aged fifty-four, to the Remington Arms Company of Ilion, New York.

He had a marketable item if only someone would recognize it. What Sholes, aided by Glidden and Soulé, had done was devise a carriage that moved one space to the left when a key was depressed, and a "pianoforte" action for the keys, all of which struck a platen at exactly the same point.

Sholes still was not thinking of his typewriter as an office machine. Apparently no one else was either. As late as 1889 *Popular Science* was still running articles and letters on "the type-writer for the blind."

Remington Arms was ripe for a new product. The close of the Civil War had put it in the doldrums and financial distress. Philo Remington, eldest son of the founder, Eliphalet, began producing typewriters in 1873 but they were not marketed until three years later. As a retail item they were a bust. Philo Remington gave up trying to popularize the machine and sold it—lock, stock, and barrel, one might say—in 1886. He was premature by only five or six years. Early in the last decade of the nineteenth century a typewriter boom took hold. Designs competitive with Sholes's mushroomed. The world of business at long last had discovered the invention.

Even though Sholes continued working on his typewriter—his final patent was granted in 1878, twelve years before his death—his name went unsung. But the Remington name, in arms and typewriters, survived. Philo paid Sholes $12,000 for the rights to his invention. It was all he ever got.

THE "ZIPPER"

That thing a woman refers to when she asks, "Will you zip me up?" was twenty years in arriving after it first appeared as a gleam in the eye of an inventor. Generically known as the slide fastener, and as the "Zipper" and other names in trade circles, it was patented in 1893 by Whitcomb L. Judson, a Chicagoan, who told the Patent Office it was "a cheap locker or unlocker for shoes." It was to take the place of laces or buttons. "My fastener," he elaborated, ". . . may also be applied to mail bags, belts, and the closing of seams uniting flexible bodies." His imagination apparently fell short of men's trouser flies.

Judson ultimately went on to fame and fortune, right? Wrong. He missed by a hair. Each tooth of his invention required three right-angle bends, so complicating its manufacture that it could not be produced economically.

Judson's idea lay there in the archives of the U. S. Patent Office doing nothing until the year 1906. Now, it so happened that in the same year Judson obtained his patent, Lewis Walker, of the Westinghouse Electric Company, saw what was billed as a "hookless fastener"—Judson's device—at Chicago's Columbian Exposition. It intrigued him, and off and on for thirteen years he tried to modify the design so it would yield to easy manufacture. He didn't succeed.

In 1906 a man named Gideon Sundback entered the picture. Sundback, later to be endowed with a doctorate in science by Allegheny College, was twenty-six years old, Swedish by birth, who had been educated in his homeland and in Germany. He held a degree in electrical engineering. Walker induced Sundback to join Westinghouse, and no sooner had the man sat down to his new desk than he was handed the patent papers for Whitcomb Judson's fastener. Could he do anything with it? Was a graduate electrical engineer, working for an electrical manufacturing company, being asked to toy with a thing to fasten—er—maybe ladies' undergarments?

Why not? Sundback saw possibilities. It took him a long seven years to solve the problem of slide-fastener design and to blueprint the machinery to produce the product.

As an outgrowth, the Hookless Fastener Company was incorporated in 1913. It had twenty employees. Sundback applied for a patent in 1914 and was granted it three years later. Zippers became a roaring success, as did other, competitive slide fasteners in succeeding years.

NEON SIGNS

Among the brilliant scientists that France has produced was one who contributed much to the world's knowledge of chemistry, whose name embellished commercial advertising manufacturers' shops on every continent, whose far-ranging imagination dreamed up an idea for producing electrical current that may yet, one day, tap the seas for energy—and who, in the end, turned out to be a born loser.

Georges Claude—remember those red, glass-tube signs, "CLAUDE NEON"?—was a chemist and physicist, born in Paris in 1871. He was educated at the École de Physique et de Chimie, and launched on a career that brought him fame, fortune, and honors. At the age of twenty-six he and a fellow chemist, named Hess, reported that the solubility of acetylene in acetone was nearly proportional to the number of atmospheres of pressure imposed. The coefficient of expansion was much lower than that of liquid acetylene, and the solution did not explode even in the presence of a red-hot wire. The discovery, at long last, made it possible to ship and store the volatile, dangerous acetylene safely.

Claude produced liquid oxygen by the expansion method, making possible its production on a commercial scale, and isolated the various gases of the air. In 1910 he experimented with electric discharge tubes containing neon, argon, helium, krypton, and xenon, and by 1920 the Claude neon-sign business, delayed by World War I, had become established. Money poured into his purse. It was Claude who invented a new and inexpensive method of producing ammonia, the cheapest form of fixed nitrogen for industry and agriculture. That was in 1917, when the Allies needed ammonia for the output of munitions, and for that he was decorated by his government. In the 1920s he became enamored of an idea for generating electricity practically for free by solar heat as it affected surface ocean water. As described in the February 1927 issue of *Popular Science:*

Prof. Georges Claude demonstrated before the French Academy of Science that . . . the temperature of sea water at various depths holds immeasurable stores of usable power. He . . . demonstrated a working model of a generator that draws power from the difference in temperature between the tepid water at the surface of tropic seas and the cold water at a depth of some 3,000 feet. In a partial vacuum, he showed, the tepid surface water will boil of its own volition. The resulting steam can be fed to a turbine, thence to a condenser which, with the aid of frigid water from the depths, increases the vacuum and consequently the efficiency of the steam plant. He declared that for every 40,000 cubic feet of water a second, there could be generated 400,000 kilowatts of power . . .

A bit less than four years later Claude sank an enormous tube of corrugated steel nearly six feet in diameter and more than a mile long into Matanzas Bay, Cuba. It was his third try. Two previous steel tubes, each costing thousands of dollars, lay lost at the bottom of the ocean. The shore end of the third tube was tied to Claude's first experimental generating station, boasting a turbine four feet in diameter. His "heat machine" developed enough power to light forty 500-candlepower lamps. Now, said Claude, he would build bigger power stations.

He didn't. His search for cheap electricity was costing him his shirt. Two other items in the news of the time illuminate Claude's persistent research. He discovered the use of fluorescein dye as a distress signal for seamen and downed aviators. The red crystals, exposed to seawater, put a patch of brilliant yellow on the surface to attract the attention of searching planes. And he constructed a huge steel ball, with portholes, for an exploration of the sea's floor.

Now Claude began to be torn by resentments. He felt that his contributions to French science had not been properly appreciated. By an unhappy coincidence, Adolf Hitler had come to power in Germany. Events marched inexorably toward Claude's downfall. World War II began. France collapsed. Claude, a bitter man, publicly urged the citizens of France to collaborate with the Nazis.

"I was convinced in 1940," he later said, "that Germany's victory was definitive."

Arrested at his home in St. Cloud, near Paris, in 1945, he stood trial for treason, was convicted as a collaborationist, and, stripped of his honors and properties, sentenced to life imprisonment. He was absolved of other wartime crimes, including an allegation that he had designed the German V-1 "flying bomb." Five years later he was released, and spent the remainder of his days in disgrace, a man whose seeds of nobility in the sciences had fallen on the barren ground of personal pique. He died in 1960 at eighty-nine.

Even his neon light lost favor. Advertisers preferred Plexiglas with fluorescent lighting behind it. But, as an accolade to Claude's genius, even today experiments go on in trying to generate electricity from the sun and seas.

AEROSOL SPRAY CANS

One day in 1949 a customer dropped by the office of Robert H. Abplanalp, who owned a machine shop in the Bronx, New York, and handed him a tin can with a funny-looking gadget on the top of it.

"Yeah," said Abplanalp, "so what is it?"

The customer, John J. Baessler, a manufacturer of washing machine meters, had a mission. He had met a chemist named Frederick G. Lodes. Lodes was hoping to persuade Baessler to make pressurized spray paint cans. But the two men had a problem. They needed a cheap, efficient valve. All they had at the moment were leaky, expensive brass valves fitted to "bug bombs" for the Army in World War II.

Baessler was paying a call on Abplanalp to buck the problem to him. Consumer-type aerosols were just coming on the market.

Baessler explained. "Doesn't work very well," said he of the brass valve he exhibited.

"We talked for several hours," Abplanalp related later. "I said, 'Leave the stuff here and I'll look at it.' I did, and got absorbed."

The idea was sound. If a valve could be devised to dispense the contents of a can (not tin, of course, but an aluminum alloy) under

the pressure of an inert gas, it would open the door to a whole new industry catering to the needs of the housewife, the home workshopper, and thousands of businesses needing a spray or stream at the touch of a finger.

Abplanalp—the name in Swiss-German means "from flat mountain"—the son of an immigrant machinist, was no novice at mechanics. At the age of ten he and his father built a miniature steam engine. He studied engineering at Villanova University in Pennsylvania but dropped out to open his own machine shop. He liked tinkering better than books. Hardly out of his teens when the United States was plunged into World War II, he served in the Army in Europe, and among the chores suiting his talents was supervising German prisoners in a Cherbourg railroad repair yard. Returning home at war's end, he found his machine shop in a financial shambles, $10,000 in debt.

He had worked his way out of that problem when the customer handed him the aerosol can. With characteristic application Abplanalp tackled the job of improving it. In three months he and his engineers designed a seven-part, leakproof valve. The trouble was that the valve cost nine cents to make, far too much for widespread use. He kept tinkering with manufacturing techniques and in the end produced one that cost only two and a half cents.

The rest is history. Abplanalp filed for a patent. Baessler and Lodes became Abplanalp's partners. Baessler put up $15,000 to get a production line started. In time Baessler and Lodes sold out, leaving Abplanalp sole owner of the enterprise.

Today a half-billion Abplanalp valves are produced annually in ten foreign countries. A billion are made at Abplanalp's Precision Valve Corporation plants in Yonkers, New York, and Chicago. They squirt or spray hundreds of products from mosquito killers to paint.

There is a cloud shadowing the future of the spray can that Abplanalp's valve made possible. Some scientists have lately expressed fears that releasing large quantities of spray cans' present gas propellant, a fluorocarbon like Freon, into the air possibly might endanger the earth's inhabitants. Rising into the upper atmosphere, they suggest, it could break down chemically and release chlorine, which could react with and destroy some of the upper-atmosphere ozone that protects earth dwellers by shielding them from harmful solar radiation. Currently this controversial hypothesis is under study by the National Academy of Sciences. Should it prove correct, spray-can makers might be forced to find another propellant gas to substitute for the Freon-type ones now in use.

The problem needn't worry Abplanalp. As this book went to press, his personal fortune was estimated at $100 million. He owned two

Georges Claude, inventor of the neon light, in 1927 proposed a solution to the world's energy crisis—producing power (right) with turbines driven by steam from the temperature difference between the oceans' surface water and that at great depth.

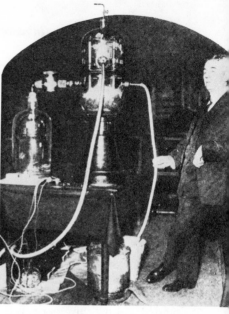

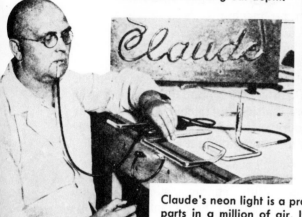

Claude's neon light is a product of a gas that occurs as only twelve parts in a million of air. It's inert, but has a peculiar property—when an electric current is passed through it in a near vacuum (above, left), it glows. After a half century of worldwide use, the tube lighting has begun to give way in many adaptations to Plexiglas with fluorescent lighting behind it. Claude, a fertile inventor who found an inexpensive method to produce ammonia for industry and agriculture, died in disgrace at eighty-nine for having betrayed his country.

The world's most popular aerosol valve got that way and made its inventor—shown here—a multimillionaire because it was cheap and simple. Robert Abplanalp saw in plastics a key to low manufacturing cost. His valves, costing 2½ cents, dispense among other things hair sprays, deodorants, laundry products, paints, wax, and insecticides.

Mathematician, philosopher, architect, businessman, writer, and maverick designer, Buckminster Fuller has been called one of the greatest minds of his time. Whole communities, he says, one day will be able to live in scientifically controlled surroundings through the use of his geodesic domes (below). They weigh only an ounce or two for each cubic foot they enclose, yet they shrug off stresses that would flatten buildings of conventional design.

Popular Science

LOW-COST SUN DOMES YOU CAN BUILD EASILY

Start your summer earlier!

islands in the Bahamas. To one of them, Grand Cay, former President Richard M. Nixon was a frequent visitor. Abplanalp likes to call himself "Big Al." The name fits. Six feet tall, he is moon-faced and beefy. A man shy of publicity, he is happiest when deep-sea fishing or drinking beer with friends. His employees call him "Bob." He makes a point of hiring the handicapped. He is interested in fish farming as a means of alleviating the world's food shortages. He is addicted to luxury cars and expensive attire. A sign on his office wall says, "Quitcherbellyakin."

Preferring trains to airplanes, he compromised on his distaste for flying by buying a seaplane—instead of a wheeled machine—to bridge the distance between Florida and the Bahamas.

As for his success, he once remarked, "Edison said genius was 99 per cent perspiration and 1 per cent inspiration. I say it's 2 per cent inspiration, 8 per cent work, and 90 per cent luck. I'm a lucky guy."

GEODESIC DOME

Richard Buckminster Fuller, the inventor of the "geodesic dome," once got mad at his wife and talked to her in a language she could not understand—mathematical formulas. "Bucky," as he is known to his friends, was fully in character. He thinks in numbers and dreams in images. Admirers, *Time* magazine once remarked, compare him with Leonardo da Vinci. He has no such illusions about himself.

"Officially," he has said, "I'm a machinist." That comes from an apprenticeship in a factory making cotton mill machinery after he was expelled from college, "officially," as he put it, "for cutting classes but actually for general irresponsibility."

For a fellow who was the bad boy of the building industry before he was thirty—he expressed a profound disgust with existing construction methods—Bucky Fuller has come a long way. While his geodesic dome is by no means his sole achievement, its subversion of age-old tenets make it his masterpiece. C. P. Gilmore, executive editor of *Popular Science* and a co-author of this book, tells about the time the late industrialist Henry J. Kaiser ordered a Fuller dome as an auditorium for a new housing development in Hawaii. Construction had just begun, and Kaiser wanted to be on hand as it went up. He boarded an airplane in California and sped westward, only to find on his arrival that the building was complete. Nineteen hours after the shining new dome was started it housed the Honolulu Symphony Orchestra for a full dress concert before an audience of 2,000.

Fuller domes go up that fast and that easily.

In 1966 *Popular Science* sold to its readers plans to build a backyard dome for five dollars, including a permit signed by Fuller.

As far back as 1917 Fuller began working out a new branch of mathematics, an extension of solid geometry which he named "energetic synergetic geometry." He figured out a way to string together a series of tetrahedrons—four-sided pyramids—in a way that balanced tension struts against compression members. He applied his theory to an extremely light dome-shaped structure. It was just as strong as much heavier, conventional buildings.

"The trouble with most buildings," he said, "is they expend most of their strength just holding themselves up."

The larger a Fuller dome was built, the stronger it became: doubling its size squared the number of strength-distributing parts. They probably are the most efficient buildings ever built, weighing only an ounce or two for each cubic foot they enclose. Yet they can withstand hurricanes.

Fuller domes dot the DEW line, the radar defense net across northern Canada. They house railroad roundhouses in Baton Rouge and Wood River, Illinois, their two-and-a-half-acre floors completely clear of supports. The Marine Corps uses small domes as mobile shelters, transported knocked down by helicopter. The world's most unusual greenhouse, St. Louis's Climatron, is housed in an aluminum Fuller dome. Another Fuller dome housed the 1959 U. S. Exposition in Moscow, and still another, a huge one twenty stories high, built of steel and transparent plastic, enclosed the U.S. exhibition at Expo 67, the Montreal World's Fair.

Gadfly of the technological world, Bucky Fuller is scientist, engineer, architect, and philosopher. He regards man as "a self-balancing, 28-jointed, adapter-base biped," an automobile as a migratory, glassed-in porch, and an airplane as a powered, high-speed room. Of stubby build, thick-necked, he was a grandnephew of Margaret Fuller, friend of Ralph Waldo Emerson, the Sage of Concord. Apparently he was fascinated by ideas from the time he became sentient. Certainly he was not interested in grubbing for money. Abruptly in 1927 he quit building prefabricated structures with his father-in-law, a top architect and educator, to devote full time to his own radical ideas. As late as 1958 he had made little money. To pay expenses he worked as a research consultant, researcher for a manufacturer, editor and publisher, naval officer, chief of the federal board of economic warfare's mechanical engineering section, and teacher and lecturer in scores of colleges and universities.

Now well into his seventies, Fuller does much of his own engineering. His imagination ranges untethered. He designed a three-wheeled, rear-engine automobile capable of 120 mph, getting 40–50 miles per gallon. He designed a vertical-takeoff, jet-powered airplane more than fifteen years before jet propulsion was taken seriously. He designed a complete, one-piece, die-stamped bathroom that could be installed in a minute, complete with a "fog gun" that shot out a stream of 90 per cent air and 10 per cent water for more efficient bathing. He created a new kind of projection for global maps that eliminated the distortion in other maps. It was the first map ever granted a patent. He designed a seven-room aluminum house to be mass-produced using aircraft construction. He designed a pyramid community that could be built in a dry dock, floated, and towered to a river or harbor to house 6,500 persons as an answer to the country's dwindling buildable land reserves.

Structures of his geodesic and other designs today are built by the thousands throughout the world. He has more than 100 licensees. Bucky Fuller has been called a Rube Goldberg who takes himself seriously, a visionary, even a nut.

Some nut!

PARKING METERS

On July 16, 1935, the good citizens of Oklahoma City, Oklahoma, woke up to discover that 150 newfangled things requiring a deposit of coins to park an automobile legally had been installed overnight on the business streets. Whoever was responsible was satanically clever. For test purposes, the devices had been put on only one side of the street in a given block and on the other side in the next block. The opposing, facing sides of the streets were free. By nine o'clock the free side of each block was filled with cars. The opposite side was empty. Merchants on the sides requiring coins got on the telephone to city hall. Some of them used language that wouldn't bear repeating.

When, that same year, the things were installed in Mobile, Alabama, a "vigilante" committee showed up with axes to chop them down. Carthage, Texas, city officials agreed to install them in their business district, but when workmen began putting them around the courthouse the sheriff chased them away with a shotgun. As late as 1948 one indignant motorist got an aroused public in his town to outlaw the devices.

What had angered the citizenry was, of course, parking meters. Those in Oklahoma City were the first ever in the United States. The idea for them came out of the head of Carlton C. Magee, then editor of the Oklahoma City *Daily News*. In the late 1920s, when Magee was a member of the chamber of commerce traffic committee, the parking problem obsessed him. In searching for a solution, he hit on the idea of a timing device to show how long a car had been parked and a coin hopper to pay for the privilege. Magee took his idea to Gerald A. Hale, a professor of mechanical engineering at Oklahoma Agricultural and Mechanical College. Hale grew so absorbed he quit teaching to enter a partnership with Magee. It was Hale who worked out the mechanism.

Now let's return to that July day in Oklahoma City. The irate telephone calls by the merchants to city hall were only the opening scene. Hale recalled the morning vividly. By 11 A.M., as shoppers came to town, the metered sides of the streets began to fill with cars, and a funny thing was happening. There was a steady turnover of parking spaces. Throughout the day the metered sections remained relatively full, but a motorist could always find a parking space. The unmetered sides had a sluggish turnover. At the end of three days merchants on the free sides of the streets were petitioning the city council to install meters on their sides, too. The lack of meters was costing them patronage.

Still, the going was slow for Magee and Hale for a decade. In 1936 only 8,000 meters were sold, and the next three years brought average sales of only 4,000. Then came World War II, and in its aftermath a mushrooming automobile population brought the parking meter into its own. Sales boomed. Today, under various trade names, parking meters in the hundreds of thousands pour multimillions of dollars into the coffers of city governments. An abomination to many motorists, the meter nonetheless has served in part as a solution to the traffic problem. Throughout the land it is a fixture of the city scene. The metered parking lot is commonplace.

A segment of the public accepts the parking meter as a challenge to its ingenuity. Chewing gum, hairpins, paper clips, and cardboard stop up coin receivers. Most meters reject slugs, but some of them can be induced to accept cheap foreign coins. Thefts of money from them are not uncommon, especially in the larger cities. Some meters are merely smashed with sledge hammers. But one problem meter manufacturers and city governments no longer have to contend with. In the beginning meters caused suits, frequently by merchants who demanded the right to park their cars free in front of their stores. The courts and legislative action have stopped that.

In some communities parking meters have created a new kind of cop—in skirts. "Meter maids" cruise around on motorized tricycles to leave their calling cards under windshield wipers when the word "VIOLATION" appears in a meter's window. The card costs money.

PENS

The story of pens—the writing kind—properly begins with an accident. In the year 1884 a man named Waterman, like every smart insurance salesman of his time, carried on his watch chain a collapsible steel dip pen and a stoppered, portable inkwell. This arrangement, as recounted by the September 1956 issue of *Popular Science,* delighted no one but dry cleaners.

The idea of a pen that could hold its own ink supply was one of writing's oldest, most elusive dreams. Archaeologists had dug up a "fountain" pen, a hollow reed into which ink was poured, from an Egyptian tomb sealed around 4,000 B.C. Crude fountain pens with built-in ink reservoirs had appeared on the American market in the early 1880s, and our man Waterman bought one. As one of his sales prospects was about to sign an application for a large insurance policy, Waterman tendered the fountain pen. Then came the deluge. The pen flooded the document, and the testy customer gave his business to a rival agent.

Lewis Edson Waterman was a native of Decatur, New York, the son of a wagon builder, Elisha Waterman. Lewis' father died when he was a small boy, and he had no formal schooling until after he was ten. Even then it was pretty scanty. He attended a seminary in Charlotteville, New York, for a short time. With his mother remarried, the family moved to Kankakee County, Illinois, and for four years from age sixteen Lewis taught school and worked at carpentry. Between the ages of twenty and twenty-four he taught school, sold books, and studied shorthand. He was so good at shorthand that just before the Civil War—he was now in his mid-twenties—he gave instruction in it. Still trying to find his métier, he went into life insurance sales. (Delicate health evidently excused him from being drafted in the war.) For all of twenty-three years he sold insurance and traveled. The concept of a fountain pen began percolating through his head and, moving to New York City in 1883, he began experimenting. The fountain pens on the market certainly didn't live up to their notices, as witness the one that cost him a customer.

He made progress. Before the year was out he applied for his first patents. They were issued on February 12 and November 4, 1884. He established the Ideal Pen Company, and soon, so well did his product sell, he also established the L. E. Waterman Company. In only three years, at the age of fifty, after a lifetime of indifferent success, Lewis Waterman had hit the jackpot.

What he had invented was a controlled leak. Capillary attraction kept the ink confined in the body of the pen until the nib was in contact with paper. This principle of ink control was used by all "fountain" pen manufacturers from that day forward.

The name Waterman became such a commonplace that neophyte airplane pilots three quarters of a century later were entering solo flight hours in their log books as "Waterman time"—which is to say, they fibbed about the actual amount of flying they did. Fountain pens got around. A British diplomat, negotiating a treaty with an Arab, a North African tribal chieftain, produced an inkwell and an old-fashioned dip pen to make the document official. Signing his name with a blotchy flourish, the diplomat proffered the pen to the tribal leader. "No, thanks," said the Arab, "I have my own." From his burnoose he drew forth a two-tone American fountain pen, inked a fingertip, and solemnly affixed his thumbprint. In World War II isolated Chinese and Burmese guerrilla outfits solved the problem of medal presentations for valor—in the absence of medals—by awarding American fountain pens.

Waterman was president and manager of his pen company until his death in 1901.

Now flip the pages of the calendar forward by forty-five years. Suddenly, almost overnight, a manual writing instrument employing a different way of applying ink to paper was in the hands of millions of persons. It was the ball-point pen.

It seems singular that only four years elapsed between Waterman's first "fountain" pen patent and a patent for a ball-point obtained by one John Loud. That was in 1888. But there it was, an idea for delivering ink to paper by way of a tiny, rotating ball bearing constantly bathed in fluid from a reservoir. It lacked the flexibility and expressiveness of the fountain pen. Pressing down on the ball bearing could produce no broad-line flourish. The mark the ball-point made was limited to the size of the bearing. But it was a brand-new concept in a finger-held writing instrument.

Nothing came of it. The ball-point's time had not arrived. There was no way to monitor the flow of ink in the manner that Waterman controlled it to a nib.

The success story of the ball-point pen didn't hinge on one man. It began some thirty years after John Loud's patent. In 1919, at the close of World War I, Ladislas Biro, eighteen, was a tired, dead-broke veteran of a defeated Hungarian army. He drifted. He studied medicine, became a sculptor and a painter. He got to be pretty good. His pictures hung in the national salon. For a time he even practiced hypnotism as a sideline. This wasn't making any money. Casting about for a new product idea, he began to wonder if there wasn't an alternative to the fountain pen. The fountain pen demanded replenishment too often. With an elder brother, Georg, he devised a pen with a ball point. It was liquid-ink-fed. On a vacation trip the two showed an experimental ball-point to a dignified gentleman they met on a beach. The dignified gentleman urged them to set up a factory in Argentina. No wonder—he was Argentina's President, Augustín Justo. By now twenty years had elapsed since the end of the war. The brothers moved to Paris in 1939. The war clouds of a second world war gathered. Availing himself of the Argentine invitation, Ladislas Biro fled to Buenos Aires, landing with ten dollars in his pocket. His brother followed. They had hard times. They had to design production machinery, get ball bearings from Sweden to tip their pens, and train workmen. By 1943 they began to produce ball-points gravity-fed with liquid ink.

The pens were a spectacular failure. They smeared. Taking a page from Waterman, the Biros adopted a capillary-action feed. It wasn't perfect, but it was better. In 1944 they sold the North American and Caribbean rights to their pen to the Sheaffer company for a cool half-million dollars.

Now a different ink compound was tried. Big headlines proclaimed that a gelatinous ink made ball-points "the successor to the fountain pen."

Other U.S. pen companies came out with their own versions of ball-points. Milton Reynolds, a salesman type, produced his own design. Starting with a capital of $26,000, Reynolds in one year racked up a net profit a hundred times that. Fancy ball-points sold for up to $25 each. A New York department store sold $100,000 worth of ball-points at $12.50 each—in one day. Advertising became absurd. Reynolds, claiming his pen would write under water, hired Esther Williams, a swimmer and movie star with more curves than a superhighway interchange, to prove it. "But," acidly asked a competitor, "will it write on paper?" Advertised another manufacturer, "This is the pen that will make ten copies." Responded a choleric rival, "But will it make an original?" Infringement suits grew like toadstools after a rain.

All this was sound and fury. The ball-point was not all that good. It was, in fact, pretty bad. The trouble was with the ink. It clogged, jammed, or skipped entirely. It wasn't water-fast. It disappeared after exposure to sunlight. A moist thumb could lift a signature from it and transfer it to a bank check or document. Forgers rejoiced. Some banks refused to honor checks signed with ball-points. So the bubble burst. Fifteen-dollar price tags were slashed to fifteen cents, but ball-points wouldn't sell.

Rescue for the industry arrived by way of another Hungarian, a chemist, Franz Seech. He had escaped from Nazi-occupied France in the war and made his way to Los Angeles. Fired from a job with a ball-pen company when disaster hit the business, Seech re-invented the ball-point. Renting a cubbyhole laboratory, he came up in 1949 with a secret ink formula. Within a year nightclub comics were joking about "70,000 words without refilling." Example: "I'm too young to die—I've still got 30,000 words left in my Paper Mate."

Naturally enough, it was a stocky, balding, flamboyant man with a penchant for double-breasted suits and bright neckties—again, a salesman type—who made the ball-point pen a household item throughout the world. He was Baron Marcel Bich (pronounced "beek"), a naturalized Frenchman born in Turin, Italy, whose business career began in a leaky shed in Clichy, a Paris suburb, in 1945. The shed produced pen holders and pencil cases. With the ball-point's ailments cured, he began producing it to sell for pennies. Ultimately, with lawsuits sorted out and marketing areas under control, Baron Bich's "Bic" pens began pouring from eighteen factories at the rate of 7,000,000 a day. That was one out of every four sold in the world. Bich engineered his entry into the American market by buying out— yup, no fooling—the Waterman company. Soon a third of U.S. sales were Bic's.

The first Hungarian in ball-points, Ladislas Biro, didn't wind up exactly as a charity case. Pocketing his half-million dollars from Sheaffer, he teamed up with an Englishman to license the manufacture of pens based on his principle, and in due course slapped an infringement suit on Baron Marcel Bich. The settlement could keep the two partners and their heirs in truffles and champagne to time eternal —6 per cent of all Bich's income.

That dull rattling sound you hear is caused by John Loud's bones turning in their grave.

CROWN BOTTLE CAP

The most factual description that can be applied to William Painter, the man who conceived of the crown bottle cap, is that he was a hopelessly inveterate inventor. Like Lord Kelvin, who was always thinking of a better way to do things, Painter was constantly looking about to improve things mechanical. His bottle cap idea came rather late in life.

Practically everyone in the civilized world uses his caps. They are the cork-lined metal crowns clamped on to a shallow boss on top of the bottle mouth. They account for the pry-type bottle openers found in all kitchen drawers, and for openers serving the same purpose, screwed to the walls of hotel bathrooms throughout the world. For almost eighty years Painter crown caps dominated the bottling industry. Only when the twist-off cap began becoming popular did the crown cap find a rival. Painter's crown cap, a simple thing that made him rich beyond the dreams of avarice, was only one of his eighty-five inventions. He was more than an inventor; he was an accomplished engineer.

An eldest son, Painter was born in 1838 on the farm of his father Edward at Triadelphia, Maryland. He was descended from Quaker stock and became a member of the Society of Friends. At seventeen he was apprenticed to a patent-leather manufacturer in Wilmington, Delaware. At twenty he patented a fare box and a railroad-car seat and couch. Four years later he patented a counterfeit-coin detector and the year after that a kerosene lamp burner. By the time he was twenty-seven he was foreman of a Baltimore machine shop. For twenty years he constructed pumping machinery. Meanwhile, he tinkered: an automatic magneto-signal for telephones, a seed sower, a soldering tool, pump valves. About 1880, bottle stoppers began intriguing him. It took him several tries to come up with what he wanted. In 1885 he patented a wire-retained rubber stopper that could be removed with one hand, and organized a company to produce it. Within four months he had thought of a better way, and patented the first single-use bottle stopper, other than corks, that ever had been offered the bottling trade. He disbanded his first company and organized the Bottle Seal Company to market his invention, much lower in unit price than his previous one. Less than seven years later he came up with the crown cap, and his company became the Crown Cork and Seal Company.

Painter not only invented the new cap but designed, as well, the machinery to make it and apply it to bottles.

Painter had factories throughout the world, and was the active head of his company until five years before his death. His final patent was granted posthumously.

XEROGRAPHY

Chester Floyd Carlson, the man who invented the dry-copying machine to reproduce printed matter, drawings, and halftones on untreated paper, would have been in an earlier day the hero of an Horatio Alger do-or-die novel.

Penniless, the son of an immigrant, itinerant Swedish barber, and the sole support of his parents at the age of fourteen, Carlson worked his way to success and died a multimillionaire. He gave away a fortune to charities.

Carlson sounds too good to be true, and he was. Despite his openhandedness when he came into money, he leavened simplicity with shrewdness. He pursued a dream so relentlessly, to the exclusion of all else, that the first of his two wives divorced him. He didn't succeed by himself. Lucky breaks, one in particular, helped him.

He was elevated to sainthood by his heirs and assigns, and little wonder. His invention was the equivalent of a machine to print money. Men around him made fabulous profits. A taxi driver who bought a hundred shares at ten dollars each in a company that acquired the commercial rights to the Carlson process wound up with a fortune of a million and a half dollars, and the Xerox Corporation that Carlson made possible is, of course, one of the Cinderella stories of American business.

Chester Carlson was the son of Ellen Josephine and Olof Adolph Carlson. His mother died while he was washing windows, sweeping out stores and offices, and acting as a printer's devil to bring money into the house. His father was too arthritic to work. Yet young Carlson managed to gain a B.S. in physics at the California Institute of Technology (and later donated millions to his alma mater). He emerged from college $1,400 in debt in the middle of the Great Depression. He received only two replies to eighty-two applications he mailed out seeking work, and settled for thirty-five dollars a week as a research engineer at the Bell Telephone Laboratories in New York. He had an immense personal drive. He studied at night to become an expert in patent law.

It was his frustration over difficulties in obtaining copies of documents and drawings that led him into experiments to obtain reproductions almost instantaneously. The only methods extant were by photography and the Photostat process, both slow. By courtesy of his mother-in-law, Carlson established a lab in a bare room behind a beauty parlor in New York's borough of Queens. There, with the help of Otto Kornei, a German refugee engineer, on October 22, 1938, Carlson succeeded after three years in producing an image by a dry process.

He inked the date and the word "Astoria" on a glass slide. He rubbed a sulphur-coated metal plate with a pocket handkerchief to give it a static electric charge. With the slide on top of the metal, he exposed it under a flood lamp for three minutes. When he dusted the plate with powder, his inked inscription appeared. He had invented the world's first process of electrostatic copying, subsequently named xerography for the Greek words "dry" and "writing."

In 1937 he had filed a patent application for purely theoretical "electrophotography," and tried peddling his idea to the fat cats of the industrial world, among them the Radio Corporation of America, International Business Machines, Remington Rand, and General Electric. Everyone turned him down with what he later described as "an enthusiastic lack of interest."

By 1944 with his own slender resources he had patented his copying machine. It still needed a vast amount of work. Ten years had elapsed since he had begun his experiments. In that same year he described his invention in a magazine, *Radio News,* and demonstrated his process at the Battelle Memorial Institute of Columbus, Ohio, a privately endowed research organization. Battelle agreed to carry on

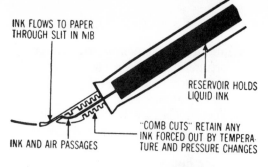

INK FLOWS TO PAPER THROUGH SLIT IN NIB

RESERVOIR HOLDS LIQUID INK

"COMB CUTS" RETAIN ANY INK FORCED OUT BY TEMPERATURE AND PRESSURE CHANGES

INK AND AIR PASSAGES

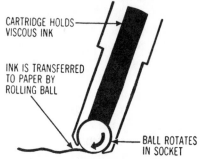

CARTRIDGE HOLDS VISCOUS INK

INK IS TRANSFERRED TO PAPER BY ROLLING BALL

BALL ROTATES IN SOCKET

Parking meters endured a rough introduction. Merchants complained. Vigilantes wanted to chop them down. Today, in hundreds of thousands, they decorate curbs everywhere and enrich city coffers.

The fountain pen was the result of an accident, and the ball-point pen was a disaster until a Hungarian refugee Ladislas Biro, re-invented it. Today the latter type is manufactured by the billions each year everywhere.

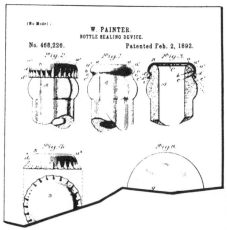

William Painter, the inventor of the fabulously successful crown bottle cap—the kind you pry off—patented scores of other things, including a counterfeit-coin detector. That was back in 1859. He was only twenty-one at the time.

The dry copying machine, shown here with its inventor, Chester Carlson, was another device that was a long time a-borning. The Xerox copier was twenty-four years from idea to financial success. At one point Carlson carried his lunch in a paper sack to save money.

Wrap Your *Christmas Gifts*
IN CELLOPHANE

Cellophane, taken for granted the world over as a wrapping, was far from being a marketable product when the idea was bought by du Pont from Jacques Brandenberger, left, in 1923. The company's researchers produced moistureproof cellophane, another type that sealed under heat and pressure, and still another that demoisturized foods.

King Gillette, inventor of the safety razor, said in his patent application his main object was to provide a thin blade that could be discarded. It was a tough goal. "If I had been technically trained," he remarked later, "I would have quit." He had to hire a man to invent the blades for him. Immensely rich in the end, he lost most of his money to poor investments and fights over control of his company.

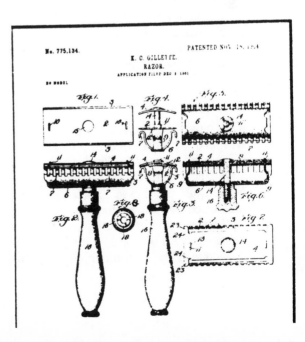

some research for him. It didn't put up a lot of money. Carlson, on his uppers, carried his lunch to work in a brown paper bag.

Then came his big break. A year after the magazine article appeared, it fell into the hands of Dr. John H. Dessauer, research director for the Haloid Company, a manufacturer of photocopy machines and the paper for them. Dessauer's company was in no great shape financially and needed an exciting new product. Haloid acquired the commercial rights to Carlson's invention. In 1948 Haloid and the Battelle institute jointly demonstrated the process publicly. The coined trade name "Xerox" entered the language.

Haloid's dry copiers were not an instant success. It was eleven years after the first public demonstration before Haloid, become the Xerox Corporation, achieved a reverberating sale with a model designated the "914" because it made copies on paper measuring 9 by 14 inches.

Carlson never went on the Haloid payroll. He remained a consultant, and by a neat arrangement with Battelle he profited enormously.

The Xerox story is told in a book by Dessauer, *My Years with Xerox* (Manor Books). As he relates, instant dry-copy reproduction has not proved an unmixed blessing. To keep from being buried in paper, hundreds of business houses put locks on their copiers. The federal government alone owns 60,000 copying machines. With each government department jealously guarding its files, 500,000 square feet of storage space must be added yearly to accommodate the output of Carlson's invention and those of competitive manufacturers. As Carlson's primary patents expired, forty-odd other companies put their own versions of dry copiers on the market.

Carlson's first crude model is on display at the Smithsonian Institution in Washington, D.C.

At sixty-two, on September 19, 1968, Carlson was found mortally ill in a seat at a New York movie theater.

He actually did become a Horatio Alger hero. Among the many honors heaped upon him was a Horatio Alger Award.

CELLOPHANE

The closest approach to any intimate glimpse of the man who wrapped the world in cellophane was an article many years ago in the *Christian Science Monitor* by a daughter, Irma:

"Struggling to open the tight, transparent wrapper on the package he had just purchased, my father turned to me in mock exasperation and asked, 'Who was the joker who invented cellophane?'

"Not every child could have answered that question, but to me it came easily. 'You, Daddy,' I said, laughing."

Jacques Edwin Brandenberger, a Swiss, was a curious amalgam of inventor, business executive, engineer, and sales pitchman. Unlike most inventors, he was a businessman of exceptional shrewdness. He knew the value of a franc. He had an upper-class elegance and a dignified reserve that was almost monastic. He disliked exploitation of his person. In consequence, few of his traits were exposed to the public except as they were reflected in his career. Anxious that Brandenberger be given his just due by history, a nephew, Dr. Ernst Brandenberger, in 1972, on the hundredth anniversary of the inventor's birth, sought circulation of a monograph on him in the United States. Jacques Brandenberger probably would have been the first to disown it. It was syrupy, poorly written, and bespoke little of the man.

He had pronounced aesthetic interests. He had a fondness for Europe's seventeenth century and for the Versailles of Louis XV in the eighteenth, and he loved to acquire antiques of these periods.

In the classic sense, Brandenberger invented cellophane (a generic noun) by stumbling on to it. He was graduated summa cum laude at twenty-two by the University of Bern with a doctorate in philosophy, but he had laid the groundwork for his forays into chemistry at the Technical Institute in Winterthur. In France and Bohemia he worked in dye houses, bleaching works, fabric-printing factories, and textile chemical plants. He began experimenting with viscose, a viscous solution made by treating wood pulp with sodium hydroxide and carbon disulfide. (Cotton linters or peanut shells would have served almost as well.) Cellophane is nothing more than viscose, regenerated cellulose, solidified as a thin sheet instead of as a thread, as in rayon.

By nine years after his graduation from the university—as the youngest man in Switzerland with a doctorate—Brandenberger had become manager of a large French textile firm and had been issued a patent for a new type of mercerizing machine.

As early as 1882 a process for making a film of regenerated cellulose by denitrating—removing from it the nitric-acid group of compounds—had been described in patent papers in the United States. Brandenberger's insatiable curiosity led him, about the turn of the century, to experiment with making tablecloths impervious to dirt and stains by treating them with a cellulose solution. He produced a smooth, sparkling cloth, but it was stiff and brittle. Then he tried coating the cloth with a thin sheet of viscose film. As a salable item, the cloth was a bust, but the sheet of film offered possibilities. He had hit on what in the end he would name cellophane. For most of ten years he experimented not with the product but with machinery to produce it, and more as a hobby than a priority item. In 1908 he patented the production process, and three years later a factory of a company named La Cellophane began turning the stuff out. Brandenberger had named it by combining "cello" from cellulose with the last syllable of the French word *diaphane,* meaning transparent.

Methodically, he protected himself by patents at home and abroad.

Possibly he had dawdled because he failed to recognize the value of his discovery. That was understandable. The transparent sheeting was too thick for ready handling in packaging, and it was expensive— $2.65 a pound. To wrap a loaf of bread in it would have cost a prohibitive two cents. It was used primarily to sheathe luxury goods, such as perfume. Because of its cost, some packagers kept their stocks of it in the company safe. Brandenberger succeeded in reducing the thickness to .0078 of an inch and the weight to .863 of an ounce per 1.196 square yards.

Here his sense of salesmanship asserted itself. He opened a select cellophane display store in the Chaussée-d'Antin, near the Boulevard Haussmann, a lively Parisian shopping district. He wrapped expensive products in cellophane. At his urging, the French magazine *L'Illustration* attached a sheet of cellophane to its 1912 Christmas issue. Cellophane had its merits. Perhaps the chief one was that in manufacture it picked up no static charge and therefore collected no dust. But as a sales item it wasn't all that good. It was permeable and later, in the United States, it failed at first as a protective cigar wrapper.

Enter now into the Brandenberger fortunes America's E. I. du Pont de Nemours & Company. Whereas in Europe Brandenberger had had his hand in everything pertaining to cellophane, from production machines, to inks for printing on it, to advertising and sales, du Pont was a different kettle of fish. For one thing du Pont operated in the hurly-burly world of intense competition. For another, this colossus of industry had a reservoir of technical talent matched in few places in the world. In 1923 du Pont was licensed to produce cellophane. It galled the nabobs of the Wilmington, Delaware, empire to buy anything abroad (which meant outside its own immediate precincts). But Brandenberger, chairman of his board and chief operating officer, had an impregnable patent position. He didn't want money. He was dumb like a fox. He wanted du Pont stock, and in return for the license he got a big chunk of it. He knew du Pont would improve cellophane.

Improve it, it did. Quite early it was sued by a knife manufacturer because his cellophane-wrapped product had rusted. So, four years later, du Pont introduced moistureproof cellophane. Then it devised a way to seal cellophane under heat and pressure. Look into the butcher departments of supermarkets today and you can see workers ironing the stuff on meats. Du Pont's Dr. Hale Charch headed the research team for these and other improvements. Du Pont reduced prices 75 per cent to compete with other flexible packing materials such as waxed paper and glassine, and other films, notably polyethylene and polypropylene. Patent suits sprang up, and lawyers jawed at each other in and out of court. When the fur stopped flying, two other American manufacturers had been licensed to produce cellophane. Gag advertising flourished. One ad pictured a stork wrapped in cellophane, with the legend, "All the best things come wrapped in cellophane." A magazine ran a cartoon of a new father looking on his child in a hospital and exclaiming, "What, no cellophane?"

Meantime, Brandenberger sat quietly at home counting his money. He had had a good life. Licensed factories in other countries were producing cellophane. He had research credits other than cellophane, including the invention of hollow-fiber artificial silk. For his efforts to promote French industry, he was appointed chevalier and made an officer of the Legion of Honor. America's Franklin Institute awarded him a gold medal—he joined Henry Ford, Orville Wright, Alexander Graham Bell, and Pierre and Marie Curie as its recipients. He died at eighty-one and is buried in his native Zurich. "I am at home in Paris," he had said, "but my home is Pfäffikon [Zurich]."

A hundred years after his birth there were more than seventy-five types of du Pont cellophane alone, with differing degrees of moistureproofness. They were further tailored to individual wrapping jobs with varying degrees of oxygen permeability, heat-sealing properties, and other characteristics. Some types were engineered to let moisture *escape* and thereby forestall mold in products they enclosed.

U.S. cellophane production in 1924 was about 500,000 pounds. The world's annual production of it as of 1972 was estimated at almost 600,000 *tons*. Three fourths of it was consumed by food industries.

RAZORS

The inventor of the safety razor and the inventor of the electric razor were brothers under the skin—both were weighed down with financial troubles.

The "safety" kind

King Camp Gillette is recognized throughout the world as the inventor of the safety razor. That's not quite accurate. First of all, at least three other "safety" razors, consisting of a blade clamped between two plates and attached to a handle, preceded Gillette's. Second, had it not been for a skilled technician in his pay who developed a process for hardening and sharpening thin sheet steel, Gillette would just have been another name in the telephone directory. He did have a better idea for a safety razor. But as he later remarked of his long search for a design and money to produce the product, "If I had been technically trained, I would have quit."

Gillette was thirty-five years old before he began tiring of his role as a bottle-stopper salesman, and cast around for something—anything —to invent and manufacture. He actually worked his way through the alphabet trying to think of something. Then, one day, standing in front of his mirror, chopping away at the stubble on his chin with a straightedge, it hit him. Why not a razor with presharpened, disposable blades, plus a guard to keep a man from cutting himself? Previous attempts at this had used a segment of a straightedge that had to be honed periodically.

The disposable blades of hardened steel proved to be the lesser of Gillette's problems. His technician finally produced them. What stood between him and riches was financing. Nobody believed in his idea. One man was foxed into buying 500 shares in Gillette's company at $.50 a share. Some years later Gillette bought the shares back for $62,500. But for the moment King Gillette was at dead center. It was eleven years before he put his safety razor on sale—in the same month and year, December 1903, that the Wright Brothers first flew at Kitty Hawk, North Carolina.

The Gillette was hardly an immediate success. Sales grew at a maddeningly slow pace. Men were wedded to their old straightedges. It took a world war to make Gillette wealthy. The U. S. Government bought his razors by the hundreds of thousands for its soldiers (profligate as always with the taxpayer's money in time of war), and the soldiers "liberated" such government property when they were mustered out. Gillette knew he had it made when, after the war, railroad Pullman washrooms installed slots above the basins to discard used blades.

Razors sold for a dollar. It was on the blades that Gillette made his money. As his patents expired he renewed them with improvements, but hundreds of other disposable blades appeared on the market. Nonetheless, Gillette led the field. The name had become synonymous with razors and blades.

Despite vast riches, King Gillette died in reduced circumstances at seventy-seven. Questionable investments and a fight over control of his company reduced his estate to only a million dollars.

The electric kind

The electric razor could be said, without great abuse of the truth, to have been the product of a sprained ankle.

Jacob Schick, who in due time turned his talents toward electric-shaver design, displayed excess energy even at the age of sixteen. He was in full charge of building a branch railroad line to a New Mexican coal mine. Come of age, he joined the U. S. Army, serving in the Philippines and Alaska. He was a hopelessly inveterate inventor. In Alaska he designed a new type of boat for the upper waters of the Yukon River that carried fifty tons of cargo and drew only a foot of water. He put various inventions on the market, among them a couple of devices for sharpening pencils, but they only provided him with fiddling money.

Retiring from the Army in 1910, he spent four years on mining explorations in British Columbia. With the temperature at forty degrees below zero, he grew annoyed with heating water to shave. Then he sprained his ankle and had to stay in camp for weeks. He killed and lived on a moose and, for want of something else to do, fretted over the shaving problem. Finally he designed a razor—non-electric—that didn't require soap and water. Off to a manufacturer went his drawings, to be returned with a rejection slip.

Back on active duty in World War I, and mustered out in 1918, he was still preoccupied with the subject of shaving. Now he decided to invent an electric razor. He was strapped for money. His wife Florence mortgaged their home in Stamford, Connecticut, for $10,000 to support them. Other inventors were on the same track. The July 1919 issue of *Popular Science* carried an advertisement for a "vibrating electric razor" called LekTroShave. Whatever happened to it is lost in limbo.

It was eleven years after the war before Jacob Schick got his electric shaver on the market. Sales rode a snail's back. In later years one of the early purchasers reported, "It shaved you with a loud buzz and an aroma of hot lubricating oil. Tiring of my perpetual do-I-need-a-shave? look and feel, I went back to my trusty Gillette."

Schicks improved. By the time Jacob Schick died in 1937 at fifty-nine, a retired lieutenant colonel, his razor had begun cutting into Gillette's market. Other electrics followed. Some had rotating blades. Some had cutters that raced back and forth like shuttlecocks. But all employed the Schick principle: like a barbershop hair clipper, a series of fixed slots to plow up the hair, a series of moving blades to snip it off.

NYLON

Just after World War II, a giant model of a woman's leg, thirty-five feet high, sheathed in a stocking, was put on public display in Los Angeles as an advertisement for a new kind of fabric. If a man named Wallace Hume Carothers had seen it, he would have been astonished, abashed, and—considering his temperament—mildly indignant. Dr. Carothers had created the fabric. He never saw the giant display

Then came the electric razors. The man pictured above shows what it was like to shave with an electric forty-five years ago. In the photo at the left is the first commercial shaver put on the market by Jacob Schick, father of electric shaving.

This (right) was an electric shaver? Well, almost. Schick used this experimental shaver, driven by a regular machine shop motor and flexible cable, to develop a cutting-head design. He obtained key patents based on information he got from it.

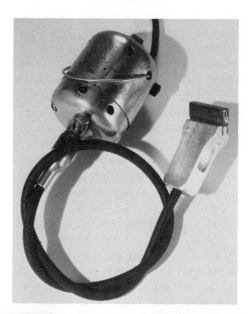

And here (below) are samples of what has happened to electric shavers since Jacob Schick first proposed the idea. Multiple heads have proliferated. Cutting-head design varies widely. Shavers come both corded and cordless. But all use Schick's basic principle. Pictured (L to R) are the Schick, Ronson Cordless, and Norelco Tripleheader.

As a substitute for silk, nylon, a wholly synthetic fiber, made its mark in World War II when the United States was cut off from the Japanese product. Nylon went into tire cord, combat clothing, and jungle hammocks. After the war this huge woman's calf (left) advertised stockings. Above is a photograph of the inventor, Wallace Hume Carothers.

Dorothy Rodgers (right), wife of the famed composer Richard Rodgers, is a columnist, a decorator, and an inventor. During World War II she found herself engaged in menial tasks, previously entrusted to servants, including cleaning bathrooms. She thereupon invented and patented (see below) a disposable swab, the Jonny Mop, which she sold to Johnson & Johnson.

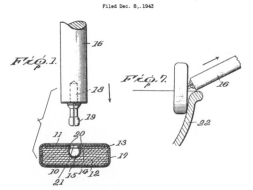

June 25, 1946.   D. F. RODGERS   2,402,577
CLEANING DEVICE
Filed Dec. 8,. 1943

because he had been dead for nine years—by his own hand. His death was a poignant footnote to a brilliant career.

Carothers was one of the greater chemical scientists of the century. It was he who directed a team of other research chemists to the development of nylon, which replaced silk for women's hosiery, and in the years that followed led to a spin-off of a whole family of other products at E. I. du Pont de Nemours & Company in Wilmington, Delaware—among them Orlon, Dacron, and Lycra. Nylon (a generic noun) went on to thousands of uses, from dress fabrics to boat sails, to ropes and parachutes, to gunstocks and steel-hard electric-shaver bearings, depending on the nature of the compounding.

Carothers was a bookish-looking bespectacled man, described by the unscientific as an egghead. If he was humorless, he made up for it in gentleness. An Iowan by birth, the eldest of four children, he enjoyed tools—anything mechanical—as a boy, and read voraciously. He sopped up *Gulliver's Travels,* Mark Twain's books, studies of the life of Edison, and works by the giants of nineteenth-century English literature. In high school he got immersed in chemistry, and converted his bedroom into a laboratory. Boyhood friends knew him as "Doc" or "Professor." He loved classical music. In later years he remarked occasionally that if he were to start over again, he would devote his life to music. He was deeply emotional and shy. He would lapse into silence when in a group of people, but give him an audience of one and his conversation sparkled. His parental forebears, of Scotch and Scotch-Irish ancestry, were farmers and artisans. Wallace Carothers was his family's first scientist.

Thoroughness marked his performance in school. On entering college he rapidly outdistanced his classmates in chemistry and the physical sciences, even though a financial shortfall forced him to work to pay for his education. From Missouri's Tarkio College and the University of Illinois he drifted into teaching at the universities of South Dakota and Illinois and at Harvard University. James B. Conant, then Harvard's president, said of him, "Although he was always loath to speak in public even at scientific meetings, his diffidence seemed to disappear in the classroom." He achieved a Ph.D. degree and the honor of the highest fellowship award offered by the Illinois chemistry department.

But inwardly he was fretting. Teaching was not his bag. He was always off in a laboratory somewhere among test tubes. At thirty-two, he had to make a choice. Du Pont was embarking on a program of fundamental—as opposed to product-oriented—research, and Carothers was offered the chairmanship of organic chemistry. If he hesitated at being swallowed up in a vast industrial complex, it was only briefly. Its laboratories offered far more facilities than a university. He was given carte blanche. He could putter around on anything he chose, and with a staff to boot. He moved into one of the scores of research buildings at Wilmington, each equipped with slides at upper windows so that workers could bid quick adieu to the premises if an experiment got out of hand.

One of his first projects was a study of a chemical group known as acetylene polymers. Research chemists had been chary of tackling polymers. They were thought to be colloidal in nature, intractable, and not subject to known physiochemical laws. Carothers laid the ghosts of that belief. Probing into acetylene polymers led to the development of neoprene synthetic rubber, widely used today in such products as gasoline and oil hose, garden hose, insulated wire, and gloves.

But Carothers' outstanding scientific achievement was in the field of linear polymers. He had long been eager to try synthesizing compounds of high molecular weight. It was known that certain molecules combined to form "giant" molecules, as in such substances as silk, cotton, and natural rubber.

Carothers had his eye on a wholly synthetic fiber. Rayon, of course, was not. It was regenerated cellulose, and had been stumbled upon by France's Count Hilaire de Chardonnet in 1878. One day while he was coating some photographic plates with collodion the bottle slipped and broke on his table. When he tried to clean up the mess some time later, the partly dried collodion stretched into long threads. With that as a start, Chardonnet worked to perfect a thread that could be produced commercially, and six years later produced his first one from a nitrocellulose solution of mulberry-leaf pulp, coagulated into filaments in heated air. His "Chardonnet silk," to become known as rayon, was the hit of the Paris Exposition in 1889.

Four decades later a Carothers assistant, Julian W. Hill, fresh from the Massachusetts Institute of Technology, put a polyester, previously synthesized in Carothers' labs, into a high-vacuum distillation apparatus. From it after several days of cooking he drew long streamers that hardened into opaque, brittle strands. They were easily broken, but if tugged on at either end they could be stretched to several times their original length. What was more, they snapped back to their original length, if not stretched beyond their high elastic limit.

Hill had synthetic giant molecules in his hand. A lack of elasticity was a major shortcoming of rayon, in which du Pont had quite a stake. Rayon came from cellulose, common in nature. Hill's substance was composed of coal, water, and air. The phenomenon demonstrated, Carothers reported, "for the first time the possibility of obtaining useful fibers from strictly synthetic materials."

Carothers was standing on the edge of immortality in research circles. His team now had a long-chain, or linear, polymer. The stretching process had aligned the molecules into long parallel bundles equivalent to those of natural fibers like silk or cotton. But while a laboratory wonder, the stuff was not commercially producible. It was rather structurally weak and had a low melting point. Four years elapsed. Carothers tried several thousand chemical combinations and produced hundreds of fibers. None was satisfactory. The atmosphere around the organic-chemical labs was gloomy. The "patient money," as du Pont's funds for basic research were called, could run out. C. M. A. Stine, du Pont's chemical director, stood staunchly behind Carothers. Let the man be, he said.

Then, one day in 1934, Dr. Carothers himself squeezed through a hypodermic needle a thread of the first fully practical synthetic fiber and turned it over to the development chemists and production engineers. A new compound had been shaken up in a test tube, and tremors were felt around the world.

Known only as "Fiber 66" until 1938, it was first used in toothbrushes. It scored its first marketing triumph—by now named nylon—as hosiery in 1940. Then came the war. In the absence of Japanese silk almost four million nylon parachutes were produced, along with airplane-tire cord, combat clothing, netting and hammocks for the jungle, and life rafts. A sex-image movie actress, Betty Grable, auctioned off once-worn stockings for as high as $40,000 each in behalf of the war effort. A pair of nylons in a soldier's pocket bought romance in London, Paris, Rome, Athens, Moscow, and, postwar, in the ruins of Berlin.

Dr. Carothers didn't live to see any of this. He was devoted to a sister, Isobel, a radio performer of some fame, and was never able to reconcile himself to her death in January 1936. He became obsessed with the thought that his life's work had gone for nothing, even though in that same year he had been elected to the National Academy of Sciences, the first organic chemist in industry to be so honored. Fits of depression, that had been descending on him, grew. On April 29, 1937, two days after his forty-first birthday, he took his own life. His colleagues said he had created a world he never saw.

Behind him were more than fifty patents. He had accomplished in nine years what most men would take a lifetime to achieve. Nylon was patented posthumously in his name. He was survived by his widow, Helen, herself with a bachelor's degree in chemistry. A daughter, Jane, was born after his death.

ELECTRIC CLOCK

The idea for clocks not actuated by weights or springs was already three quarters of a century old when Henry Ellis Warren, a graduate of the Massachusetts Institute of Technology, began addressing himself to electric clocks.

The Dictionary of Inventions and Discoveries, edited by E. F. Carter, dates the "devising" of electric clocks from 1840, when England's Sir Charles Wheatstone is of record on the subject. In the next few years several inventors proposed or patented electric clocks. The first U.S. patent for an electric clock was taken out by an A. Hull of Lloydsville, Ohio, in 1873.

So Henry Warren didn't invent the electric clock. The earlier idea of a gnat-power motor to turn the hands was sound. The trouble was that an electric clock wouldn't keep good time, and the problem lay in regulating the frequency of alternating current purveyed by generating stations. The frequency had to be rigidly maintained, and clock motors had to be made synchronous with the dynamos that produced the current, if clocks were to be accurate.

Warren was a natural inventor. At his death he held a hundred patents. As a boy he rigged up a gas engine to run his mother's sewing machine, and an automatic chicken feeder. His first patent after his graduation from MIT was a method of taking temperatures by a "thermophone" at a distance or underwater.

The electric-clock problem fascinated him. He worked on it in his first laboratory, an unused hen house. Direct current was, of course, out of the question for clock actuation. The current had to be cycled for synchronous operation. That posed the problem. Electricity was supplied from a large number of generating stations, varying in size. There was no standard frequency—the number of complete to-and-fro cycles of current per second. Moreover, the stated frequency ran a discrepancy of a cycle or two above or below in actual delivery. This made little difference in the operation of motors or lamps. But a motor-driven clock could be off by many minutes a day if it was designed for sixty cycles and the current feeding it was fifty-nine or sixty-one.

Warren invented a master clock to monitor generator output. It detected a thousandth-of-a-second variation in generator revolutions, and hence of frequency. Today the accuracy of master clocks in the U.S. is checked regularly by radio signals from the Naval Observatory in Washington, D.C.

Warren's synchronous "Telechron" electric clock for the consumer was a useful application of the uniform timing of successive cycles of electrical pulses from a generator. It certainly didn't complicate matters for him when U.S. grids adopted sixty-cycle current output—with sixty seconds in a minute and sixty minutes in an hour.

His first master clock was installed at the Boston Edison Company in 1916. He himself estimated that within ten years twenty million persons were using electric clocks. Warren founded the Warren

Telechron Company, and was its president from 1914 to 1943. General Electric purchased a half-interest in the firm in 1929 and full control in 1943.

Among his other inventions were an oilless clock, a device used on astronomical telescopes to track stars automatically, and fire-control mechanisms for guns. From 1919 to 1940 he was a consulting engineer to General Electric. He received awards from the American Institute of Electrical Engineers and the Franklin Institute. He died at eighty-five.

PAPER BAG

Margaret E. Knight—"Mattie" to her friends—was not in her early years the kind of little girl who played with dolls. As quoted by Robert W. Lovett in *Notable American Women 1607–1950,* edited by E. T. James and J. W. James (Belknap Press of Harvard University Press, 1971). "I never cared for the things that girls usually do." She was famous in her neighborhood for her kites and sleds. Born in York, Maine, she and her family moved to Manchester, New Hampshire, and it was there that she produced her first invention. It was a contrivance to shut down a textile loom automatically when a steel-tipped shuttle accidentally fell out. It was designed to prevent injury to workmen. She was only twelve years old. She didn't patent the thing.

A big, strongly built woman with a gentle voice as she matured, Mattie Knight began looking with curiosity at paper bags. She did not invent the paper bag. Whoever was responsible for that is lost to history. She only made it practical by devising machinery to produce it with a flat bottom. It was only an improvement on existing manufacturing methods for producing bags. But every shopper who loads up at the supermarket today is indebted to her. She was thirty-two when she took out the patent for this, her first registered invention.

Her output of ideas was impressive. She invented a dress and skirt shield, a clasp for holding robes, and a spit, and obtained a half-dozen patents or assignments on shoe-making machines. Undaunted by the complexity of ideas she tackled, she even designed, and patented, a sleeve-valve automobile engine as an alternative to the poppet valve.

At her death in 1914, at seventy-six, she was described in one obituary as a "Lady Edison." That was stretching a point, as even she probably would have said. She was not even the first woman to be granted a U.S. patent. That honor went to Sybilla Masters in 1715 for a system, credited in that age of male chauvinism to her husband, for pulverizing maize. A year later she obtained a patent for "working and staining in straw." In the following century, in 1809, a Mary Kies obtained a patent for straw weaving with silk or thread.

But Mattie Knight made her mark for her sex. Apparently it didn't do her much good financially. Her personal estate was appraised at $275.05.

JONNY MOP

A more successful inventress than Mattie Knight—financially at least —is the wife of the world-famed composer Richard Rodgers. Author of two best-selling books about her own houses beautiful, *My Favorite Things* and *The House in My Head,* co-author with her daughter Mary of a book, *A Word to the Wives,* and, again with Mary, of a monthly column for a women's magazine, decorator, hostess extraordinary, Dorothy Rodgers has several profitable patents to her credit. During World War II she found herself engaged around her home in menial tasks normally entrusted to servants not then available. Those tasks included cleaning bathrooms; necessity indeed became the mother of invention for she thereupon conceived of a disposable swab, which she patented and sold to Johnson & Johnson. The Jonny Mop made her a small fortune before her patent, number 2,402,577 ("Cleaning Device"), ran out in 1963. "A desideratum in devices of this character," reads the patentese in a paragraph of the application, "is . . . maximum ease of disposability with minimum impairment of cleaning capacity."

As often happens to inventors, Mrs. Rodgers had to fight for her rights in court; her suit against the giant company for unpaid royalties in dispute ended in arbitration which she won by an unanimous vote of the arbitrators.

Jonny Mop was not her first or only invention. In the late thirties she conceived of what she calls a "people-cooling device"—a bracelet for ladies, a watch strap for men, holding dry ice. When her collaborating chemist died she abandoned the idea. Eighteen years later another inventor patented a similar device. Mrs. Rodgers invented a method of making dress patterns so they can be altered on a sewing machine and reused. She sold the idea to McCall Patterns and collects an annual fee from that company. An educational device of hers was patented and sold to the Ideal Toy Company. One of her most dramatic inventions was a device to rescue children accidentally locked in refrigerators, a fairly frequent disaster which appalled her. Even though the cost of the improvement was less than a dollar, no refrigerator manufacturer would touch it, possibly because of the morbid implications of the need this lady inventor wanted to fill.

CHAPTER 3

Alexander Graham Bell— The Man Who Always Wondered

ONE AUGUST morning in 1906, at his summer retreat in Nova Scotia, Alexander Graham Bell was roused from a dream about kites—his latest scientific preoccupation—with the news that a grandson had been born. Still half asleep, Bell dreamily asked: "Can it fly?"

What sort of man was this? One who combined a soaring imagination with an insatiable need to know (Bell's son-in-law, David Fairchild, once said "Wondering to him was almost a passion.") Together with a bulldog persistence, these qualities shaped an extraordinarily successful, multifaceted career.

Bell was one of the most idolized men of his time, a world traveler, society lion, and hobnobber with the great. The invention of the telephone alone would have assured him all this. But there was much, much more. A list of the things Bell invented or helped develop is wonderfully varied: a hydrofoil boat that held the world's speed record for ten years; a phonograph; a "vacuum jacket" that was the precursor of the iron lung; air conditioning; a telephonic bullet probe; scientific sheep breeding; the audiometer; a light-beam telephone; man-carrying kites; an airplane.

And his activities outside the realm of invention were both abundant and rewarding to his fellowman. He helped establish *Science* magazine; was the second president of the National Geographic Society and launched its successful magazine; and was a regent of the Smithsonian Institution. He was an early sponsor of the Montessori method of early childhood education in this country. And throughout his life, he was a gifted speech teacher, devoted to the problems of the deaf. (Whenever he was asked to list his occupation, the father of the telephone answered, "teacher of the deaf.") Toward this goal, he gave some half million dollars in charity.

All in all, one might think, enough to satisfy any man—even a

Alexander Melville Bell, Alexander Graham Bell's father in 1868 was a successful professor of speech and elocution, and had just published *Visible Speech*, a pioneer attempt to reduce all speech sounds to symbols.

A dapper sixteen, Alexander Graham Bell became a pupil-teacher in elocution and music in a school at Elgin, on the Scottish coast. He spent several years there.

Eliza Grace Bell, née Symonds, was Aleck's mother and a talented miniature-painter. Deeply religious, she was some ten years older than her husband, who wrote he never saw her frown.

Bell launched his American career by becoming a teacher of the deaf. This 1871 photo shows him (top row, right) with his pupils at the Boston School for the Deaf.

titan. But the great irony of Bell's long and singular life is that for most of it he was haunted by a baseless fear; that his supreme achievement, the telephone, had come so early (at age twenty-nine) it would rob the rest of his work of real meaning. "I can't bear to hear," he wrote in 1879, "that even my friends should think I stumbled upon an invention and there is no more good in me." Perhaps, for Bell, if fame could not be the spur, fear was.

Alexander Bell (he gave himself the middle name of Graham on his eleventh birthday) was born in Edinburgh, Scotland, on March 3, 1847 . . . the same year as Edison. Aleck was named after two previous Bells, prophetically, for rarely has a great man's lineage been so visible in his own life.

Aleck's was a family of Scottish speech specialists and actors. His grandfather, the first Alexander Bell, was a stage comedian, then prospered giving speech and elocution lessons. He published a book on stammering, and one called *The Practical Elocutionist* that used symbols to show phrasing and stress. By the time he was forty-eight, an account of one of his public recitations referred to him as "the celebrated Professor of Elocution."

One of Grandfather Bell's sons was David Charles Bell, who became a teacher of speech and a Shakespearean actor. Aleck's uncle David struck a young George Bernard Shaw as being "by far the most majestic and impressive looking man that ever lived on this or any other planet." (All the Bell men seemed to have had compelling physical appearance, magnetic personal presence, and magnificent voice.)

Aleck's own father, Alexander Melville Bell, was an internationally known teacher of speech and elocution, a phonetician who invented "Visible Speech." This was an influential pioneer system for representing, on paper, any speech sound in any language, using symbols for the placement and movement of throat, tongue, and lips. Alexander Melville may even have inspired the character in Shaw's *Pygmalion* who transmutes base cockney into noble English—Professor Henry Higgins.

Aleck's mother, née Eliza Grace Symonds, was the daughter of a naval surgeon. A painter of miniatures, living with her widowed mother in Edinburgh, she was thirty-four when she met Alexander Melville Bell in 1843, ten years older than he. And she was already quite deaf, relying on an ear tube to hear at all. (You can see it lying coiled in her lap in the portrait photo in this chapter.) Remarkably, she was also a talented pianist; she could monitor her playing only by using the mouthpiece of her ear tube to pick up the vibrations from the piano's sounding board. In outlook, she was much different from Aleck's father—deeply religious and observant where he was careless of the strict Scottish Sabbath rules and somewhat skeptical—but their

Bell's "harmonic telegraph" (above) gave him a clue to the principle of telephony when he heard its steel reed twang. But his first telephone (below) of 1875 couldn't make words intelligible.

Bell's backer Gardiner Greene Hubbard urged him to develop the harmonic telegraph. Bell stubbornly invented the first successful telephone instead.

In the time-hallowed version of the telephone's first words," Bell spills battery acid, cries "Mr. Watson, come here—I want you!" Tom Watson (right) says he heard every word.

marriage seems to have been blissfully calm. After she died in 1897, Alexander Melville Bell wrote: "She was so kind, so gentle, so loving, that during the fifty-two years of our companionship, I never saw a frown on her sweet face."

In his early childhood, at least, Aleck's predilections and talents seemed strongly molded by his mother. He was a pious little boy, even taking his father to task for not being sufficiently reflective on Sundays. He became so adept musically that his mother retained a well-known pianist, Auguste Benoit Bertini, to give him lessons. For a while, both master and pupil dreamed of a great concert career. Aleck eventually went other ways, but never lost his love for the piano.

Like so many other brilliant men, Aleck had a lackluster record in school. With his older brother Melly (Melville James) and his younger brother Ted (Edward Charles) he attended the Royal High School. He hated Latin and Greek, was stultified by the rote work in mathematics, and never ventured to take any science courses at all. Outside school, however, Aleck was developing a lively interest in the natural world. He collected plants (but strongly resisted labeling them with their correct Latin names). He dissected animals. He learned to prepare and develop the clumsy glass photographic plates of the day. And, around age fourteen, he produced his first real invention, at the instigation of a friend's father, who owned a flour mill called, coincidentally, Bell's Mill. The problem was to remove the husks from wheat before it was ground. When Aleck found that a stiff-bristled nail brush would do the job, and remembered seeing a device at the mill that used rotating paddles, he melded the two ideas, suggesting a rotary brushing wheel. His friend's father had one built, and it worked so well he used it happily for years.

In 1862, the fifteen-year-old inventor made a move that he later described as "the turning point of my life." Leaving school after only four years instead of the full six-year curriculum (would it be merely facetious to call him a Royal High School dropout?), he joined his grandfather in London. Alexander Bell, seventy-two, was still teaching speech and elocution, a practice he immediately extended to young Aleck, whose declamatory gifts he burnished with joint readings from Shakespeare. He insisted also on transforming the adolescent's dress. Soon Aleck was turned out in full London gentleman's regalia, including kid gloves, top hat, and cane. Though he chafed somewhat at the restrictions of town life in London, his exposure to the magnificent old man gave him a new sense of independence and a seriousness of purpose he had never felt before. When he returned home after a year's visit, he had been "converted . . . from a boy somewhat prematurely into a man."

Before the trip back to Edinburgh, Aleck was taken by his father to the London workshop of the eminent electrical experimenter Sir Charles Wheatstone. Years before, Wheatstone had made his own contribution to the centuries-old effort to produce a "speaking machine"—a mechanical device that could mimic the human voice—and it was this that had led Alexander Melville Bell to his door. Wheatstone trotted out his venerable model, an improvement over an eighteenth-century design, and it dutifully though creakily delivered a few simple words and sentences. Once home, Aleck and Melly together built their own "speaking machine" by duplicating the human vocal apparatus out of assorted materials. Modeling their organs carefully from real ones, they assembled a tin tube throat; a rubber larynx; gutta-percha jaws, teeth, pharynx, and nasal cavities; rubber lips and cheeks; a rubber palate stuffed with cotton; and, most ingenious of all, a wooden, rubber-covered tongue in six segments that could be raised and lowered individually by levers, so as to shape and position the whole tongue naturally. For lungs, the boys relied on their own.

Through trial and error, Aleck learned how to adjust tongue, lips, and palate to get the desired sounds. Shakespeare was well beyond the machine's capacity. But its wailing "mama" was so lifelike that a neighbor solicitously inquired after "the baby's" welfare. The whole endeavor was an ideal one for a novice inventor to chew on. Moreover, it gave Aleck a sound and permanent grounding in the mechanics of speech production.

Clearly, it seemed, Aleck was to pursue the family intoxication with the spoken word. In 1863, a stately sixteen, he took a one-year job as teacher of elocution and music at Weston House, a boarding school for "young gentlemen" at Elgin on the northern coast of Scotland, and was a considerable success there. Returning from Elgin in the summer of 1864, he was plunged, with his brothers, into demonstrations of his father's revolutionary phonetic alphabet, "Visible Speech," which had finally been finished after a quarter-century's effort.

He took classes at the University of Edinburgh, returned to Weston House as an assistant master, and pursued his own researches into the puzzles of speech, investigating the exact pitch of vowel sounds with the aid of tuning forks set resonating in front of his mouth. When Aleck reported on his work to Alexander Ellis, a noted phonetician, Ellis told him that he was in fact independently duplicating an identical set of experiments that had been carried out by the illustrious scientist Hermann von Helmholtz. Ellis also mentioned that Helmholtz had used electromagnets to keep a number of tuning forks resonating simultaneously, and that he had been able to create vowel sounds by changing the loudness of the forks. Apparently, Bell somehow assumed that Helmholtz was actually transmitting the sounds from one point to another, via electricity. From this totally mistaken impression, the idea of telegraphing speech over a distance took root in his mind. It bore fruit ten years later, in the telephone.

For the next few years, Aleck continued to teach and to learn. In 1868 he began for the first time to teach deaf-mute children to speak, using his father's Visible Speech system. He began to experiment with electricity and telegraphy. With his mounting skill and experience, he became a partner in his father's practice, which had moved to London on the death of his grandfather. He took courses in anatomy and physiology at London's University College.

But the family successes were blighted by illness. Ted had died of tuberculosis in February 1870. In May of that year Melly—well established in a career essentially parallel to that of all the male Bells—died of the same disease. Aleck's father had been pondering emigrating to the Americas, where he saw rich opportunities. Besides, he had been much impressed by the bracing climate in Ontario on previous travels. The deaths of two of his sons within months, together with what seemed to be poor health in the remaining one, decided him. In July 1870, the family, including a reluctant Alexander Graham Bell, sailed for Brantford, Ontario. There, both his health and spirits quickly revived.

Now came another entrance of that theme of deafness which was to resound so importantly in Aleck's life. Sarah Fuller, head of the Boston School for Deaf Mutes (later the Horace Mann School) had been much impressed by Melville Bell's lectures on the use of Visible Speech in teaching the deaf. In 1871, Aleck went to Boston to teach at the school, where the success of his efforts confounded the prevailing idea that little more could be done for deaf-mutes than to teach them sign language. Shortly after, he also taught at the Clarke School for the Deaf in Northampton, where in a few weeks he taught children more than 400 English syllables.

One of the eminent Yankees much impressed by Bell's work was Gardiner Greene Hubbard, a successful businessman and lawyer, president of the Clarke School, and extremely active in the education of deaf children. His daughter Mabel had been left stone deaf by a bout of scarlet fever when she was five years old. Hubbard could not bear the thought of the traditional deaf-mute education, with its reliance on sign language, for his little girl, and managed to have her trained to speak by teachers using oral methods. The founding of the Clarke School was a direct outgrowth of his experience. Meeting in April 1872, Hubbard and Bell thus had much in common, and became good friends. They had, in fact, more in common than they were at first aware of. Hubbard was a patent attorney specializing in mechanical and electrical inventions; he was particularly intrigued by

Alexander Graham Bell at twenty-nine, a black-bearded
young man, has a confident air, as well he might have.
It is 1876, the year his telephone is successfully demonstrated and patented, but before its commercial application. In this year, the telephone is offered for sale to
Western Union, but it is declined. The following year, he
married Mabel Hubbard, whose father, Gardiner Greene
Hubbard, was one of his backers. His wedding gift to
her: most of the interest in his patents.

telegraphy. In a master stroke of serendipity, Bell had been thrust together with a man almost uniquely suited to become his father-in-law.

Aleck's reputation flourished. In the fall of 1872 he settled in Boston, opening a school for the training of teachers of the deaf. In 1873, he became Professor of Vocal Physiology and Elocution at Boston University, and continued a lively private practice. One of his pupils was George Sanders, a five-year-old boy, born deaf, the son of a prosperous Salem leather merchant. George was to profit greatly from his long tutelage with Bell; and Bell was to profit from the friendship of George's father.

For both Sanders and Hubbard quickly became financial backers of Bell's "hobby"—his electrical researches, when they learned of his extracurricular experiments. Still stimulated by his previous exposure to Helmholtz's work, Bell was resolved to develop what he called a "harmonic telegraph." This instrument would, he hoped, simultaneously transmit tones of different pitches over a single wire, and then unscramble them at the receiving end, using sets of tuning forks. If successful, it would be the basis of a true multiple telegraph—one capable of transmitting many messages at a time over a single line. The multiple (or multiplex) telegraph was the Holy Grail of the Western Union Telegraph Company and of hordes of inventors, including Thomas A. Edison; it was obviously worth a fortune to the man who perfected it. When both Hubbard and Sanders offered to subsidize Bell's work, he agreed, with the proviso that all three share equally in the eventual rewards, if any.

Bell was a genius at invention, but he was not a gifted craftsman. Realizing that he lacked the manual skill to assemble the equipment for his various experiments, he went for assistance to the workshop of Charles Williams, on Court Street in Boston, which turned out commercial equipment and fabricated all sorts of electrical apparatus to order. It was a mecca for electrical inventors—Edison had tinkered there some years before. Bell was assigned a bright young man—a mainstay of the shop—to help him. The young man, whose name was Thomas A. Watson, described that first meeting in a 1913 address delivered before the third annual convention of the Telephone Pioneers of America: "In the early winter of 1874 I was making . . . some experimental torpedo exploding apparatus. That apparatus will always be connected in my mind with the telephone, for one day when I was hard at work on it, a tall, slender, quick-motioned man with pale face, black side whiskers, and drooping mustache, big nose and high sloping forehead crowned with bushy, jet black hair, came rushing out of the office and over to my work bench. It was Alexander Graham Bell."

Bell had already conceived, but not tested, the basic principle of his telephone, probably during the summer of 1874. Now he confided it, early in 1875, to his new friend and disciple. In Watson's words: "One evening when we were resting from our struggles with the [telegraphic] apparatus, Bell said to me, 'Watson, I want to tell you of another idea I have, which I think will surprise you. . . .' I have never forgotten his exact words; they have run in my mind ever since like a mathematical formula. 'If,' he said, 'I could make a current of electricity vary in intensity, precisely as the air varies in density during the production of a sound, I should be able to transmit speech telegraphically.' He then sketched for me an instrument that he thought would do this, and we discussed the possibility of constructing one. I did not make it; it was altogether too costly, and the chances of its working too uncertain to impress his financial backers . . . who were insisting that the wisest thing for Bell to do was to perfect the harmonic telegraph; then he would have money and leisure enough to build air castles like the telephone."

Bell sought encouragement also from Joseph Henry, elder statesman of American science, and director of the Smithsonian Institution in Washington. Bell reviewed his experiments and demonstrated some of his apparatus, learned which of his work was original and which was following on well-trodden paths, and diffidently revealed his plan to transmit speech electrically. Henry proclaimed that it was "the germ of a great invention" and urged Bell to develop it himself, rather than simply publish the concept. When Bell accurately disclaimed the necessary knowledge of electricity, Henry pointedly told him: "Get it!"

Although these words filled Bell with new resolve, they clothed an unconscious irony. Soon after the telephone had made its successful appearance, a leading electrical scientist, Moses G. Farmer, commented to Watson: "That thing has flaunted itself in my very face a dozen times within the last ten years and every time I was too blind to see it. But if Bell had known anything about electricity he would never have invented the telephone." And in later years, Bell himself came to agree.

The moment of discovery actually came on the sweltering afternoon of June 2, 1875, in a garret over the Williams electrical workshop. Bell in the receiving room and Watson in the transmitting room were patiently trying to overcome their harmonic telegraph's maddening foibles. The steel organ reeds (substituted for tuning forks) needed constant retuning by means of an adjustment screw. Sometimes, if a reed were screwed down too tightly, it stuck to the pole of the electromagnet beneath it instead of being free to vibrate. When one of Watson's reeds, in the transmitting room, stopped vibrating,

The Centennial Exposition of 1876 in Philadelphia offered Bell the chance to exhibit his inventions (inset, right), including the voice-powered and battery-powered tele-

Battery-powered "liquid transmitter" (below) had sent the telephone's first words. Sectional view (left sketch) shows its construction. Vibration of diaphragm made wire bob up and down in liquid, varying resistance to current.

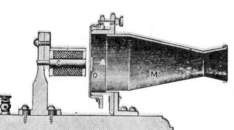

Voice-powered telephone (above) served as transmitter or receiver. Sectional view (upper sketch) shows design. Voice vibrates diaphragm D of transmitter and similar diaphragm in receiver.

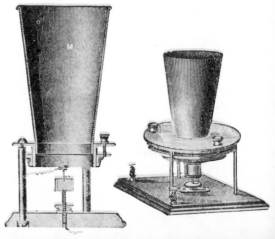

phones shown on opposite page, below. Emperor Dom Pedro of Brazil, hearing Bell over the telephone, exclaimed in astonishment, "My God, it talks!"

Centennial Exposition judges made Bell prove his invention was not merely a mechanical "lover's" or "tension" telephone, which transmitted sound over a taut wire, like these in ad from *Popular Science*, July 1882.

Watson plucked at it to free it, and as nothing happened, kept on plucking it. An account of the day published in *Popular Science* describes what happened next: "Suddenly there came a shout from Bell and he rushed in excitedly from the next room. 'What did you do then? Don't change anything. Let me see!' "

Listening to the receiving reed at the other end of the line, Bell heard a completely different sound from the usual transmitter whine —the twang of a plucked reed complete with its timbre, the complex set of tones and overtones that give character to sound. He at once realized that the plucked reed, screwed down too tightly to fulfill its normal, make-or-break, telegraphic function, had instead acted as a diaphragm, and sent continuous, but fluctuating current over the line. In Watson's words: "The circuit had remained unbroken while that strip of magnetized steel by its vibration over the pole of its magnet was generating that marvelous conception of Bell's—a current of electricity that varied in intensity precisely as the air was varying in density within hearing distance of that spring. That undulatory current had passed through the connecting wire to the distant receiver, which, fortunately, was a mechanism that could transform that current back into an extremely faint echo of the sound of the vibrating spring that had generated it, but what was still more fortunate, the right man had that mechanism at his ear . . . The speaking telephone was born at that moment."

An accident. But, as Pasteur once wrote, "Chance favors the prepared mind." Everything in Bell's background had prepared him for this chance brush with glory. And he instantly seized the opportunity. Contrary to electrical dogma, an induced electric current *could* be strong enough to be useful. And surely he could devise diaphragms better suited to speech than the steel reeds. "All the experimenting that followed that discovery," says Watson, "up to the time the telephone was put into practical use, was largely a matter of working out the details." Within days, the first, crude membrane diaphragm telephone transmitted the faint murmur of Bell's voice to Watson, although the words themselves couldn't be made out. It was not until the following March—March 10, 1876—that Watson heard "a complete and intelligible sentence." That was, of course, the immortal "Mr. Watson, come here. I want you." In fact, whether Bell actually spilled the now legendary battery acid, and whether, indeed, these were the exact words Bell used, is totally, and immaterially, uncertain. What is clear is that this model of the telephone, one that used a battery and a variable resistance instead of a magneto transmitter, was the first really successful one. And a powered, variable-resistance transmitter made possible the enormous success of the future telephone industry. Three days before, Bell had received his first telephonic patent—possibly the most valuable patent in history.

The news of his discovery was soon broadcast in a way that could not have been better arranged by the most audacious of publicity agents. Again, happy coincidence smoothed the way. That year, 1876, was the year of the great Centennial Exhibition, held in Philadelphia and attended by notables from all over the world. Gardiner Hubbard, Bell's old friend, backer, and soon-to-be father-in-law, was one of three members of the committee on the Massachusetts science and education exhibit. He pressed Bell to participate; the result was that the state's exhibit included a table labeled "Telegraphic and Telephonic Apparatus By A. Graham Bell," which included both the variable-resistance and magnetic versions of the telephone. But Bell resisted going to the exhibition himself; he was immersed in school matters. Mabel, his fiancée, practically had to drag him to the railroad station, because he had, as he wrote his mother the next day, "not the remotest intention of leaving Boston." But, moved at seeing the young girl (she was eighteen) "pale and anxious," Bell got on the train. "What I am going to do in Philadelphia," he wrote, "I cannot tell."

What he did there is history. It is well described in the first in a remarkable series of *Popular Science* articles on the early telephone, written by Fred De Land starting in 1906. (Bell commented that the writer, whom he had never met, "seems to know more about me and what I have done than I know myself.")

Sunday, June 25, 1876, was oppressively hot. It was the day a group of experts including the famous English scientist Sir William Thompson, later Lord Kelvin, was to judge the electrical exhibits. Bell's modest table was tucked in a remote corner of the sweltering exhibition building, by a flight of stairs, and before the moist and exhausted judges reached it they had run out of both time and energy. They probably would simply have not bothered, except that one of them recognized Bell, and insisted on seeing his exhibit. The fact that this person was Pedro II, the portly Emperor of Brazil, was probably of some influence with the other judges. Luckily, again, Dom Pedro had visited Bell at the Boston School for the Deaf just eleven days before, and had formed a warm impression of him. De Land writes: "His Majesty spoke so enthusiastically about the telephone, that, tired as the judges were, they concluded to investigate thoroughly its merits."

First, Sir William listened with the sheet-metal diaphragm of a receiver to his ear as Bell, at the far end of a gallery, sang and spoke into one of his electromagnetic transmitters. The first words Sir William clearly made out were "Do you understand what I say?" Amazed, he ran to tell Bell that he had indeed understood. When

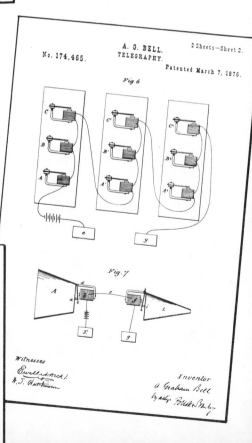

A. G. BELL.
ELECTRIC TELEGRAPHY.

No. 186,787.

2 Sheets—Sheet 1.

Patented Jan. 30, 1877.

Fig. 1

Fig. 2

Fig. 3

Attest

Inventor
Alexander Graham Bell

Bell filed the second basic telephone patent in January 1877 to cover many new developments that had improved his invention. This box phone with a protruding tube was both transmitter and receiver. It used a "quick-acting" horseshoe electromagnet having coils with soft-iron cores fastened to its ends. Bell stayed up nights to work out the patent's details.

This may well be the most valuable patent ever issued (right). Bell's first telephone patent of March 7, 1876, is actually titled "Telegraphy." Fig. 6 shows his idea for a harmonic telegraph; the voice-powered telephone appears in Fig. 7. The only claim to having invented a telephone is the fifth item (below), the last item of the patent, which sufficed to prove Bell originated the telephone.

A. G. BELL.
TELEGRAPHY.

No. 174,465.

2 Sheets—Sheet 2.

Patented March 7, 1876.

Fig. 6

Fig. 7

Witnesses

Inventor
A. Graham Bell

174,465

ducting-wire orhood of the the conduct-magnet both tion in each

ndulations in the vibration inductive ac-otion of the ghborhood of

ndulations in gradually in-istance of the

circuit, or by gradually increasing and diminishing the power of the battery, as set forth.

5. The method of, and apparatus for, transmitting vocal or other sounds telegraphically, as herein described, by causing electrical undulations, similar in form to the vibrations of the air accompanying the said vocal or other sound, substantially as set forth.

In testimony whereof I have hereunto signed my name this 20th day of January, A. D. 1876.

ALEX. GRAHAM BELL.

Witnesses:
THOMAS E. BARRY,
P. D. RICHARDS.

At a sensational demonstration in 1877, Bell proved the long-distance worth of his invention by transmitting speech and music over telephone wires between Salem and Boston. The Boston *Globe's* account was the first newspaper dispatch via telephone. With the proceeds from the next such lecture, Bell bought his wife this silver telephone model (right).

This first commercial telephone had a round opening that served as both transmitter and receiver, requiring the user to shift it adroitly from mouth to ear. Developed by Bell in 1876, it went into service in 1877 when a banker leased two of the instruments, and attached them to a line between his office in Boston and his home in Somerville, Massachusetts.

Pioneer desk telephone set of 1877 had a primitive voice-powered transmitter and a duplicate that served as a receiver, at opposite sides. Photo at Smithsonian Institution by *Popular Science* appeared in magazine's seventy-fifth anniversary issue of May 1947.

Some early phones that saw actual service (1878–79) include these versions (from left): mahogany phone of subscriber to first exchange, in New Haven; phone with a bell (Central transmitted a squeal before); set with two duplicate phones, for talking and listening; and plain and fancy wall phones.

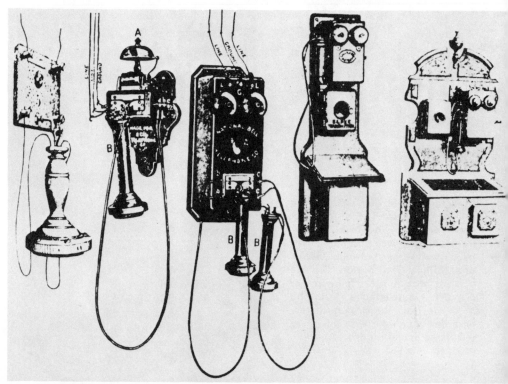

By paying extra, a well-heeled subscriber received two telephone instruments and enjoyed the luxury of using one for talking and one for listening. Normally, the instrument (right) served as both transmitter and receiver, and the user had to say the equivalent of "over" to signal the other party to speak.

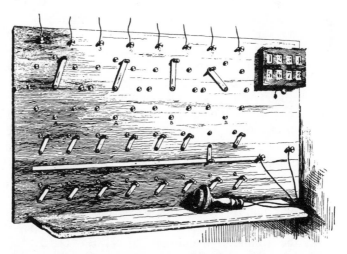

First telephone exchange opened in New Haven in 1878, with switchboards like this one, which had eight lines. Original thirty subscribers included physicians, dentists. Operators were boys whose high jinks led to replacement by women.

Dom Pedro took the receiver, he heard Bell reciting "To be or not to be," leaped from his chair, and shouted, "I hear, I hear," and soon Bell, still spouting Hamlet, saw Dom Pedro galumphing toward him at what he called "a very un-emperor-like gait."

The telephone had made a stunning impact. One of the experts, Professor George F. Barker of the University of Pennsylvania, wrote: "I was greatly astonished and delighted to hear *for the first time* the transmission of articulate speech electrically. The mode of operation of the instrument was obvious at once, as soon as it was exhibited: it was one of those marvelously simple inventions that causes one to wonder, on seeing it for the first time, that it had not been invented long before."

And Professor T. Sterry Hunt, an eminent Canadian scientist, after dining with Sir William Thompson at the end of that great day, wrote to Bell: "He [Thompson] speaks with much enthusiasm of your achievement. What yesterday he would have declared impossible he has today seen realized, and he declares it the most wonderful thing he has seen in America. You speak of it as an embryo invention, but to him it seems already complete; and he declares that, before long, friends will whisper their secrets over the electric wire."

Sir William spoke prophetically. More trials followed at the exhibition, and Bell received a Centennial award. The government published reports by Sir William and by Joseph Henry, chairman of the judges. Professor F. A. P. Barnard, president of Columbia University, said he was confident that "the name of the inventor of the telephone would be handed down to posterity with a permanent claim on the gratitude and remembrance of mankind."

In the summer of 1876, Bell successfully transmitted between various points near his parents' home in Brantford, Ontario—the first real long-distance telephony. The distances: four or five miles. Bell and Watson (who gave up his job at the Williams shop and received a one-tenth interest in all Bell's patents) continued experimenting, and conducted more long-distance trials. On February 12, 1877, Bell gave a tremendously popular public demonstration at Lyceum Hall in Salem, where he spoke over an eighteen-mile telephone connection to Watson in their laboratory in Boston. Watson could be heard by those in the hall, shouting, "Hoy! Hoy!" (This, incidentally, was the form of telephonic address Bell used all his life, resisting "hello" to the end.) Bell happily transmitted to Boston the news story dictated by a reporter for the Boston *Globe*. Next day, the paper published it, under the trumpeting headline: "SENT BY TELEPHONE. The First Newspaper Dispatch Sent by a Human Voice Over the Wires." Two young Japanese pupils of Bell proved, beyond any doubt, that the telephone could "talk Japanese."

The telephone's father speaks over the first long-distance line
between New York and Chicago at its 1892 formal opening.
The 950-mile-long line was a single circuit, made of wire so
thick it weighed more than 400 tons; the cost of its copper
was $130,000. The ceremony, in the New York offices of
AT&T, began with a cornet solo, before an audience of some
one hundred reporters, company officials, and politicos. Bell
is shown talking to William Hubbard in Chicago; Hubbard
was Bell's wife's cousin, and had assisted him at the Centennial Exposition in Philadelphia, 1876.

The first cash Bell obtained directly from his invention was a profit of $149 gained from a demonstration-lecture to a packed house in Salem. With $85 of it, he had a silver miniature of the telephone made for Mabel. Commercial development of the telephone followed very rapidly, and in July 1877, Alexander Graham Bell, with silver and perhaps even golden prospects assured, married Mabel Hubbard. As a wedding gift, he turned over to her about 30 per cent of the shares in the newly formed Bell Telephone Company, all that he owned save ten shares, which he kept for sentimental value. It was to prove a gift worthy of a rajah. Thanks to Gardiner Hubbard's business acumen (it was he who insisted on leasing, not selling telephones) and an insatiable demand for the remarkable new device, the Bells went by easy stages from being comfortable, to being well-off, to being rich. By 1881, a mere five years after the laboratory prototype of the telephone first spoke, the Bells were worth about a million dollars, with an income of about $37,000 a year. This came about despite the fact that patent litigation to establish the true authorship of the telephone dragged on for eighteen years. (After 1881, Bell had nothing to do with the development of the telephone business.)

So there Bell was, just thirty years old, world-famous inventor of the sensation of the day, and with a sizable fortune on the horizon. Another young man might have been quite bowled over. But for Bell, the only real effect seemed to be on his weight. Two months before the wedding, Mabel had written to Alexander's mother, jokingly, "I am beginning to learn that my happiness in life will depend on how well I can feed him." On their nuptial day, the six-foot Bell was a slender 165 pounds. A few months later, Mabel wrote from Scotland, where they were sojourning, "Aleck is perfectly happy with his Edinburgh rolls, Scotch oatmeal porridge and red herring . . . In fact Aleck is growing tremendously stout, and can hardly get his wedding trousers on now." In the fall, his weight reached 201 pounds, and by Christmas he had outgrown his trousers. Next summer—214 pounds. He never again sank below 200, and ballooned in later life to an imperial 250.

Even when he was close to seventy and suffering from diabetes, he could not resist the lure of forbidden food. When his doctor, summoned to treat an attack of acute indigestion following a wee hours raid on the refrigerator, taxed Bell for the folly of devouring cold potatoes, macaroni and cheese, and Smithfield ham, the inventor replied that it was the best meal he'd enjoyed in an age.

Bell had other idiosyncrasies that tried Mabel's patience for the forty-five years of their remarkably happy married life.

For his wife, by far the worst of these was his nocturnal behavior. Bell was a classic case of the night owl. His natural preference was to retire at about 4 A.M., after a night of solitary strolls, and perhaps piano playing, and to sleep through the whole morning. (His breakfast, which he didn't mind eating ice-cold, was simply left on a tray near his bed.) He once wrote Mabel, in expiation of his irritating behavior, "to take night from me is to rob me of life."

Only fellow night owls can properly sympathize with his incredible difficulty in waking up in the morning. His daughter Elsie—born in London, 1878—said that her father was "the soundest sleeper I have ever known . . . He was so hard to awaken that he often stayed up all night in order to be on time for an early-morning engagement." In 1898, on a tour of Japan, he was summoned to appear before the Emperor at ten in the morning, in full formal dress. Bell looked forward to the whole affair with unmasked loathing. On the fatal morning, his valet managed to oust him from bed, deck him in the hated outfit, and launch him in the appropriate direction. After a brief audience, Bell returned home and tumbled wordlessly into bed. When he woke at 2 P.M., he demanded to know when the consul was coming to conduct him to the Emperor.

Bell blamed some of this behavior on sleeplessness caused by very frequent headaches. Many resulted from heat, to which he had a great aversion, and which also caused him annoying rashes. (Bell became an early exponent and practitioner of home air conditioning.) But most of his headaches seemed to be of the "tension" variety, arising when his work was not going well.

Mabel could also never quite reconcile herself to her husband's preference for dark and stormy weather (he shunned the sun) nor to a strain of aloofness, a kind of perpetual questing for solitude. "I often feel like hiding myself away in a corner out of sight," he wrote to Mabel one month after his brilliant success at the Philadelphia Centennial Exhibition. Even though he came to be the cheerful and staunch patriarch of a large clan, his son-in-law David Fairchild could say of him with justice, after Bell died: "Mr. Bell led a peculiarly isolated life; I have never known anyone who spent so much of his time alone." Perhaps this aloofness, the solitary walks at night, the weekend flights to an isolated houseboat at his summer estate in Nova Scotia, his endless piano playing in an otherwise silent house—perhaps this was characteristic of the inventor's mind. And perhaps Bell himself summed it up best when he wrote ". . . I somehow or other appear to be more interested in *things* than people . . ."

Bell did indulge one bizarre but harmless eccentricity. This lover of trees and mountains, lakes and rocks, rain and wind could not suffer moonlight to fall on him, or any of his loved ones, while he slept. So on nights of the full moon, before going to bed, he tiptoed round the sleeping house, drawing curtains and arranging screens to shield his family from its baleful rays.

The Graphophone competed with Edison's phonograph in the early days of recorded sound. It was developed by a trio: Alexander Graham Bell, Chichester A. Bell, and Sumner Tainter. The instrument, shown above with accessories and right, used a cardboard cylinder coated with wax, and a stylus that incised a groove of varying depth in the wax. This yielded better recordings than those of Edison's indented tinfoil cylinders. Edison later switched to wax phonograph records.

Chichester A. Bell, whose name appears on early Graphophone patent (right), was Aleck's year-younger cousin, amateur musician, boxer, friend of George Bernard Shaw, who modeled role of doctor in *The Doctor's Dilemma* after him. He also was an expert in chemistry—the reason Alexander invited him, with Sumner Tainter, to form the Volta Laboratory Associates in 1880.

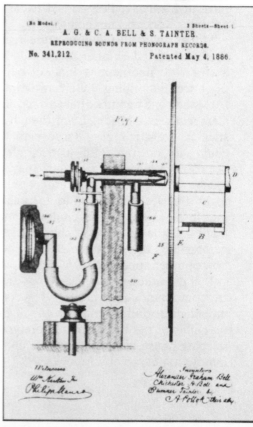

PRODUCTION OF SOUND BY RADIANT ENERGY.*

By ALEXANDER GRAHAM BELL.

IN a paper read before the American Association for the Advancement of Science, last August, I described certain experiments made by Mr. Sumner Tainter and myself which had resulted in the construction of a "*Photophone*," or apparatus for the production of sound by light ; † and it will be my object to-day to describe the progress we have made in the investigation of photophonic phenomena since the date of this communication.

In my Boston paper the discovery was announced that thin disks

Bell reported on his light-beam telephone or "Photophone" in this *Popular Science* article of June 1881. Originally it relied on the fact that selenium's electrical resistance varied with the intensity of light falling on it. In the drawing, a lampblack photophone transmits speech over a span of 130 feet.

Bell is pictured in 1884 in the study of his elegant mansion, one of the largest and costliest Washington, D.C., houses of its time. (It was built in 1879 for $100,000). An inventory of the Bells' assets in 1883 showed that they had, albeit narrowly, become a millionaire family.

None of this character analysis, of course, explains why Bell, his fame and fortune assured at age thirty, did not simply enjoy life as a lionized genius and take it easy. For forty-five years he never stopped working hard at his twin careers of inventing and teaching the deaf. One key was certainly his enormous curiosity, his constant wondering! (In 1879, he bought a copy of the Encyclopaedia Britannica with the intention of reading it from beginning to end.) Another was probably his fear that the invention of the telephone was to be the pinnacle of his career, making the rest of his life a long anti-climax.

In this fear, Bell was justified. But what an anti-climax!

Until his death at age seventy-five, Bell's restless spirit ranged over a dazzling array of subjects, from magazine publishing and progressive education to aviation and eugenics. He never stopped inventing. But none of the things he developed in those forty-five years ever came close to being another telephone. At least, not in posterity's opinion. About one of them, Bell himself thought otherwise. It was the Photophone.

Bell was aware, in 1878, of a recently discovered and intriguing property of selenium, a gray, crystalline element. In a lecture to the Royal Institution in London that year, he said: "It has not long been known that the electric resistance of selenium varies under the action of light. . . . If you insert selenium [in a circuit with a telephone and a galvanic battery] and throw light upon it, you change its resistance and vary the strength of the current you have sent to the telephone."

In 1879, Bell hired another alumnus of Williams' electrical workshop. He was the twenty-five-year-old Charles Sumner Tainter, whose recent experience included work with optical instruments. The Bells set up in a house in Washington, D.C., and Bell and Tainter started working together on selenium devices in a laboratory nearby. Although Bell had originally sought a new variable-resistance transmitter for the telephone, to supplant Edison's new carbon-button transmitter, he was soon overcome by a vision of a more sweeping kind: "the reproduction of speech by the agency of light." In February 1880, the same month his second daughter, Marian, was born, Bell and Tainter successfully transmitted speech over a beam of light. They inserted a selenium cell of a great sensitivity (which they had developed) into a telephone circuit. Sunlight was reflected from a mirror onto the cell. A speaking tube was connected to the mirror so that voice vibrations made the mirror quiver, thereby varying, or modulating the light beam. In this way, the electric output of the selenium cell accurately mimicked the speaker's voice. But the difference between this and other telephonic transmitters was that no wire was needed to connect speaker and listener. In an 1880 *Popular Science* article, "On the Production of Sound by Light," Bell wrote

The Bell family in 1885 included Mabel, Aleck, and their daughters Elsie and Marian, who was called "Daisy." Elsie had been born in 1878, in London. She married Gilbert Grosvenor soon after he became editor of the *National Geographic Magazine*. Marian, born in 1880 in Washington, married David Fairchild, a botanist. The Bells also had two sons who died within hours of their premature births.

that he had spoken via photophone between points 700 feet apart.

Bell was in raptures: "I have heard articulate speech produced by sunlight! I have heard a ray of the sun laugh and cough and sing! I have been able to hear a shadow, and I have even perceived by ear the passage of a cloud across the sun's disk." He called his new invention the Photophone, and forecast great things for it: "Can imagination picture what the future of this invention is to be! . . . In general science, discoveries will be made by the Photophone that are undreamed of just now."

But the scheme had many practical handicaps, which others saw, even if Bell did not. For one thing, the range was generally limited to several miles, a distance reached in 1897 by using an arc light instead of a sun-reflecting mirror. But aside from some eventual use by the military—the Photophone was secure from wiretappers—it simply had no takers. In the 1890s, Bell had switched to the name "Radiophone," suggested by the French scientist Ernest Mercadier, because the device worked with radiant energy. (It was not to be confused with the twentieth-century radiophone to talk by radio.)

Despite the world's indifference to his brain child, Bell insisted that the photophone was his finest invention. Even at the end of his life he called it "the greatest invention I have ever made . . . greater than the telephone."

But Bell was diverted from his photophone disappointments by work in a completely different—and much more profitable—field, the phonograph.

In 1880, the French Government awarded Bell the rarely bestowed Volta Prize for his invention of the telephone. Named after Alessandro Volta (inventor of the battery's forerunner, the voltaic pile), the prize was given for distinguished achievement in the science of electricity, and carried with it not only tremendous prestige but the resonant sum of 50,000 francs—about $10,000. With it, Bell decided to establish a sort of inventors' association—the Volta Laboratory Associates—in Washington, consisting of himself, Tainter, and the the newly enlisted Chichester A. Bell (from England). "Chester" Bell was his year-younger cousin, son of Uncle David Bell, and a professor of chemistry; Bell wanted his chemical expertise, especially, for his photophone researches.

By 1881, the Volta Associates were gradually phasing out work on the photophone in favor of experiments on the phonograph, in the hope that there was a great deal of money to be made in improving Edison's crude device, then literally no more than a toy. Their principal contribution to the tangled history of the phonograph was the technique of engraving the original impression on wax, rather than Edison's method of indenting tinfoil (the indentations were

eradicated with a few playings). They also contributed to the development of the flat disc. From their shares in the patent and other rev-
enues deriving from this work, Tainter and Chichester Bell gained
financial independence for the rest of their long lives.

Bell's share, more than $200,000, he had set aside in a trust fund
for work of help to the deaf. Most of this money was used to maintain
the Volta Bureau, set up at the Washington laboratory specifically to
continue his researches on deafness. The bureau later merged with an
organization Bell founded and endowed with $25,000 in 1890—the
American Association for the Promotion of the Teaching of Speech to
the Deaf.

Work during the Volta Laboratory period was punctuated by two
tragedies, one national, one personal. Each led directly to a Bell invention aimed at saving lives. The first was the death of a President,
the second, the death of Bell's son.

On July 2, 1881, less than four months after taking office, President James A. Garfield was shot in the back as he walked through
Union Station in Washington. The assassin was a deranged citizen,
Charles J. Guiteau, who had been pestering the White House for a job
for weeks and afterward insisted that he had wanted to eliminate a
"traitor" and secure the presidency for Chester A. Arthur, the Vice-
President. The wound was not immediately fatal, but the bullet had
lodged too deep for easy detection, and it had to be removed. Bell had
previously worked on methods of metal detection by electricity, using
an induction balance—a circuit that canceled out the interference
caused by currents induced in a telephone line. Metal in the vicinity
of the balance could upset it and cause an audible tone in the line.
Bell had been summering in Massachusetts, but he immediately
offered to devise a bullet detector based on these principles, and, with
Sumner Tainter, returned to Washington to work furiously at the
Volta Laboratory, in the July heat he so detested. When they had succeeded in producing a model with a working range of three and a half
inches, Garfield's doctors asked them to try it.

On July 26, Bell and Tainter took their jury-rigged assemblage of
coils, condensers, and batteries to the sickbed of the President at the
White House. The doctors tried the apparatus, but without success. A
second trial with a much improved version, on August 1, also failed.
Returning to Boston, Bell tried a new tack, and invented the telephonic needle probe. This device used two electrodes in a series circuit
with a telephone receiver. One electrode was a flat metal plate placed
on the patient's skin; the other was a fine needle sheathed with shellac
insulation except at its tip. When the needle probe touched metal, the
operator heard a click in the receiver. Although Tainter demonstrated
the probe successfully to Garfield's doctors (using a bullet hidden in a

The chateau-like main house of the Bells' summer estate was completed in 1893 at Baddeck, Cape Breton Island, Nova Scotia. Its name — Beinn Bhreagh — was Gaelic for "beautiful mountain."

The extraordinary tetrahedral kites of Bell were described in a *Popular Science* article (1903) by his son-in-law, Gilbert H. Grosvenor. Here the man-carrying kite Mabel II, designed with an open space large enough for a passenger, is shown at Baddeck, first supported on boats (left) and then rising into the air as it is towed (below). Bell was convinced that he could achieve powered, heavier-than-air flight; but the Wrights beat him to it.

Nicknamed "Casey" after poetry's baseball "hero," Frederick W. Baldwin, a mechanical and electrical engineer born in 1882, was practically adopted by the Bells around 1906. He became Bell's assistant and collaborator in developing Bell's ideas on tetrahedral construction along commercial lines. His first project was designing and building a giant tetrahedral observation tower atop Beinn Bhreagh. He also joined with Bell in experiments with hydrofoil boats.

Members of Bell's Aerial Experiment Association (1908) in this *Popular Science* photo include, from left, "Casey" Baldwin, Lieutenant Thomas E. Selfridge, Glenn H. Curtiss, Bell, Douglas McCurdy. Last man, Augustus Post, is a guest. Group aimed to produce a practical flying machine, with Bell's tetrahedral man-carrying kite to be finished first, then other designs. Third AEA plane, Curtiss' *June Bug* (below), flew 6,000 feet in 1908.

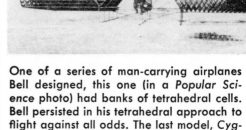

One of a series of man-carrying airplanes Bell designed, this one (in a *Popular Science* photo) had banks of tetrahedral cells. Bell persisted in his tetrahedral approach to flight against all odds. The last model, *Cygnet III,* was actually mounted on the running gear of a Curtiss plane; it "flew" 12 inches.

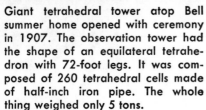

Giant tetrahedral tower atop Bell summer home opened with ceremony in 1907. The observation tower had the shape of an equilateral tetrahedron with 72-foot legs. It was composed of 260 tetrahedral cells made of half-inch iron pipe. The whole thing weighed only 5 tons.

Called a hydrodrome, the HD-4 skimmed the waters of Bras d'Or Lake at 70 mph, fantastic in 1919. Seen with Bell aboard (above) and at speed (below) in these photos from a *Popular Science* article, the pioneer hydrofoil was developed by Bell and Casey Baldwin. Its speed record stood for ten years.

slab of raw meat) they decided not to use it. Garfield was probably beyond help anyway, with a severe infection no doubt caused by the ham-fisted probing of his wound by a whole legion of unsterilized physicians. The President died on September 19.

But Bell's invention went on to save other lives. Physicians learned of it, and began using it. One of them told Bell that the inventor's name would "hereafter be coupled with Jenner, Wells, and Harvey as suffering humanity's greatest benefactors." Until the development of X-ray machines, the telephonic needle probe was used to locate bullets on a wide scale; in the Sino-Japanese War of 1894–95, the Boer War of 1899–1902, and in the First World War, it saved many lives. In recognition of his services, the University of Heidelberg gave Bell an honorary doctor of medicine degree in 1886.

In the midst of the frantic effort to save Garfield's life, Bell's son Edward was born prematurely on August 15, developed difficulty in breathing, and died a few hours later. (A second son, Robert—the last—was also born prematurely, died on November 17, 1883.) Part of Bell's response was to invent what he called a "vacuum jacket," an uncanny anticipation of the iron lung that years later kept so many polio patients alive. The vacuum jacket was a metal cylinder that hermetically sealed a victim (it was designed primarily for those rescued from drowning) up to his neck. A pump would force air out of the cylinder, and atmospheric pressure would push air into the victim's respiratory system. Then the pump would force air back into the cylinder. Bell actually demonstrated a working model of the vacuum jacket in 1882, but nothing ever came of it. As in many other of Bell's ideas, there seemed to be a wild disregard of the practical, which in this case would have suggested to most other men that the easiest way to administer artificial respiration to a drowning man was the old but uncomplicated laying on of hands.

One other invention of this period had an essentially medical function—the audiometer. Bell got the idea, in 1879, for a device that would reveal partial hearing in those thought completely deaf, and would also detect some hearing impairment where none had been suspected. Using a telephone receiver and induction coils whose separation could be varied, the audiometer generated tones of known and repeatable frequency and intensity, so that an individual's hearing ability could be measured quantitatively. (One of the standard units of sound measurement, the decibel, honors the audiometer's inventor.) The value of the instrument was soon apparent. In 1885, Bell reported to the National Academy of Sciences that more than 10 per cent of 700 school children screened with the audiometer proved to have some hearing loss.

And now the care of the deaf would dominate Bell's life. In 1887, a six-year-old girl, stricken deaf and blind at the age of a year and a half, was brought by her father for Bell to help. The little girl sat on his knee and sensed his compassion. Years later, Helen Keller wrote, "But I did not dream that that interview would be the door through which I should pass from darkness into light." It was Bell who launched Helen's education with the "miracle worker," Annie Sullivan. He remained her constant friend and supporter for the rest of his life.

Bell's preoccupation with the deaf led him directly to a study of inheritance and eugenics. His study on inherited deafness, published in 1883, together with a monumental follow-up subsidized by him and published in 1895, may represent Bell's most important scientific, as opposed to technological contribution. He also embarked, in 1889, on an experiment in scientific sheep breeding that was to last more than thirty years. He was trying to produce a strain of twin-bearing sheep, but failed.

It is not practical to breed sheep in the nation's capital. But in 1886 Bell had bought land near Baddeck on Cape Breton Island, Nova Scotia, and from then on the magnificent site served as his summer retreat. He called it "Beinn Bhreagh," Gaelic for "beautiful mountain." In 1893 he completed the main house, a large, sprawling, comfortable mansion in a rather confused, French chateau style, with splendid views over the Bras d'Or Lakes. The estate included the whole of a large headland, and it was on these rambling meadows that Bell's recalcitrant sheep grazed. Beinn Bhreagh was also the locale of experiments that would make a more considerable impact.

Bell had many ideas for inventions in the 1890s. There was a scheme to make printing impressions from photographs. A device that could provide fresh water for men adrift at sea by condensing fog or moist air. A boat with a revolving hull to overcome drag. A way of using selenium to see with electricity. He even coiled a wire around his head and connected it to a similar loop around an assistant's, and then waited to see if their thoughts might leap the gap—an ESP phone, perhaps. It didn't work. None of these ideas was pursued with any real tenacity, nor with sufficient application to the technical problems that had to be solved if fancy were to become reality.

From 1891 on, Bell was gripped by a furious resolve to create a self-powered heavier-than-air flying machine. Bell had always been fascinated by flight. As a small boy in the Scottish hills, he had watched, with awe, the incomprehensible comings and goings of the birds. Even on his honeymoon in England, Bell had made sketches of birds on the wing. And Watson, in later years, remembered that from his earliest meeting with Bell, "he discussed with me the possibility of making a machine that would fly like a bird."

Then, in 1891, Bell caught flying fever in earnest, and it rekindled all his old yearnings. He caught it from an old friend, physicist Samuel Pierpont Langley, secretary of the Smithsonian Institution, who was deeply committed to heavier-than-air flight and was already building and testing models. In June 1891 Bell wrote, "Langley's flying machines . . . flew for me today. I shall have to make experiments upon my own account in Cape Breton. Can't keep out of it. It will be all UP with us someday!"

Over the next several years, Bell somewhat randomly tested—mostly at Beinn Bhreagh—models of helicopters, designs of wings and propeller blades, propulsion systems that included steam jets at the tips of a pinwheel rotor and gunpowder rockets. Bell witnessed (and photographed) the successful flight of Langley's sixteen-foot-long, steam-powered, propeller-driven model, which was catapulted from a houseboat on the Potomac. Bell supported Langley's work, personally and in print, despite the fact that the two were, in essence, rivals. In an interview for *McClure's Magazine* in 1893 he said: "I have not the shadow of a doubt that the whole problem of aerial navigation will be solved within ten years . . . I am able to speak with more authority on this subject from the fact of being actively associated with Professor Langley . . . in his researches and experiments."

In 1898, however, Bell became convinced that the way to powered, heavier-than-air flight was through man-carrying kites, because their stability promised safety. From then on, Bell poured large amounts of time, money, and effort into a dead end, building bigger and bigger kites. After 1902, the kites had a cellular construction, based on the tetrahedron. They had great strength and stability, and enormous drag. (Ironically, long after Bell's kites were abandoned, the tetrahedral construction principle flourished as the progenitor of space frame architecture.) In December 1905, Bell managed to loft a wind-powered, man-carrying kite he called the *Frost Wind*. It carried an extremely nervous 165-pound "pilot" about thirty feet in the air. Of course, the Wright Brothers had already achieved their first powered flight two years before. And in the fall of 1905 Bell learned from eyewitness report that the Wrights had made a sustained flight of *thirty* minutes. Nevertheless, he resolved to go his own way and fit an engine to one of his slow-speed, man-carrying tetrahedral kites.

In 1907, Bell formed a group at Beinn Bhreagh that was to have a profound influence on the future of aviation. He called it the Aerial Experiment Association (AEA). Its members: Frederick W. ("Casey") Baldwin, a young engineer who joined Bell as an assistant in 1906; Douglas McCurdy, another young engineer; Lieutenant Thomas E. Selfridge, who died a year later in an army trial of the

Wright aircraft—the first aircraft fatality; Bell; and Glenn H. Curtiss. Curtiss was a motorcycle racer and maker of motors for both cycles and dirigible balloons. Bell assembled the group for one purpose: to develop a flying machine. They were to try his approach first, then each member could have a whack at his own design.

Here is Glenn Curtiss' account, from a *Popular Science* article of 1927: "Professor Bell thought that Chanute, the Wrights and all the rest were wrong in trying to fly flat planes. Safety in flight, he assured me, was to be found in the development of the tetrahedral kite."

The group did indeed build a kite, the 3,400-cell *Cygnet,* which, unmotorized, carried Selfridge up to a height of 168 feet after being towed on Little Bras d'Or Lake. In 1908 the association moved to Curtiss' shop at Hammondsport, New York. Curtiss received a telegram from Bell saying, "Start building. The boys will be down next week." In Curtiss' words: "That was like Professor Bell. We hadn't decided what to build, or how to build it, but he wanted something built right away. Incidentally, he could not build anything himself. I never saw a man less handy with tools . . . But he had a wonderful way of getting his ideas across to the man who had the mechanical skill to carry them out." Curtiss also noted that Bell had come to be plagued by his own invention; muffle the telephone as he might, it persisted in waking him from his priceless noon slumber. "Little did I think, when I invented this thing, that it would some day rise up to mock me," complained Bell to Curtiss.

At Hammondsport, the AEA held the first successful public flights of self-powered, heavier-than-air machines—three of them, in fact. All were biplane designs. The first, the *Red Wing,* crash-landed during its second flight, probably for lack of lateral control; it did not incorporate the Wright brothers' wing-warping method. Bell directed that the tips of the upper wing be provided with hinged ailerons (or little wings) that moved up and down, but always opposite to each other. As a *Popular Science* story on the AEA planes explains, "by leaning toward the upper side when the machine began to tip the air pilot's body pressed a lever which moved all the ailerons simultaneously—down on the lower side, up on the higher side. Thus, with different air resistance at opposite wing tips, the craft came back to an even keel."

The next three planes designed and made by the AEA all used the new lateral control device to good advantage. The *White Wing* flew 1,017 feet in nineteen seconds. Curtiss' *June Bug* won the *Scientific American* trophy, on July 4, 1908, for the first heavier-than-air flight of more than one kilometer. And the last plane produced by the AEA, the *Silver Dart,* was the first heavier-than-air craft to fly in Canada, at Beinn Bhreagh. On March 31, 1909, its mission brilliantly achieved, the AEA disbanded according to plan. McCurdy and Baldwin got the *Silver Dart,* Curtiss the *June Bug.* The five associates also came away with a joint patent covering the aileron, which became the basis of a long fight with the Wrights (see Chapter 7). Eventually, the AEA patents came to be worth some two million dollars. To subsidize the unique effort of the AEA had taken all of $35,000 from Mabel Bell, plus $3,000 put up by Bell for mimeographing expenses.

Incredibly, Bell persisted in his quixotic quest for tetrahedral flight, despite the stunning success of his own "boys" and himself with biplanes. This determination to breast the mainstream of aviation may have been vanity, a simple belief in the superiority of his original idea, or a crotchet of advancing years. (By this time Bell, with his snowy white hair and whiskers and his ample figure, looked like a cross between Santa Claus and an energetic polar bear.) In any event, he built several more multicellular craft (he called them "aerodromes," the name Langley had used for his ill-fated plane in 1903). In March 1912, just after his sixty-fifth birthday, the *Cygnet III* rose from the ice-covered surface of Baddeck Bay. It was the first and the last self-powered, man-carrying tetrahedral kite to do so. It was airborne for a total distance of one foot. Finally, Bell had had enough of flying. Through the air, that is.

Flying on the water—with hydrofoil boats—was to occupy Bell for many of his remaining years. He and Casey Baldwin began experimenting with hydrofoils in 1908, originally as a help in getting their water-launched aerodromes into the air. But their interest quickly focused on hydrofoil boats. (This kind of craft has "wings" submerged in the water. When the boat starts moving, the lift produced by water moving past the foils raises the hull clear of the water, and the boat "flies" on the foils. Drag is greatly decreased.) In 1911, both Baldwin and Bell rode in a new Italian hydrofoil boat on Lake Maggiore "at express-train speed," actually, about forty-five mph. This stimulated the design and building of their first "hydrodrome," the HD-1, which by 1912 got up to fifty mph (before it crashed), and looked like a midget, bi-winged seaplane. The HD-2 and HD-3 both proved disappointing.

Then the Great War broke out. Bell tried to interest the Navy Department, without success, in the HD-3. Reasoning that the only real contribution to the United States military success he could make was in the realm of hydrofoils, he and Baldwin started work on the HD-4. (Bell had become a U.S. citizen long before).

And the HD-4 was a winner. As pictured in a 1920 *Popular Science* article, she had a sixty-foot-long torpedolike hull, with "two outrigger hulls or pontoons connected with the main hull by means of a deck shaped like the wing of an airplane." Mounted atop each out-rigger was an airplane propeller driven by its own 350-hp Liberty engine, supplied by the Navy. "At high speed," the story reported, "the hull of the craft is entirely clear of the water, and is supported on small steel plates arranged in groups like the shutters of a venetian blind . . . one set on each side . . . one at the stern . . . and a fourth set at the bow. The faster the boat goes, the higher she rises from the water, so that she automatically reduces or reefs the submerged hydrofoil surface to just the amount required to carry the load."

On September 9, 1919, the five-ton HD-4 set a world's marine speed record of 70.86 mph. Though the craft performed flawlessly, the Navy finally decided its design was too radical for military use. In 1921 it was dismantled, but its speed record stood for ten years. In 1922, Baldwin and Bell received joint patents covering various hydrofoil features. They were Bell's last patents.

In the last year of his life, Bell weakened visibly. His diabetic condition was growing worse, and he began to look haggard from losing weight. But his remarkable imagination never flagged, and he speculated on, and even experimented with, a rich variety of projects —some new, some revived from past years. There was the photophone again, a hydrofoil naval towing target, fresh water from the sea, solar heating (by using fluids circulating on rooftops). In an interview for *American Magazine* in 1921, he said, "There cannot be mental atrophy in any person who continues to observe, to remember what he observes, and to seek answers for his increasing hows and whys about things." Traveling with Mabel through the Caribbean in the winter of 1922, he even climbed down an underwater observation tube in the Bahamas.

Then, just at the end of July 1922, at his beloved home in Bad-deck, Bell weakened suddenly. Weaving in and out of consciousness, he rested in his bed on a sleeping porch, with a view of his "Beautiful Mountain." At two of a hushed and luminous morning, on August 2, 1922, as Mabel called his name, he raised his lids and smiled. She implored him not to leave her. His fingers spoke into her hand a sign for "no." Then he died.

Bell was buried where he wished to be at the top of his mountain on August 4, at 6:25 P.M. All telephone service throughout the United States was suspended then, for one minute. There is no monument, simply a marker, set into a rock, with Bell's name, the dates of his birth and death, his calling—"inventor"—and the words he had specifically requested: "Died a Citizen of the United States."

He might have included in his epitaph some words from an interview he gave in 1902, about the life of an inventor: "It is pretty hard and steady work. But then, it is my pleasure, too."

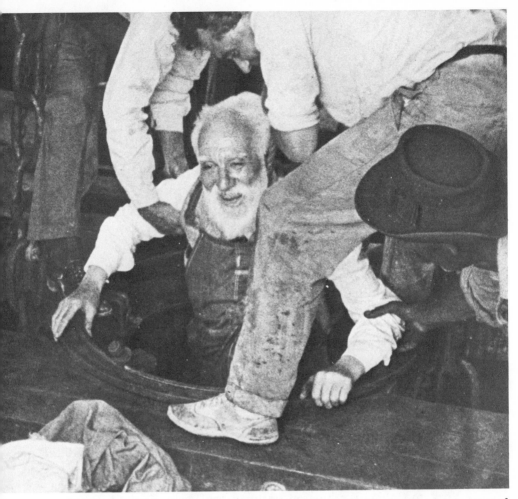

Bell had been interested in underwater research all his life. In this picture, one of Bell's last portraits, he is being helped out of an underwater observation tube in the Bahamas; he and Mabel had been taking a tour of the Caribbean in the winter of 1921–1922, and Bell was seventy-five. On August 2, 1922, he died.

Alexander Graham Bell Museum, in his beloved Baddeck, Nova Scotia, displays highlights of his accomplishments to streams of visitors. It houses exhibits spanning the whole of his career, including the first telephones, the Photophone, his extraordinary tetrahedral kites, and his aeronautical experiments with Curtiss and others.

CHAPTER 4

Kodak and Polaroid— From Eastman to Land

MODERN photography owes its shape to two remarkable men, one distinctively of the nineteenth century, the other of the twentieth . . . both inventive geniuses, both brilliant entrepreneurs, both averse to publicity and, ironically, camera-shy. Their names: George Eastman and Edwin H. Land.

It is difficult not to set his name down as George Kodak. Seldom has an inventor come to be so inextricably linked with the trademark and company name he founded. And seldom has such fame been so merited. For George Eastman was the prime mover in a true revolution. Almost solely by his own efforts, he transformed what was once the awkward craft of photography, limited to a patient and skillful few, and made it accessible to the millions.

George Eastman was born on July 12, 1854, in Waterville, New York, to George Washington Eastman and Maria Kilbourn Eastman, whose families had arrived in America before the middle of the seventeenth century. (The old homestead, built around 1770, has been moved to the grounds of Eastman House in Rochester.) George's father, a penmanship teacher, founded the first commercial college in Rochester, New York. But he died when George was eight, and the family—George, his mother, and two sisters—had a hard time of it. His mother took in boarders to make ends meet. In school, George was an indifferent student but a gifted ballplayer (he was an outstanding catcher for an amateur baseball team after he left school). The cramped family finances forced George to quit school at fourteen to take a job as messenger for an insurance company, at three dollars a week. For five years he plugged away, studying accounting during the evenings, keeping scrupulous accounts of every penny earned and every one spent—the first year he managed to save thirty-seven dollars. At age twenty, in 1874, he got a bookkeeping job as a junior clerk in the Rochester Savings Bank, where, with the magnificent salary of $800 a year, he was able to save really significant amounts—

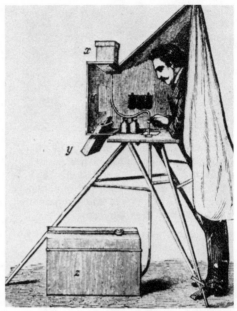

Photography before Eastman: Wet plates used in the 1870s had to be coated, exposed, and developed while still wet. So a photographer, like this amateur, had to carry a cumbersome outfit, including a darkroom, on his back. In the field, he set up this "dark tent" (right), to prepare and develop the negatives.

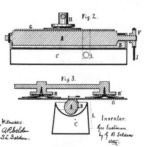

Wet plates were swept aside by the introduction of gelatin-bromide dry plates. In 1879, George Eastman received a British patent for a process and an emulsion-coating machine for mass-producing dry plates. The American patent, shown here, was granted in 1880.

This kerosene "safelight" with a ruby red front glass served for the developing of dry plates in a darkroom of the 1880s. The side door could then be opened for full light, to inspect the resulting pictures.

Eastman's introduction of roll film opened photography to the masses. This first Kodak, marketed in 1888, contained enough film for one hundred pictures. It was the progenitor of "Brownie" box cameras.

Eastman introduced the first folding Kodak in 1890. It could produce forty-eight 4-inch by 5-inch pictures from a single loading, but was fairly compact when closed.

The early Kodak cameras, like the one this modish photographer (circa 1890) is using, had to be returned to Rochester to have the film developed, prints made, and the camera reloaded. Total charge for this service, including one hundred prints: $10.

One of the more ingenious wrinkles to be introduced in the steadily growing line of Kodak cameras was the unique feature of the Autographic models, introduced in 1914; the photographer could identify the film permanently at the time the picture was taken, by writing on the film with a stylus.

The range of Eastman cameras in 1917 is shown by this trio, drawn from *Popular Science* ads. The No. 2C Autographic Kodak Jr. was a slender camera that would fit the pocket, yet take 2 7/8-by-4 7/8-inch pictures. It had a ball-bearing shutter with speeds up to $\frac{1}{100}$ of a second, and an f/7.7 lens. Price—$19. With the Premo film pack model, you opened the back and dropped in a pack of twelve cut films. After each exposure, you pulled a black tab to uncover the next film. The Graflex camera was a true single-lens reflex. The image was reflected by a mirror onto a ground glass, where it could be viewed. The mirror swung out of the way just before exposure.

No. 2C Autographic Kodak Jr.

Premo film pack camera for cut film.

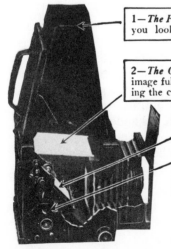

1—*The Focusing Hood* into which you look to see the picture.

2—*The Ground Glass Screen* where you watch the image full negative-size—focusing it exactly, adjusting the composition up to the instant of exposure.

3—*The Swinging Mirror* which reflects image in full negative-size onto the ground glass screen.

4—*The Focal Plane Shutter* gives not only a wide range of speeds but also FULL-timed, uniform exposure of the entire plate.

Single-lens reflex Graflex.

enough to help finance his future ventures in photography.

George became involved with photography in a completely casual way. He had latched onto the idea of visiting Santo Domingo, and when he mentioned his plan to a co-worker, he was advised to take along a photographic kit to make a pictorial record of his trip. George readily agreed, and, at age twenty-four, he set about equipping himself.

This was no easy task. "My layout," said Eastman about this 1878 venture, "had in it a camera the size of a soap box, a tripod which was strong and heavy enough to support a bungalow, a big plate holder, a dark tent, a nitrate bath, and a container for water," together with a quantity of heavy and fragile glass plates. A cartoon of 1923 jokingly portrays a boyish Eastman staggering along in front of the Rochester Savings Bank under a great heap of equipment and chemicals. A local wag asks: "Goin' campin', George?" and the reply is "Nope. Just goin' out to take a snapshot."

But it really wasn't at all funny. If you wanted to go afield to take pictures in 1878, you needed the stamina of a Nepalese Sherpa. The cause was the basic process of photography, the so-called wet-plate process. In 1851, an English sculptor, Frederick Scott Archer, had found a way to bind light-sensitive sodium salts to a glass plate, doing away with the earlier daguerreotype and calotype. He coated a glass plate with collodion—a syrupy liquid made of cellulose nitrate in ether and alcohol—to which a salt of iodine, potassium iodine, for example, was added. When the wet plate was dipped into a silver nitrate solution, the resulting reaction coated the plate with light-sensitive silver iodide in suspension. But the plate thus made had to be exposed immediately, while it was still wet. And it had to be developed and fixed on the spot, then instantly washed and dried. Thus the photographer had to carry with him not only the plates and chemicals he needed, but also a collapsible darkroom that he could set up in the field. Obviously, photography was not a hobby to be lightly tackled.

So complex was the whole business, in fact, that George Eastman took lessons at five dollars an hour to learn to use what he called his "packhorse load" of equipment. Eventually, he decided not to go to Santo Domingo after all, but to Mackinac Island. The trip apparently went well enough except for one mishap. He had wrapped his underwear around a glass container full of silver nitrate to keep it from breaking, but it leaked—and he had to replace his underwear.

Eastman quickly became engrossed in his demanding new avocation, avidly reading everything he could on the subject. From British magazines he learned that photographers overseas were experimenting with ways of making the new dry plates. The process had been invented by the English physician and photographer Dr. Richard Leach Maddox, in 1871. He coated glass plates with gelatin instead of collodion, with silver bromide replacing silver iodide, the whole forming an emulsion that was left to dry. The dry plates could be prepared in advance, then exposed and developed at the photographer's pleasure. Using a formula from one of these magazines, Eastman started preparing his own dry plates. His immediate aim was to lighten his own photographic work by doing away with the "packhorse load." But he was soon struck with the commercial possibilities of supplying ready-made dry plates to other photographers— primarily professional portrait photographers.

His family's continuing poverty, and his fierce desire to alleviate it, goaded him to several years of hard and initially unrewarding experimentation, conducted after a day's work at the bank, mostly in his mother's kitchen. Often, he was so exhausted he would sleep in his clothes on the kitchen floor, next to the stove. Finally, he perfected a device for coating glass plates and a gelatin emulsion that could be used with it. In 1879, he sailed for England, then the center of the photographic world, and obtained his first patent, "An improved process of preparing gelatin dry plates for use in photography and apparatus thereof." (He received the corresponding American patent the following spring.)

In April 1880, with $2,500 received from the sale of his English patent, Eastman leased the third floor of a loft building on State Street in Rochester, and began to make dry plates for sale. On January 1, 1881, he went into partnership with Henry A. Strong, a local buggy whip maker who was one of his mother's boarders, to form the Eastman Dry Plate Company. Come March, the young venture had six employees on its payroll. Later that year, Eastman resigned from the bank to devote full time to the dry plate business.

As with many other budding technologies, disaster threatened, often from almost trivial causes. The business nearly failed when dry plates in the hands of dealers and photographers went bad, losing their sensitivity to light. Eastman recalled the plates, closed his plant, and went to Europe with Strong to learn how to make a more stable emulsion. There he found that the problem was not his formula, but rather a defective shipment of gelatin. With a new supply, the partners replaced the bad plates, and the business was saved.

It was obvious that Eastman was on the right path. An 1881 *Popular Science* review called "Progress in Photography" stated that the new process offered "considerable advantages." Yet heavy glass plates were still a clumsy and limiting medium. The same review confidently predicted the development of the roll film camera, which only awaited the invention of a flexible support for the gelatin emulsion.

That was precisely what Eastman had in mind. In 1880, a small

A usually camera-shy George Eastman, age seventy, poses for *Popular Science* in the garden of his Rochester home in 1924. He is using his recently introduced Ciné-Kodak 16mm movie camera—the first movie camera produced for amateurs, to fulfill his dream of "movies in the home." Edison had used Eastman's roll film, the first really flexible film medium, in his motion-picture system. The Ciné-Kodak 16mm required five years of research. Eastman contended he was simply "an amateur photographer."

A little-remembered system of color-movie photography, called Kodacolor, was introduced in 1928. It used a peculiar, ribbed film, and required the movie-maker to place a three-color filter, shown below, over the camera lens. The cumbersome system was replaced, in 1935, by introduction of the enormously successful Kodachrome film.

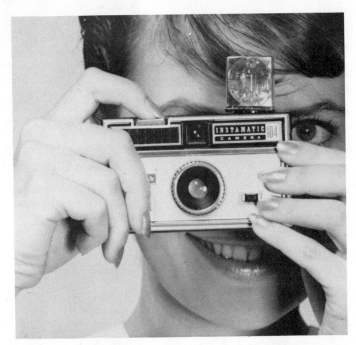

Kodak further simplified photography for the amateur with its Instamatic system in 1963. The camera is loaded simply by dropping a film cartridge into it. Evolution of light-producing devices culminated in "flash cubes," and "magicubes" like the one on the top of the Instamatic camera above. They consist of four flashbulbs on a single base, in plastic cube.

The easy-loading Instamatic concept was extended to home-movie projection in 1969 with a new breed of machines that automatically played and rewound movie film in cartridges.

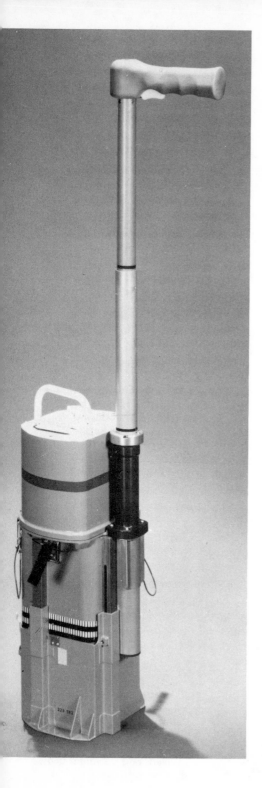

Moon soil is illuminated by flash lamp, shown in action above, built into the special camera.

Close-up photo of lunar soil is one of stereo pairs brought back. Lumps are intriguing metallic spangles.

The technical genius of the company George Eastman founded reached new heights, literally, with this special camera, built for NASA, to be used by the Apollo astronauts. It made extreme close-ups, in color and stereo, of the lunar soil. At left, the camera with its handle fully extended for use on the moon; top, a view of its business, or taking, end; above, one of the close-ups it made of the lunar surface.

four-by-five camera with a lens, tripod, and a starter supply of a dozen Eastman dry plates cost $12.25. The business grew, converting to a $200,000 corporation called the Eastman Dry Plate and Film Company in 1884. But Eastman knew that glass plates represented an obstacle to the spread of photography that had to be shattered, even though he had not as yet conceived the idea of making it a medium for the masses.

The first concept he tried, in 1884, was Eastman Negative Paper, a light-sensitive paper that could be made transparent enough for printing, after it was exposed, by bathing it in hot castor oil. Eastman and an associate invented a mahogany roll holder that permitted photographers to use rolls of the paper film in their regular dry plate cameras—the beginning of a new era of freedom in photography.

But the new medium was not really satisfactory—the grain of the paper appeared too obtrusively in the final print. So Eastman announced, in 1885, Eastman American film. In this film, the paper served only as a carrier for the light-sensitive gelatin emulsion, from which it was separated by a thin layer of plain, soluble gelatin. After exposure and development, the image-bearing gelatin layer was stripped away from the paper. Then this thin film negative was transferred to a sheet of clear gelatin and given a protective coating of collodion.

Now came a critical turning point, for Eastman and for photography. Commenting about this period in later years, he said: "When we started out with our scheme of film photography, we expected that everybody who used glass plates would take to films, but we found that the number who did so was relatively small, and in order to make a large business we would have to reach the general public." With what turned out to be profound intuition, Eastman decided to inveigle the public with a new kind of camera, which would capitalize on his film inventions. This was the Number One Kodak Camera, introduced in 1888.

With this camera, the revolution was truly launched. Here for the first time was a photographic instrument anyone could use successfully, without having to master an arcane art. It was a simple, fixed-focus box camera, relatively small and light enough not to demand a tripod during shooting. It came loaded with enough Eastman American roll film to make 100 snapshots. With film, a shoulder strap, and case, it sold for twenty-five dollars. When the user had exposed all the film, he returned the camera with ten dollars to Rochester, where the film was developed and printed, a new roll of film was inserted in the camera, and the whole package returned. For the first time, a total novice in photography could take pictures virtually without effort. With this camera began the immortal slogan (coined by Eastman) "You press the button—we do the rest."

The trade name Kodak soon became one of the most familiar in the world. Its origins are testament to the distinctiveness—some might say quirkiness—of George Eastman's personality. He needed a name that was easy to spell in any language and was meaningless in all, so it could be trademarked. In later years, Eastman explained how he had chosen "Kodak." "I devised the name myself . . . The letter 'K' had been a favorite with me—it seems a strong, incisive letter . . . It became a question of trying out a great number of combinations of letters that made words starting and ending with 'K.' The word 'Kodak' is the result."

Amateurs who essayed this new form of painless photography were enthralled. Another man might have stopped there, at what seemed the pinnacle. Not Eastman. In 1886, he had hired a young chemist named Harry M. Reichenbach to do research into film—one of the first instances of an American industrialist hiring a full-time research scientist. In 1889, the research bore fruit. Eastman introduced the first commercial transparent film, with a flexible base of cellulose nitrate. It was coated on glass-topped tables 200 feet long and 42 inches wide. Soon after, another inventor—Thomas Edison—seized on the new flexible film to realize his dream of a practical motion picture system.

In the same year, 1889, a new corporation was formed—the Eastman Company—capitalized at $1 million. In 1890, a folding Kodak appeared. And in 1891, the transparent film was further refined, so it could be loaded into the camera in daylight. No longer did happy snapshooters have to interrupt their hobby while they waited for the camera to be returned to the Rochester plant; rolls of film could be purchased everywhere, and the camera loaded by the photographer. The company's slogan was changed to "You press the button, we do the rest (or you can do it yourself)."

The business was growing very fast. In 1892, it became the Eastman Kodak Company of New York, with a capitalization of $5 million; a year later, Eastman was a millionaire. In 1895, the pocket Kodak Camera was introduced, made in part of aluminum, with a little window in which the numbers for successive exposures could be read. In 1898 came the Folding Pocket Kodak Camera, only an inch and a half thick and six and a half inches long, with an all-metal case —perhaps the progenitor of all modern roll-film cameras. And in 1900, Eastman's dream of photography for every man was realized with a triumph of mass production: the first Brownie, sold for a dollar and using film costing just fifteen cents a roll. Just a year later, Eastman Kodak Company of New Jersey was formed with a capitalization of an impressive $35 million. George Eastman, now forty-six, was a very wealthy man.

Edwin H. Land's first major invention—the foundation of the great Polaroid empire—was a flat plastic sheet capable of polarizing light. Two overlapping sheets of the material could be used as a light "valve" by rotating one of them, as demonstrated above with his polarizing screens.

In this illustration from a 1936 *Popular Science* article on Land, the young inventor (he was twenty-seven) demonstrates what he believed would be the chief application of polarizing screens: ending headlight glare for night driving. Both headlights are fitted with polarizing screens; Land is masking one of the headlights with a second screen whose optical axis is "crossed," or perpendicular to the first's. This screen would be in the windshield of the other auto.

Polaroid demonstrated this system for full-color, "3-D" movies at the 1939 New York World's Fair. The twin images that were to be combined for stereo were taken by the twin-lens movie camera. A projector polarized the images with opposing optical axes and cast them slightly out of register on the screen. The viewer watched through correspondingly polarized spectacles, which were colorless.

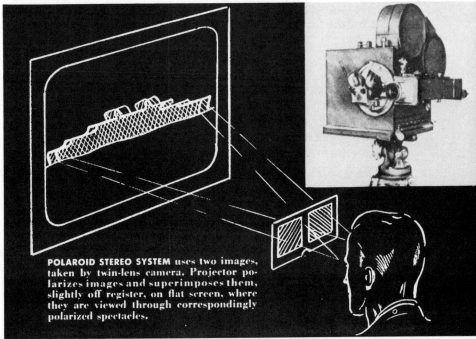

POLAROID STEREO SYSTEM uses two images, taken by twin-lens camera. Projector polarizes images and superimposes them, slightly off register, on flat screen, where they are viewed through correspondingly polarized spectacles.

The remarkable growth and emerging dominance of his company, one of the great American industrial success stories, was for the most part due to the technical innovations Eastman and his scientists brought to an appreciative public. But it was undoubtedly helped by his business skills, including an unflagging dedication to details. Marion B. Folsom, one of Eastman's assistants (and later a Secretary of Health, Education and Welfare), recalled that his boss once rejected a chart with the notation "I don't like the way the draftsman makes his *R's*." Eastman maintained a strict separation of colored pencils for use by his various departments: blue for sales, brown for credit, red for accounting, and green for himself.

Nevertheless, Eastman had great faith in the men he had carefully selected for his company. His philosophy is exemplified by an incident on an African safari, whose details he had planned to the last iota. Equipped with the latest Kodak movie camera, he was filming the charge of a furious rhino, which came straight at him. Everyone in the party hightailed it for safety, except Eastman and his hunter, who dropped the rhino just five paces from the still imperturbably filming inventor. When asked why he hadn't run, Eastman replied, "Well, you have to have trust in your organization."

In 1923 came an achievement that opened a whole new market for Eastman, one he was particularly pleased with. This was the development of a home movie camera and projector, made possible by Kodak's new 16mm reversal movie film on a non-flammable (safety) base—cellulose acetate. Eastman told a *Popular Science* interviewer next year about the Ciné-Kodak motion picture camera, "This little machine represents five solid years of research. People have been talking for several years about 'movies in the home' as an interesting possibility for the future. Now that the Ciné-Kodak is here, the future has arrived."

By this time, Eastman was one of America's wealthiest men. He may also have been extremely lonely. He never married. He had always been somewhat diffident, somewhat aloof, apparently without really close friends. He built an impressive mansion in Rochester, but after his mother's death in 1907 he lived in it quite alone. A 1929 *Popular Science* article on Eastman's sponsorship of a thirteen-month calendar—one of the great interests of his later years—describes the house as a "magnificent Georgian mansion . . . a great hall paved with tessellated marble, strewn with costly Oriental rugs, banked with flowers . . . a leather upholstered library where the array of paintings and statuary so engrossed us that we hardly noticed that the organ had ceased playing. . . ."

Eastman's endeavors as a philanthropist virtually amounted to a second career. Carefully, methodically, intelligently, he gave away

almost $100 million. This career began when his salary was sixty
dollars a week, with a fifty-dollar contribution to the Mechanics Institute of Rochester, which was the recipient of his first really large
bestowal, in 1899, of $200,000. He was at first so shy about his
philanthropy (or perhaps about his wealth) that he donated $2.5
million to MIT in 1912 under the name of Mr. Smith, a gentleman
who figured in MIT song and legend for years after. The grants to
MIT eventually reached $20 million before his identity became
known.

One of Eastman's favorite charities was the dental clinic. He not
only founded the Rochester Dental Dispensary (he gave it $3.8
million), but gave dental clinics to Rome, Stockholm, London, Paris,
and Brussels! Eastman explained this remarkable preoccupation as
follows: "I get more results for my money than in any other philan-
thropic scheme. It is a medical fact that children can have a better
chance in life with better looks, better health, and more vigor if the
teeth, nose, throat, and mouth are taken care of at the crucial time of
childhood."

He loved music, and founded the Eastman School of Music at the
University of Rochester (which eventually received a total of $51
million). He liked, however, to belittle his own musical talents by saying that when he had been very young, he bought a flute and tried for
two years to play "Annie Laurie" on it, without success. In later
years, he claimed, he could not even recognize the tune when it was
played for him.

In his seventies, he had successfully disposed of the bulk of his fortune. The great enterprise he founded no longer depended on any one
man. He had no close ties to any living person. In 1932 at the age of
seventy-eight, his health failing, he sat down and wrote a note that
expressed the man's essence: "My work is done. Why wait?"

And he shot himself.

Edwin H. Land's official biography, published by Polaroid Corporation, is remarkably terse. It reads:

EDWIN H. LAND
President, Director of Research and
Chairman of the Board

Residence
Brattle Street, Cambridge, Massachusetts 02139
Born
May 7, 1909, Bridgeport, Connecticut
Education
Norwich Academy, Harvard University

In 1947, Land saved the fortunes of his fledgling company by introducing a system of instant photography to stunned optical scientists. Here he demonstrates a portrait camera that does what his production model was to do in 1948. The 8-by-10-inch print shown was developed fifty seconds after it had been exposed.

The picture-in-a-minute concept was first made available to consumers in this Model 95 Polaroid Land camera. It produced sepia prints, 3 ¼ by 4 ¼ inches.

Film in the Model 95 was advanced by pulling the leader through a slot. A single control set both shutter speed and lens opening. Camera cost $89.75.

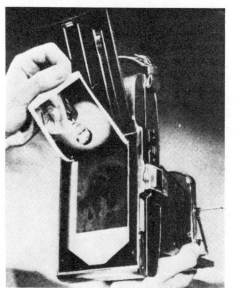

Instant photography in full color? Most experts thought it an impossibility. But Land developed color Polaroid Land film in 1963, and by 1967 had introduced this low-priced, color camera, the Model 210. At $49.95, it took an eight-exposure color film pack, and had an automatic electronic shutter.

Dr. Land (the Dr. stemmed from his honorary degrees) receives the Presidential Medal of Freedom from President Lyndon Johnson for his service on the President's Science Advisory Committee. Award was made by President Kennedy.

The Polaroid SX-70, introduced in 1973, marked the fulfillment of Dr. Land's thirty-year quest for "absolute one-step photography." Within two seconds after you press the button, the SX-70 ejects no-mess color print that develops, clean and dry, outside the camera. Colors of the resulting picture are more stable than achieved before.

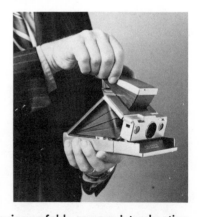

The SX-70 combines remarkable technical triumphs, not the least of them the design of a prism-less, folding, single-lens reflex that slips into a pocket. One tug on the viewfinder housing unfolds camera into shooting position. Each film pack contains its own battery, which powers all the camera's functions. A plug-in GE FlashBar gives ten shots.

That is all the personal background. The remainder of the biography consists of eighty-plus lines listing his honorary degrees, fellowships and honorary memberships, awards, and academic and civic activities (including stints as scientific adviser to Presidents Eisenhower and Kennedy). For Land is almost as famous for his reticence and reclusiveness as for his singlehanded invention of "instant photography." For years, he was almost impossible to interview, so that many of the anecdotes that are associated with him may be apocryphal. What is not in question is his standing as an inventor and an industrial pioneer. A vice-president of Land's arch rival, Eastman Kodak Company, has said: "Someday Edwin Land will be ranked with Thomas Edison and Alexander Graham Bell . . . and George Eastman."

The son of a merchant, Land attended Norwich Academy, where he was a stellar debater, a member of the track team, and an outstanding physics student. In 1926, a freshman student at Harvard University, he was strolling down Broadway in New York City one night when he was dazzled by oncoming automobile headlights. In what can only be called a flash of inspiration, he thought that polarized light might be used to eliminate headlight glare and make night driving safer. (Plane polarized light vibrates in a single plane, instead of in all planes about an axis. It is thus possible to screen out most polarized light by using a polarizing material oriented in another plane.) Scientists knew that various minerals could polarize light, but no one had succeeded in making filters to do it in a convenient and predictable manner. Land took a leave from Harvard to pursue his experiments in polarization. He experimented in a rented room in mid-Manhattan, and also in a physics lab at Columbia University, which he surreptitiously entered via an unlocked window at night. In 1928 Land achieved his first success—the first practical light-polarizing material in the form of synthetic sheets. In 1929, he returned to Harvard with his polarizer and a wife, the former Helen ("Terre") Maislen. In 1932, he introduced his polarizers at a special Harvard colloquium and took another leave to produce them. (He never returned to formal education—his doctorates are all honorary.) After five years of work, Land formed what is now called Polaroid Corporation, with backing from a galaxy of Wall Streeters—James P. Warburg, Averell Harriman, Lewis Strauss, and other similarly gold-plated investors. One of the principal aims of the new company was to persuade Detroit of the merits of Land's original dream—putting polarizing sheets in the headlamps and windshields of every car on the road to eliminate the hazards of glare in night driving. But the automotive industry, in the years from 1937 on, has steadfastly declined Land's proposals, for reasons that have never been made clear. (It is

Dr. Edwin H. Land: His formal education stopped when he dropped out of Harvard to pursue his investigations of polarizing materials. His theory of photography: "the process must be nonexistent for the photographer, who by definition need think of the art in taking, not in making, photographs."

Instant movies from Polaroid? It's the next logical step. This artist's concept (based on Polaroid patents) of an instant movie-film cassette appeared in a 1974 issue of *Popular Science*. In this concept, development takes place inside the projector after the film has been exposed. The film never leaves the cassette; the projection light is angled through the film from the side.

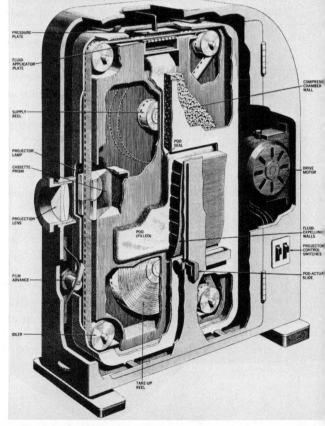

possible that the idea, even at this late date, is not dead.)

There were, however, other uses for Land's invention, and the company prospered. Polaroid sunglasses, which significantly cut glare for drivers, aviators, fisherman, and others were a tremendous success— the company still sells some twenty-five million pairs of Polaroid lenses a year. Polarizing screens became available to photographers. During World War II, the company boomed with sales to the military. But in 1947, with the end of government contracts, Land's company needed resuscitation, and Land had the answer.

Back in 1943, Land had vacationed with his family in Santa Fe, New Mexico. Like any other proud daddy, he took pictures of his daughter, Jennifer, aged three. But Jennifer demanded to see the results on the spot. This experience planted the germ of an idea that became an obsession—to invent a system of instant photography. Within hours, Land later recalled, he had fixed on the camera, the film, and the chemistry that would yield a picture immediately on exposure. It took four years to reduce his ideas to practice (one of his associates claimed that a hundred Ph.D.s could not have repeated Land's accomplishment in ten years of unremitting labor). In 1947, he astounded a gathering of optical scientists with a demonstration of "instant photography" and next year offered the first Polaroid Land camera for sale.

It cost $89.75, and produced sepia-toned prints of somewhat indifferent quality, but it did so in just a minute after the photographer had snapped the picture. The camera was an instant success, and Land kept barraging the public with a constant stream of improvements and innovations.

Edwin Land has said on several occasions that if you can state a problem it can be solved. A risky proposition, but one that Land has so far managed to demonstrate fairly well. He told stockholders' meetings that soon after that famous picture-taking session with his daughter he had solved all the problems of instant photography—all except the ones that took from 1943 to 1972.

The basic method in Land's revolutionary system, from the Model 95 on, was to encapsulate the special developing chemical within the film package. Once exposed, the film was shoved through rollers that rupture pods containing the chemicals, and development was quickly completed.

But Land's dream of what he called absolute "one-step" photography required some thirty years for realization—during which Polaroid Corporation grew to become an enormously successful business and made him a multimillionaire. In 1950 came black-and-white film; in 1955, fast films; by 1960, fifteen-second prints, ultra-high-speed film, and automatic exposure cameras; in 1963, an incredibly complex color film.

And in 1972, the camera followed that seems at last to do what the insatiable Dr. Land wants—the SX-70. Described in a *Popular Science* story as "perhaps the most fiendishly clever invention in the history of photography," the SX-70 was the pocketable camera Polaroid's engineers had wrestled to design for years. Fully automatic, it produced clean, dry plastic-coated color prints at the touch of a button, one every couple of seconds if the photographer wished. Among the many startling technical innovations, each film pack contained its own water-thin battery. And the camera eliminated one of the chief deterrents to using the Polaroid system—fastidious photographers no longer had to deal with messy, chemical-laden scraps.

Land's immersion in every detail of his company's workings is legendary. The development of the SX-70 is no exception. One story circulating at Polaroid concerns the seemingly endless efforts to perfect the color response of the SX-70 film. Land snapped a picture of one employee who was wearing a shirt of distinctive color. Unhappy with the result, Land demanded—and got—the shirt off the man's back until he could get the film's rendition right.

Those who know him cannot believe that Land will stop here. No one knows for sure what surprises the prestidigitator of Polaroid has next in store. Would instant movies be asking too much?

CHAPTER 5

Thomas Alva Edison— 1,093 Patents!

DOWN the track in front of the railroad station at Mount Clemens, Michigan, rumbled a heavy boxcar coasting toward a switch.

Squarely in the way of the deadly tons of metal in motion, oblivious to his peril, stood a little three-year-old boy—the son of stationmaster James Mackenzie. Somehow the tot had eluded the eye of his father, who was chatting with a young friend at the time, and wandered out on the track.

First to catch sight of the tragedy in the making was Mackenzie's fifteen-year-old visitor. One horrified look was enough to send him sprinting toward the little boy, in a life-or-death race with the oncoming boxcar. He *had* to win it—and by a split second he did, barely in time to snatch up the stationmaster's son and lunge out of the car's way. It was so close that a wheel of the car grazed the heel of his shoe.

The youthful hero of that rescue was Thomas Alva Edison—who in later years would become famous as America's greatest inventor of them all. On that summer day in 1862, his job was selling newspapers and candy on the Grand Trunk Railway's daily train from Port Huron, Michigan, to Detroit and back. During the long stops for freight-car switching, that the train made at Mount Clemens, he had struck up a friendship with the stationmaster, and watched in fascination as Mackenzie expertly pounded his telegraph key. Now fate had made him Mackenzie's benefactor.

What do you say to a fifteen-year-old who has just saved your little boy's life, heedless of risk to his own? How can you possibly find a way to express your gratitude? Any conceivably fitting reward in money was beyond the power of Mackenzie, a man of modest means. Instead, what came to him instinctively was to make a gift of the most valuable thing he possessed: his skill as a telegraph operator. Would young Edison, he asked hesitatingly, accept Mackenzie's offer to teach him to be a professional telegrapher?

It couldn't have been a happier inspiration. The words were sweet music to the youthful vendor of papers and candy. And so began three months of evening lessons at Mount Clemens that would be the turning point of Edison's career, by kindling his interest in things electrical. Mackenzie proved a gifted teacher—and Edison so apt a pupil that, his lessons completed, he was qualified and ready for a "pro" telegrapher's job.

The chain of events that put young Edison on the Mount Clemens station platform in the nick of time to forestall a tragedy had begun in the morning of February 11, 1847, when a lusty squall announced his arrival in the world at his parents' Milan, Ohio, home.

His father Samuel Edison, a headstrong six-footer, was a Canadian exile. Samuel had been a pioneer settler of a timberland Ontario community named Vienna—where he met and married an equally strong-minded woman, Nancy Elliott, the schoolteaching daughter of a Baptist minister. Samuel's part in an abortive 1837 attempt to over-throw the Canadian Government, sparked by a home rule con-troversy, forced him to flee that country in a hurry. His wife and their four Canadian-born children soon followed.

They found haven in another frontier settlement safely across the border in Ohio, the Great Lakes port of Milan. Here Samuel himself built them a seven-room frame and brick house, and set up a mill to turn Canadian lumber into shingles. To swell the income from the successful enterprise, he helped to build the region's "plank road" (now Route 601). Meanwhile the family grew, and the seventh child of Samuel and Nancy was Thomas Alva Edison.

Childhood escapades foreshadowed that the newcomer to the fam-ily would sometimes be a problem:

At about six, Thomas Alva "experimented" by building a fire inside his father's barn, behind their home. The barn burned down. In those pioneer days when a fire's menace was everyone's business, public outrage could be satisfied only by a public whipping in the village square—meted out by the constable, a *Popular Science* writer said (although another source gave the role to Edison's own father).

Another disastrous experiment was inspired by the boy's misguided conviction, after watching a balloon inflated, that you could rise like a balloon yourself by swallowing enough effervescing Seidlitz powders to inflate yourself with gas. Cautiously he decided to forgo making the initial trial on himself; instead, he persuaded the Edisons' not too bright chore boy to accept the great honor of becoming the first human balloon, and encouraged him to down great quantities of the fizzing potion. Instead of ascending, the hapless subject became

From the Laboratory of Thomas A. Edison
Orange 17 Aug 14 19..

Dear Canty

In reply to your question, let me say that I was the first person to speak into the first phonograph. The first words spoken by me into the original model and that were reproduced, were "Mary had a little lamb" and the other three lines of that verse.

Yours sincerely

Thos A Edison

Edison was only thirty-one at his career's peak—as vividly brought home by his youthful appearance then, in this portrait printed in *Popular Science* in 1878. That year, he received his patent for the world's first phonograph, which had just played back his historic trial recording of "Mary Had a Little Lamb." In a later letter to a friend (right) he verified that these were his talking machine's first words.

Brick-and-frame home at Milan, Ohio, was birthplace on February 11, 1847, of Thomas Alva Edison, son of Canadian-born shingle-mill owner Samuel Edison, Jr., and Nancy Elliott Edison, a former schoolteacher. Thomas was their seventh child. In 1854 the big family moved to Port Huron, Michigan.

Early portrait of Edison was this photo when he was three and a half years old. One of his earliest recollections went back about to then: in 1850 or 1851, six covered wagonloads of campers at Milan were on their way to join the gold rush in California.

Edison's strong-minded mother, incensed when his teacher called him "addled," championed his refusal to return to the Port Huron school—and tutored him herself. He always fondly remembered her standing up for him.

At about seven, Edison poses with an older sister, Harriet Ann ("Tannie"). She was the fourth of his brothers and sisters to die at an early age.

Edison at fourteen was a newsboy and candy "butcher" on Grand Trunk trains between Port Huron and Detroit. On one trip he saved a life.

While his train stopped here, fifteen-year-old Edison saw stationmaster Mackenzie's little boy about to be struck by a rolling boxcar—and risked his own life to snatch the tot to safety. His reward from the grateful father, lessons in telegraphy that made him a crack operator, played a major part in shaping Edison's future career.

violently ill—and Edison's mother, this time, punished him with a switching.

But it was she who took his part at a crucial moment in his young life. The family had moved to Port Huron, Michigan, in 1854 and the following year saw eight-year-old Edison enrolled in a one-room school there, conducted by a parson. Within three months the boy proved a misfit. Formal grammar school teaching in nineteenth-century style, enforced by the teacher's leather strap, utterly failed to kindle Thomas Alva and he sank to the bottom of his class. It came to a head when he chanced to overhear his instructor, baffled by his poor showing, call him "addled." Shattered by his teacher's inept misjudgment, convinced he really was a dunce and a miserable failure, he rushed home in tears—and refused to go back.

For all his life he gratefully remembered the uplift to his crushed spirits when his mother, hearing his story, angrily stood up for him and yanked him out of the reverend's dreary classes. Nancy Elliott Edison was a qualified schoolteacher; she herself would see to tutoring her unjustly maligned son!

Each morning from then on, as soon as her housework was done, she coached Thomas Alva in the three Rs. Most important of all, she succeeded in teaching him the why of learning—and inspired the inquisitive boy with a lasting love of it.

At nine he had read Hume's *History of England*,. Gibbon's *Decline and Fall of the Roman Empire,* and a history of the world. But the real treat for him was his first science book—Richard Green Parker's *Natural and Experimental Philosophy,* on elementary physics. Within a year he'd tried out for himself almost every experiment it described.

The quiet cellar of his home became his laboratory and retreat. Soon it held rows of bottles of chemicals, too—all of which he labeled "POISON" so no one would molest them, said a *Popular Science* account.

Samuel Edison, his athletic father, thought his son a bit queer not to be out playing games with other boys. But sports didn't interest Thomas Alva; his home lab did.

So did the locomotives of the Grand Trunk Railway, with their ornate bands of brass, and painted woodwork. When the line opened a machine shop at Port Huron in 1859, twelve-year-old Edison became a regular hanger-on, and a rail buff. Often he was able to wheedle a brief ride in a locomotive cab with the engineer. On red-letter days, an indulgent one let him take the controls himself. He'd watched them so closely that he didn't need to be told how.

The daily train between Port Huron and Detroit needed a newsboy. Thomas Alva coveted the job. His father and mother gave their permission; Samuel Edison himself applied for the position for his son, and got it.

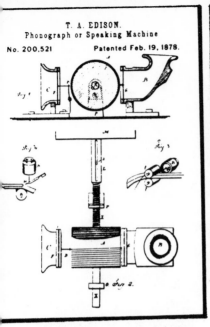

T. A. EDISON.
Phonograph or Speaking Machine

No. 200,521   Patented Feb. 19, 1878.

T. A. EDISON
Electric-Lamp

No. 223,898.   Patented Jan. 27, 1880

Edison went on to become the champion U.S. inventor. The phonograph (above) and incandescent electric lamp (right) were among his most famous feats of wizardry.

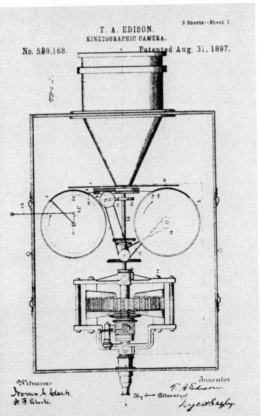

T. A. EDISON.
KINETOGRAPHIC CAMERA.

3 Sheets—Sheet 1.

No. 589,168.   Patented Aug. 31, 1897.

Witnesses

Inventor
T. A. Edison
By his Attorneys
Dyer & Seely

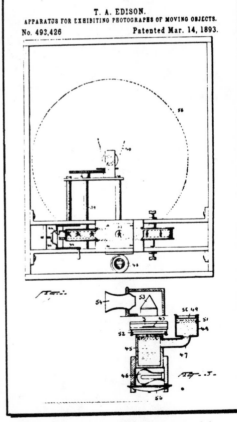

T. A. EDISON.
APPARATUS FOR EXHIBITING PHOTOGRAPHS OF MOVING OBJECTS.

No. 493,426   Patented Mar. 14, 1893.

A movie pioneer, Edison contributed ingenious and practical forms of a motion-picture camera (left) and viewer (above). In all, he made more than one thousand inventions, many of them illustrated on pages of pictures in this chapter.

Nobody wanted Edison's first patented invention—this electric vote recorder that he conceived at twenty-one, while a telegrapher in Boston. He took it to Washington to demonstrate to Congressmen, who spurned it. His lesson learned, he thenceforth stuck to ideas meeting real needs.

Dramatic success in fixing a broken-down ticker for gold prices, on a New York visit, gave Edison a new job— where he devised improved models like this one, called a printing telegraph. In 1871 he went into business for himself, in Newark, manufacturing and selling his much-in-demand gold tickers and stock tickers.

At fourteen, Thomas Alva was peddling papers and candy on the three-hour train run, leaving Port Huron daily at 7 A.M., and ending the return trip from Detroit at 7:30 P.M. His gainful venture matured him fast. A jaunty young entrepreneur, whose amiable self-reliance won him friends all along the way, he earned up to eight or ten dollars on a good day.

The train's long layover in Detroit, from ten to four-thirty, gave him the privilege of browsing for hours in the Detroit Public Library —the largest and most fascinating he'd ever seen. As if fearful of missing anything, he'd start with the first book on a library shelf and devour them all, one by one. "I didn't read a few," he liked to recall, "I read the library."

His prospering business as the train's newsboy enabled young Al, as he was called, to hire assistants—ultimately four of them, according to a *Popular Science* biographical sketch of Edison in 1878. To occupy the spare time he thus gained en route, he obtained permission to set up a chemistry lab in his train's baggage car. He also installed there a small printing press he'd bought secondhand, together with some type, in Detroit. By early 1862 he was the writer and publisher of the first newspaper printed aboard a train, called the *Weekly Herald,* and made up of local news and gossip.

These baggage car pursuits came to an untimely end one day, when a lurch of the car on rough roadbed threw a jar of phosphorus sticks from its chem-lab shelf, spilling the water that had covered them. Exposed to the air, the phosphorus ignited, and set the car's wooden floor afire. An irate conductor, after helping to put out the fire, summarily evicted Edison and his belongings from the baggage car— including his chem lab and printing press, too.

Edison himself later refuted a widely told myth that the conductor had boxed his ears so severely as to cause the deafness that afflicted him from his youth. By Edison's own version, his hearing actually became impaired when a friendly trainman was trying to help him out of a perilous predicament:

Laden down with papers, he'd tried to board his train as it was pulling out. He barely got a foothold on the rear step—and teetered there, in imminent danger of falling off, as the wind whipped his papers and the train gathered speed. Spotting his plight, the trainman yanked him aboard by the part of his anatomy within nearest reach— his ears. It may have saved his life; but Edison felt something snap in his head, he said, and always believed his deafness dated from that day. Those who knew him learned to raise their voices so he could hear.

Notwithstanding the baggage car fire, he kept his Grand Trunk job. And so it came about that he was chatting with station agent Macken-

zie during a train stop, the following summer, when he had the opportunity to save a life himself.

When the reward of Mackenzie's tutoring turned Edison into a
"pro" telegrapher, he began his new occupation as the Port Huron operator. Before long he contributed an original twist of his own.

An ice jam in the winter of 1862–63 broke the telegraph cable
across the St. Clair River, cutting off communication between Port
Huron and Sarnia, Ontario. Edison had a locomotive brought up to
the Port Huron dock, and its whistle began to startle residents' ears
with a succession of short and long toots—dots and dashes of the telegraph code. A telegraph operator across the river quickly got the
idea. A Canadian locomotive started whistling back—and the three-
quarter-mile distance was bridged by this emergency acoustic
telegraph—a *Popular Science* writer facetiously called it a pioneer
"wireless telegraph"—until the cable could be repaired.

Better opportunities for a telegrapher followed in other cities—and
Edison reached the big-league circuit of his profession when, in 1868,
a job opened for him as a Western Union operator in Boston.

On reporting for duty in the Boston telegraph office, the callow
twenty-one-year-old newcomer could sense that he was in for a hazing
from his citified fellow operators—and he couldn't have been more
right. By their prearrangement, a torrent of dots and dashes was soon
coming over the line to him from a crack New York operator, sending
press dispatches at his top speed. Coolly Edison transcribed a dizzy-
ing stream of messages. At length the grueling pace began to tire the
New Yorker himself—and Edison broke in to gibe at him, "Send with
your other foot." Finally the veteran key-pounder, the terror of many
a novice before, conceded defeat with a wondering, "Say, who are
you?" Replied the new man, "I'm Tom Edison—shake!"

Early in Edison's career as a telegrapher, this account should pause
to note, signs had begun to appear of his inventive talent—often for
decidedly informal ends:

In 1863, when he was a seven-to-seven night operator for the
Grand Trunk line at Stratford Junction in Canada, long hours and
infrequent messages were apt to leave a telegrapher drowsy. To make
sure he stayed awake, a rule required him to transmit the word "six"
at regular half-hour intervals. Edison circumvented the regulation by
devising a notched wheel actuated by a clock, that would automatically transmit a "six" over the main circuit at each appointed time.
Then he could doze in peace. He was finally caught at it—when
another operator found he didn't respond to signals between the
"sixes"—but got off with a reprimand.

The Grand Trunk line had given Edison a railroad pass for a free trip to his new job in Boston, when he lacked the fare himself, in return for a method he had originated of making one of their underwater cables do the work of two.

In Boston, where his telegraphic prowess soon earned the respect of his office mates, he found a way to deal with an infestation of cockroaches—the result of the Western Union office's having once been a restaurant. Edison glued two parallel strips of tinfoil along the wall, with a narrow gap between, and wired one strip to each pole of a powerful telegraph battery. When a cockroach walked up the wall and across the gap between the charged strips, it was instantly electrocuted. A newspaper printed a story about Edison's electric cockroach-zapper. His office manager, unhappy about the image it gave the place, made Edison remove it.

The young telegrapher's penchant for inventing was undiscouraged. It gained fresh inspiration when he happened upon the Boston electrical workshop of Charles Williams, Jr., then a factory for early fire alarms. It was also a mecca for inventors as famous as Alexander Graham Bell, who did much of his work on the telephone there. Edison, too, obtained quarters in the Williams shop, where he could perform spare-time experiments and enjoy the opportunity to hobnob with other inventors.

Their inspiration planted the seeds of an ambition to swap his career as a telegrapher for one as an inventor—backed at first by funds from friends, in return for a part interest in his ideas. But he'd test his success at it before burning his bridges.

In 1869 he obtained his first patent, for an electrical vote recorder. It could be used advantageously, he believed, to speed up the voting of Congressmen on a pending measure; by pressing buttons at their desks, all would register their votes at once, and no time-wasting roll call would be needed.

Like many an inexperienced inventor, Edison had begun with a device whose prospective customers would be few indeed—and mistakenly supposed they would welcome it. When he journeyed to Washington and demonstrated a model of his vote recorder to a congressional committee, his idea met with an icy reception, by a *Popular Science* account. Congressmen wise in the ways of practical politics told him why—filibusters and delays in counting votes were time-honored means of killing off unpopular legislation. (History would prove Edison's first patented invention precisely 104 years ahead of its time; it was not until 1973 that the House of Representatives did install an electronic vote-counting system, of a modernized design that of course resembled Edison's only in purpose.)

Then and there, Edison learned better than to waste time, effort, and money on an invention that nobody wanted.

Romance blossomed for Edison and a Newark girl, Mary Stilwell, who helped him in experiments. They were wed in 1871, when Edison was twenty-four. Photo of him (above) was made near that time; of her (right), about twelve years after their marriage.

Edison's "electric pen" (foreground) was forerunner of mimeograph. Vibrating needle point perforated paper to make a stencil. Motor ran on wet cells.

In hundreds of experiments, as pictured here, Edison perfected ways to transmit two to six telegraph messages at once over a wire—a long-sought goal.

Five years after his marriage, Edison moved from Newark to this home in Menlo Park, New Jersey, where he built a new laboratory and factory. From this lab, destined to become world-famous, came his phonograph and his incandescent electric lamp.

Two-story frame building below was Edison's Menlo Park "lamp factory." His family and lab assistants surround him in 1879 group picture at right. Beside him are his two children Marion and Thomas, Jr. (nicknamed "Dot" and "Dash"). In top row is his white-haired father, Samuel Edison.

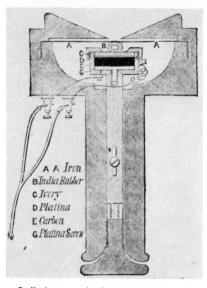

A A *Iron*
B *India Rubber*
C *Ivory*
D *Platina*
E *Carbon*
G *Platina Screw*

Bell invented the telephone, but Edison first gave it a ruggedly practical transmitter—the "carbon-button" type above, the prototype of the kind you use today.

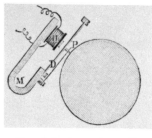

Among other telephone inventions Edison pioneered an automatic message-taker (above) to put an incoming phone call on a phonograph cylinder to play back later. He designed a *non-electric* telephone (right) to transmit voices through gas in a gas pipe!

A battery of smoking kerosene lamps produced the carbon for Edison's telephone transmitters. His first successful one had used lampblack, and Edison single-mindedly clung to that source.

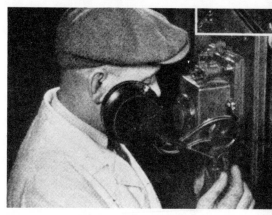

Edison got around Bell's telephone-receiver patents for rival interests, with his weird "motograph" above. A rotating chalk drum actuated the diaphragm through a frictional contact. It wasn't good but it was extremely loud.

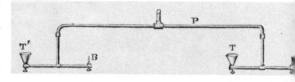

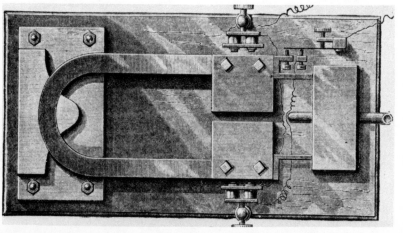

"Harmonic engine," an Edison novelty of the 1870s, was a battery-powered electric motor, whose vibrating tuning-fork arms worked a tiny pump, compressing air to drive a sewing machine or other light machinery.

His second patent was for a stock ticker, a radically improved version of one put in service in New York in 1867 by an inventor named E. A. Callahan. A stock ticker essentially was a printing telegraph; and Edison's type eliminated need for an operator at the receiving end. Its simplified circuitry also dispensed with much of the wiring of the Callahan system.

An Edison installation with thirty subscribers was soon in operation. But the members of his small company had conflicting business ideas; and the venture ended with a telegraph company's purchase of the patent rights—a deal in which Edison's share, when the proceeds were divided, was meager.

Meanwhile he'd kept his job in the Boston telegraph office. But his heart wasn't in it—he'd caught the fever of inventing. Much as a prospector clings to the hope of striking it rich, and an unlucky gambler persists in believing his next bet will be a winner, Edison was undiscouraged by the limited success of his inventions so far—and his stock of fertile ideas gave him better reason.

He couldn't wait to get to his niche in Williams' shop, and took time out at his job, for experiments to test promising inspirations. He got away with it.

But a reckless dispute with his no-nonsense boss—over the unacceptably tiny handwriting he capriciously adopted to transcribe stock market figures—got him banished from Western Union's press wire and relegated to sending only. That did it, and he resigned. He published his declaration of independence in a telegraph trade paper by announcing, at twenty-one, that he'd now devote all his time to inventing.

A "duplex telegraph" that would simultaneously send messages in opposite directions was his next innovation. With a borrowed $800 he staged a demonstration of it between New York and Rochester in April 1869. The exhibition was a flop because the New York operator didn't understand Edison's detailed written instructions, *Popular Science* said.

Now flat broke and in debt, Edison managed to borrow barely enough more to buy a ticket for a trip by boat to New York, to try his luck in the big city. He arrived without enough in his pocket to pay for a meal, let alone a night's lodging. Passing a warehouse, he saw a tea taster at work and asked if he might sample a cupful; that was his breakfast. He looked up a telegraph operator he knew, who proved to be out of work, but lent him a dollar; apple dumplings and a cup of coffee came out of that. Edison found no New York opening at Western Union and trudged on to the Broad Street office of the Gold Indicator Company, which furnished 300 brokers with the latest quotations of the price of gold—more coveted than paper money, just after the Civil War—over a telegraph system like those used for stock tickers. Its electrical engineer, Franklin L. Pope, had heard of Edison's stock ticker in Boston. But the best Pope could do for the wayfarer was to let him use a cot in the basement battery room for sleeping quarters.

With all odds against success in Edison's seemingly foolhardy journey to New York without funds, capricious fate took a hand and suddenly threw him his big chance. An uproar in the company's transmitting room brought him running to see what was happening.

That day, the price of gold was fluctuating wildly, under pressure of heavy speculation. And that was the moment when the Gold Indicator Company's central transmitter conked out, like a TV set going dead just at the instant of a touchdown play. Within minutes, messengers from the hundreds of subscribers were there, clamoring that they were getting no figures.

The head of the company, S. S. Laws, stood staring helplessly at the stalled transmitter, apoplectic as he envisioned the ruin of his $300,000-a-year business. Pope, beside him, was too panicked by the emergency to be of the slightest aid. Only one person in the big room —Edison, who'd studied the machine at first sight—noticed that a tiny contact spring had fallen into its gears and jammed them. Calmly he told Laws and Pope that he saw the trouble. "Fix it! Fix it!" Laws fairly screamed at him.

Out came the troublemaking spring and, with a few deft touches, the transmitter was quickly put back in order and running again. At once, Laws hired Edison, at the best salary he'd ever had, to help Pope keep it that way. A few weeks later, when Pope left to take another job, Edison took over Pope's at what was then a comparatively princely $300 a month.

Had high finance been Edison's dish, he'd have fancied his grandstand-seat view of a historic example. Scheming to make a killing of millions, two notorious "robber barons" of the day, Jay Gould and James Fisk, set out to corner the gold market, and then sell their hoardings at a fanciful price. During the convenient absence of President Grant from Washington, they purchased $10 million worth of gold and drove up its price to 144. Their goal was 200, and on a "Black Friday" in September 1868 they suddenly acquired $28 million worth more of the precious metal. The audacious plot might have succeeded, but for the President's hasty return and his order to sell $4 million of the U. S. Treasury's gold reserve to check the decline of the dollar's value. The price of gold plummeted back to 132, and a business panic was averted.

Actually Edison was too busy refining the printing telegraph to take much note of the earthquake-like tremors in the financial world, recorded as if by a seismograph on the Gold Indicator. He patented a further improvement in his own name; and another, together with Pope. Then he and Pope formed an independent new company in Jersey City to manufacture and rent a gold printer that undersold a Western Union rival. A third member of the company, the publisher of *The Telegrapher,* contributed free advertising, and one third of the company's profits went to each. Thus, when Western Union bought the company's gold printer for $15,000 to eliminate its competition, Edison got $5,000. The short-lived company dissolved amicably when Edison felt he was contributing more than his share of the actual work, in return for his partners' business ability.

Edison accepted an invitation from Western Union's head, General Marshall Lefferts, to join its technical staff. Their "gentlemen's agreement" said nothing whatever about a salary, and was vague indeed on what Edison would be paid for any inventions he came up with. Nevertheless, naïvely but rightly, Edison was confident he'd get a square deal. Even in a day when sharp business practice was widely the rule, it was to Western Union's best interest to encourage its talented recruit to keep on laying golden eggs for them.

Within a few weeks, Edison showed bug-eyed Western Union officials a "Unison" stock ticker system that, all agreed, would make every other obsolete. Its built-in novelty was a means to synchronize all brokers' tickers automatically—by stopping every ticker at once from time to time, correcting any deviations of individual tickers from the others, and setting them all going again simultaneously.

To seal Western Union's acquisition of this prize, General Lefferts saw it was time to make a settlement with Edison, and suggested the inventor name an appropriate price for his creation. In Edison's opinion it was worth $5,000, but he hesitated to say so; as *Popular Science* told the story, he'd have been willing to settle for less and, instead of replying, asked Lefferts himself to propose a figure. When Lefferts asked how $40,000 would do, Edison struggled to regain his composure—and replied it would be agreeable to him.

It was Edison's first big money for an invention—coming only a year after he had arrived penniless in New York.

It was also the first payment he'd ever received by check. Not understanding what a bank teller was saying when he handed the check back, Edison mistakenly feared it was no good, and hastened back to Lefferts for an explanation. The general enjoyed a hearty laugh and explained Edison was supposed to endorse the check; to make sure there was no further difficulty, Lefferts sent his secretary along with Edison to identify him.

This time the bank teller couldn't resist an unworthy prank upon one so incredibly unaware of what to do with a $40,000 check.

Then came something new to the world—Edison's phonograph! His first one, above, made and played back a recording on tinfoil, wrapped around a cylinder turned with a hand crank. At right, old print shows Edison (far right, foreground) demonstrating machine to a group of enthralled listeners.

Enthusiastic story about Edison's "Talking-Machine," featured on cover of April 1878 Popular Science, printed these engravings (insets) to illustrate how the phonograph worked. Flywheel helped user to turn hand crank at uniform speed.

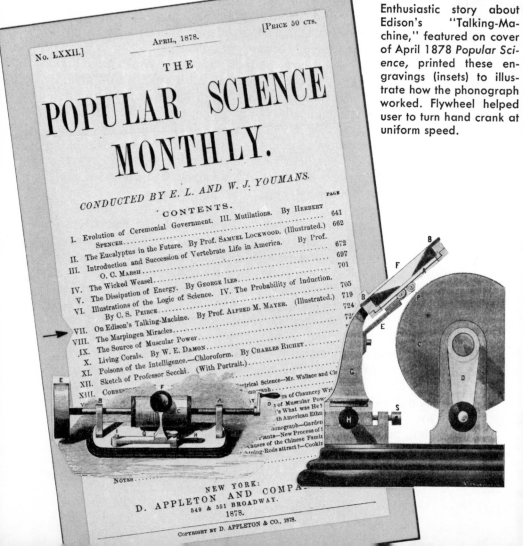

No. LXXII.]   APRIL, 1878.   [PRICE 50 CTS.

THE

POPULAR SCIENCE
MONTHLY.

CONDUCTED BY E. L. AND W. J. YOUMANS.

PAGE

CONTENTS.

NEW YORK:
D. APPLETON AND COMPAN
549 & 551 BROADWAY.
1878.

COPYRIGHT BY D. APPLETON & CO., 1878.

At left, Edison directs 1902 experiment in recording piano music, with long horn leading to piano's sounding board. Below is a cabinet-type Edison phonograph of 1915 that played wax-cylinder records it stored.

Edison's final major advance in sound recording was this forty-minute disc of 1926, a long-play record years ahead of its time, held by company official. Inventor's son, Charles Edison, looks on at left.

Edison had put off refining his original phonograph, until competition spurred him. Then, in seventy-two hours, he and staff produced 1888 wax-cylinder model at right and below.

Solemnly the teller cashed it with a stack of tens and twenties a foot high. Edison somehow managed to stuff all the bills into the pockets of his suit and overcoat, hurried home—and sat up all night to guard his treasure from thieves. Haggardly he returned next morning to Lefferts for advice. Taking pity on Edison's ignorance of money matters, the Western Union head made amends for his sleepless night by seeing that he was shown how to open a bank account and deposit his money there for safekeeping.

It was only the start of Edison's return for his invention. He received a Western Union order, worth half a million, for more than 1,000 of his stock tickers to be manufactured over the next several years.

Edison's agreement with Lefferts had made no commitment to work for Western Union exclusively. Naturally they would get first crack at his telegraph ideas, for which they were his best customer—but he had many other projects up his sleeve, in which they wouldn't be interested. A needed laboratory to perfect them all could well be combined with a factory to fill Western Union's order—and now, for the first time in his life, Edison had the money to set up the combination. He chose Newark for the site.

Unaccustomed to thinking big, he began in 1870 with a small lab and factory, and just a few employees. Again and again, he had to move his Newark enterprise to larger quarters, and increase his working force, as the venture prospered.

This "Newark period" of Edison's career, from 1870 to 1876, was only a curtain raiser for achievements that were to follow. Nevertheless it saw a succession of triumphs that would do credit to any other inventor in his whole lifetime.

Edison solved a classic problem that Alexander Graham Bell had long and vainly wrestled with—how to send many telegraph messages at once over the same wire. Edison's "duplex" telegraph had been just a start. Now he came up with a "quadruplex" system capable of sending four messages over a line at once, two in each direction. It was called "the most important contribution to telegraphy since Morse," and was credited with saving millions in contructing U.S. telegraph lines, in a biography by historian Lawrence A. Frost. For good measure, Edison produced a "sextuplex" telegraph, a six-messages-at-once system.

Pioneering in exploring other possible innovations in telegraphy, he obtained patents whose titles give an idea of their far-out variety: recording telegraphs, automatic telegraphs, chemical telegraphs, solutions for chemical telegraph paper, Roman-character telegraphs, and even "telephonic or electro-harmonic telegraphs"—which had been Bell's futile approach to a multiplex telegraph system, although Bell's telephone had been an offshoot of it.

Among non-telegraphic inventions was his "electric pen," whose vibrating, motor-driven point perforated paper with handwriting, and permitted multiple copies to be made from the inked paper. It became known worldwide as the mimeograph when he sold it to a Chicago firm to be put on the market.

When his ideas called for unavailable materials, Edison developed the materials too—for example, paraffin paper, which later became a familiar wrapping for things like bread and candy.

Romance entered Edison's life when he was smitten with the attractive young Newark girl Mary Stilwell, who assisted him in his paraffin paper experiments. The attraction was mutual, and she became Mrs. Edison on Christmas Day in 1871. They had three children. Their first two, a girl and boy christened Marion and Thomas, Jr., acquired the nicknames "Dot" and "Dash."

In 1876, twenty-nine-year-old Edison moved from Newark to set up a bold enterprise that was new to the world and would make him famous—an "invention factory," at Menlo Park, New Jersey.

Running his Newark stock ticker plant to fill Western Union's big order had been necessary—first to repay his investment in its equipment, and then to build up a nest egg for future ventures. But Edison had chafed at the demands of manufacturing work on his time—which he increasingly felt was a waste of his special talents as an inventor. He envisioned a new workshop, divorced from the task of turning out endless copies of inventions already made, and designed exclusively for perfecting the multitude of new ideas that constantly came to him.

The virgin site he selected was the crown of a knoll overlooking a flag stop on the Pennsylvania Railroad, twenty-four miles from New York. Here he erected his own two-story workshop. Painted white, the twenty-five-by-one hundred-foot frame building looked to a *Popular Science* reporter of 1878 "for all the world like a country meetinghouse, minus the steeple, and with the addition of a porch." The whole second floor was Edison's laboratory. The ground floor held a small front office, a modest library, a museum-like array of models of Edison inventions in glass cases, and a well-equipped machine shop, powered by a ten-horsepower steam engine.

Up until now, Edison had been little in the public eye, for his inventions in specialized fields like telegraphy had been far from the ken of the man in the street. If a visitor to the lab on the hill chanced to encounter a boyish-looking fellow with rumpled hair, and ask to be shown in to see Mr. Edison, he might be taken aback to find he was addressing the inventor himself.

Inventions that would come next—like Edison's phonograph, and his incandescent electric lamp—would turn his name into a household word, and earn him the sobriquet of the Wizard of Menlo Park.

A pricked finger led Edison to the phonograph, which came about in a backhanded sort of way.

Edison was working toward inventing the telephone when Alexander Graham Bell beat him to it. Graciously Edison conceded he'd been "fairly anticipated"—but Bell's success, instead of ending Edison's efforts, inspired him to experiment with further telephone ideas.

Tinkering with a laboratory hook-up of a telephone transmitter and receiver, Edison attached a sharp point to the receiver's diaphragm, to gauge the strength of its vibrations with his fingertip; he could sense its loudness better that way, than with his impaired hearing. Singing into the transmitter, he was impressed when the force of the receiver's vibrating point pricked his finger. If it could do that, he reasoned, it should be able to indent a lasting impression of the sound on a surface such as tinfoil, moving past the point.

What would happen, he pondered, if this "record" of a sound were now *retraced by a point attached to a diaphragm?* Edison felt sure that the original sound—say, a speaker's voice—would be re-created and made audible. So sure, in fact, that he confided his belief to a friend and lecturer, Edward H. Johnson. Apparently neither of them fully realized the possibilities of the idea; Edison's first modest thought was of applying it in a "telephone repeater," which would record words spoken over the limited distance they could then be heard via a telephone line, and mechanically repeat the words into another telephone line to take them farther.

Johnson added the "telephone repeater" plan to lectures he was giving on Edison's inventions—and found it fascinated his listeners. Newspaper reports of Johnson's talks credited Edison with the idea of a "talking machine." Shown the clippings, Edison agreed, "They are right. That is what it is—a talking machine!" Now it was up to him to make good on his words, by building one.

To his skilled machine shop foreman, Swiss-born John Kruesi, Edison handed a crude sketch of a simple piece of mechanism, marked "Make this." Further instructions, modifying the sketched design a little, seemingly followed. When Kruesi was done, Edison had a little machine consisting of a spirally grooved brass cylinder, turned by a hand crank, and moving slowly lengthwise as it rotated. At each side of the cylinder was a diaphragm with a stylus, like the one that had pricked his finger. In turn, each stylus could be brought against a sheet of tinfoil that Edison wrapped around the cylinder and fastened in place. The cylinder's lengthwise movement on a threaded shaft made the stylus follow the grooves.

On December 6, 1877, Edison sat before the device, set one of the points against the tinfoil, started turning the hand crank, and loudly recited the nursery rhyme "Mary had a little lamb. . . ." Then he reset the cylinder to the starting place, set the other point against the tinfoil, and turned the crank again. His assistants clustered around him to see what would happen.

Back from the tinfoil came the words Edison had just spoken—so clearly, that the voice was unmistakably his own. *"Mein Gott im Himmel!"* exclaimed awestruck Kruesi.

At thirty, Edison had invented the phonograph. When he applied for a patent it was granted in short order; the Patent Office found his device so original that nothing even like it had ever been proposed before. As word spread of his sensational talking machine, he was invited to demonstrate it to the National Academy of Sciences; to the secretary of the Smithsonian Institution; and to President Hayes himself, who sat up listening to it until three in the morning at the White House.

Of course the wavering pitch of a hand-cranked phonograph needed correction, and adding a flywheel to the shaft proved an inadequate solution; a constant-speed source of motive power must turn the cylinder. Back in his laboratory, Edison overcame the difficulty with a steam-powered phonograph—driven by a belt through the floor to the machine shop below, a *Popular Science* reporter observed in 1878. Since not everyone had a steam engine handy, spring motors and electric ones would follow. And tinfoil would give way to wax cylinders, for records. But perfecting the phonograph had to wait its turn, for Edison was off on another project.

When the phonograph had intervened, Edison was already at work on a basic improvement for the telephone. Bell's first battery-powered transmitter, which had a vibrating electrode dipping into a conductive liquid, was a delicate instrument best suited to tender handling in a laboratory. Edison envisioned a more rugged kind for home or office —a button of solid material, whose varying electrical resistance in response to pressure from a vibrating diaphragm, would likewise send the required undulating current over a telephone line.

The big question was, a button of *what* material? Seeking one that answered to his specifications, Edison vainly tried every chemical in his laboratory—some 2,000 in all, said *Popular Science*'s 1878 reporter. Finally an assistant brought him a broken lamp chimney with a thick encrustation of lampblack. Edison scraped off the sooty substance, molded it into a button—and found he had the very thing. His "carbon-button" telephone transmitter turned out to be the prototype of the kind used to this day.

Western Union wanted it, for a telephone system competing with Bell's, and asked Edison to name his price. History repeated itself and

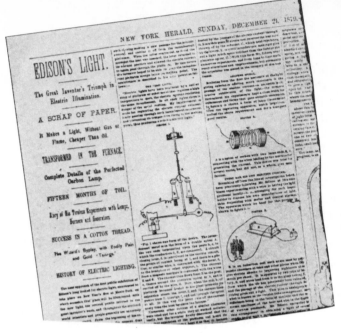

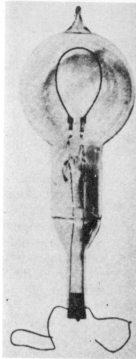

T. A. EDISON
Electric-Lamp

No. 223,898.   **Patented Jan. 27. 1880**

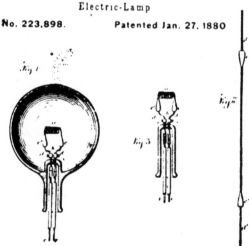

First practical incandescent electric lamp, above, was Edison triumph of 1879. New York *Herald* hailed it in big story above left. (It got one paragraph, no picture, in *Popular Science* at the time!)

Patent for Edison's lamp was granted the following year. Coil filament it showed was more advanced than looped form used for many years.

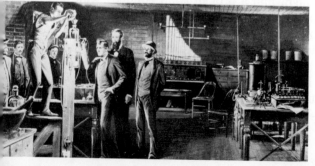

Furnace turned cotton, paper, a whisker, into carbon in Edison's quest for best material for incandescent-lamp filaments.

Edison watches a pumped-out bulb readied for test. At back of lab is organ he played for songfests with staff during breaks in work.

Whisker from red beard of old friend James Mackenzie (left) made filament for one Edison lamp. More-successful bulbs used bamboo (center) and "squirted" cellulose (right).

Besides his lamp, Edison perfected a lighting system—including primitive meter (right) and "long-waisted Mary Ann" dynamo (far right).

First electric-lighting plant, pictured in old engraving, introduced Edison system to New York in 1882. At start, powerhouse lit a total of fourteen thousand lamps.

Edison, who was thinking of $25,000 but hesitated to ask so much, proposed they make an offer. William Orton, who by then was Western Union's president, said, "One hundred thousand dollars." It was a deal, with a curious proviso requested by Edison that Orton was happy to accept: Edison would rather be paid in seventeen yearly installments, than all at once. It made sense to him because he knew he'd be tempted to spend the lump sum much sooner on his experiments, and then have none of it left.

Edison had expected his move to Menlo Park to give him plenty of opportunity to develop his ideas. Actually his inspirations now came so fast that they got in the way of each other.

A visit to a maker of arc lamps in 1878 kindled Edison's interest in electric lighting. Arc lamps, the only electric lights of the day, were too dazzling to use indoors. Incandescent lamps looked to Edison to be the thing—despite many others' earlier and unsuccessful attempts to produce practical versions.

The challenging problem was to keep an incandescent lamp filament from burning up when it was heated white-hot by the passage of electric current through it. Experiments convinced Edison that the answer was to exclude the air's oxygen from contact with the hot filament, by providing a high vacuum in a lamp bulb—the higher, the better.

The best vacuum pump available was a type called the Sprengel pump. While awaiting one he ordered from England, he was able to borrow a Sprengel pump from Princeton College. Improvements of his own enabled such a pump to remove all but one millionth of the air in a lamp bulb.

Like others before him, Edison tried lamp filaments of platinum, but he saw more promise in a filament of inexpensive carbon, which could be made by carbonizing a huge variety of raw materials in a furnace—and the hunt was on for the best, in the inventor's typical way of trying anything and everything.

What he considered his first successful incandescent lamp had a filament made from cotton sewing thread. As he and his assistants took turns standing watch, starting on October 16, 1879, it burned for forty-five hours—and then failed only when the voltage was deliberately raised to see how much it could stand. Edison saw a life of 100 hours in sight. An almost immediate switch to a filament of carbonized Bristol board proved a step in the right direction.

When Edison was wrestling with a major problem like his incandescent lamp, his day at the laboratory knew no quitting time and he worked on, far into the night. A few steps would have taken him home to bed—but, when weariness overcame him, he preferred to curl up on a bench for a brief nap and then be at it again. It was a

Fifty years later, at a New York broadcast studio, a receiver with the Edison tube below was proved able to pick up a radio program.

"Edison effect" discovered by inventor led others to radio vacuum tubes—which Edison just missed inventing, though he did make vacuum tubes he exhibits here.

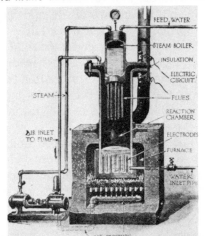

Edison invented fuel cells, to turn fuel directly into electricity, decades ahead of his time. One of his concepts, above, reacted steam with heated iron powder.

Beautiful Mina Miller, above, became the second Mrs. Edison in 1886, two years after the death of his first wife. He bought a new home for her, left, overlooking West Orange, New Jersey. The next year he moved his laboratory to West Orange—and Edison's fabled Menlo Park days were over.

tribute to the fanatical devotion he inspired in his closest aides, who had the satisfaction of taking part in creating his wonders, that they were willing to follow his example.

An unorthodox fixture of his laboratory was a pipe organ—on which Edison was "more than a fair performer," his assistant Francis Jehl wrote in *Popular Science*. After a midnight snack brought in by his night watchman, he and his men were wont to join in a rousing song fest, with Edison at the organ. Sometimes his expert glass blower, Ludwig Boehm, entertained them with German songs on his zither.

Edison invited the public to a demonstration of his incandescent lamp on New Year's Eve, 1879. The Pennsylvania Railroad ran special trains to Menlo Park. Some 3,000 people came to see the Wizard's latest marvel—and it was a show to remember.

White snow on the ground reflected the radiance of the new electric bulbs in lampposts, all along the half-mile way from the station up the road to Edison's laboratory, which was ablaze with electric light. So were Edison's home, and Sarah Jordan's boarding house near his lab, the home of many of his aides. They were the first residences ever lit by electric light. In all, more than 400 bulbs were wired up, and fed with current from a big generator in a special building near the lab.

Edison himself showed the milling visitors around, and encouraged them to lay loose bulbs, with conducting rods attached, across feeder mains in his laboratory and watch them magically light up. After the big show, his men found eight bulbs gone—some of the visitors had been irresistibly tempted to pocket them as souvenirs of the historic occasion.

Away from Menlo Park, at that time, incandescent electric bulbs would be useless, for lack of electric wiring to plug them into. The next goal Edison set himself was to build a great central lighting plant for New York City, with electric mains leading to wiring installed in the buildings of customers. Since such a system was unprecedented, Edison had to design everything for it from scratch—the generators, the underground mains, the lamp sockets (which by now held bulbs with filaments made from bamboo fibers, as they would be for ten years), and such practical details as electric meters to gauge a customer's bills for the electricity he used. The monumental task was completed by September 4, 1882, when Edison's pioneer central station on Pearl Street in New York City went into service.

Those were the highlights, but by no means the full story, of Edison's accomplishments during the "Menlo Park period" that marked the peak of his career. It would take a book to detail all his inventions and patents during those eventful years.

A picturesque feature of the final ones was America's first electric railroad, which grew to a three-mile experimental line. Using one of his "long-waisted Mary Ann" dynamos as a motor, Edison built a forty-mile-an-hour passenger locomotive that pulled a trainload of ninety people—and a slower freight locomotive for heavier duty. One rail of the track conducted electric power to the locomotive, and the other rail formed the return circuit.

The trials were enlivened by an accident when Kruesi, who was driving, overenthusiastically rounded a curve at full forty-mile-an-hour speed and the locomotive jumped the track—catapulting him face down beside the roadbed, and another man somersaulting into underbrush. Fortunately no one was hurt, a *Popular Science* account said, and the engine was set back on the tracks as good as ever. But it proved too early to interest the Northern Pacific or other U.S. railroads in electrifying their systems, and Edison's forward-looking vision of electric railways led nowhere at the time.

Married life had set well with Edison. The untimely death of his wife Mary in 1884, from typhoid fever, left a great void in his scheme of things. Sympathetic friends saw to it that he met likely successors, and the matchmakers scored when he was introduced to charming, cultured Mina Miller. Although only twenty, and eighteen years Edison's junior, she was wise beyond her years in the ways of inventors—being the daughter of a successful and wealthy Ohio one herself.

Edison taught her the telegrapher's Morse code, which could be transmitted just as well by a squeeze of the fingers as by a telegraph key—and they found a new use for the versatile means of communication. Holding hands, they could exchange sweet nothings in complete privacy, no matter who else was present. One day Edison summoned up the courage to ask her, in Morse, if she would marry him. Her answer was two pairs of dots for *Y,* a single dot for *E,* and three dots for *S.*

They were married in February of 1886, when Edison was thirty-nine. In time they would have three children; and one of these, Charles, would become a future governor of New Jersey.

To Edison it was time for a complete change of scene. He bought a palatial new home, called Glenmont, in the Llewellyn Park neighborhood of West Orange, New Jersey. Within a year, he moved his laboratory from Menlo Park to its final site in West Orange, where its newly built three-story brick building would soon be the nucleus of a cluster of structures housing Edison enterprises.

The story of Edison's ventures at West Orange from 1887 to 1910 almost defies being told in chronological sequence, because major events in so many of his endeavors stretched out into overlapping periods. Even at the expense of jumping about in dates, it seems bet-

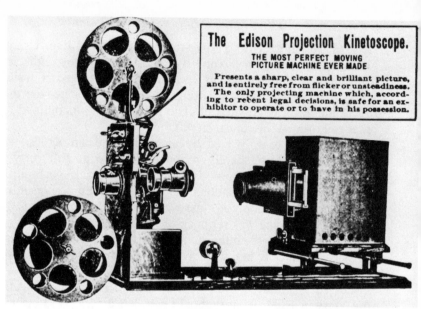

The Edison Projection Kinetoscope.

THE MOST PERFECT MOVING PICTURE MACHINE EVER MADE

Presents a sharp, clear and brilliant picture, and is entirely free from flicker or unsteadiness. The only projecting machine which, according to recent legal decisions, is safe for an exhibitor to operate or to have in his possession.

Edison's "projection Kinetoscope," above, based on Armat theater-screen projector he acquired, created the storied nickelodeon, or five-cent theater, at left. Views in Sears, Roebuck catalogs immortalized both of them.

Peepshow-type Kinetoscope, Edison's earlier version, had eyepiece for individual viewer. First "parlor" of coin-operated machines opened in New York in 1894.

With his motion-picture camera, Edison became an early filmmaker. He staged productions in world's first movie studio, above, which he built in West Orange.

Edison even made first sound movies. As boxers in studio vied before his camera, a recording horn (left foreground) made a phonograph record.

Electric-train experiments on ⅓-mile track, among Edison's last at Menlo Park, met with mixed success. Passenger version above, on one trial, jumped track on curve at 40 mph. Electric locomotive, right, could pull ninety-passenger train; another, though slower, could haul weighty loads. None ever went into commercial service.

Least-remembered of Edison's ventures, because fortune cheated it of well-deserved success, was his iron-mining enterprise of the 1890s near Ogdensburg, New Jersey. It got as far as the excavation of this huge open pit for ore.

Big mill at site, above, ground rock to powder and concentrated lean but excellent magnetite ore into black briquettes resembling burnt hamburgers, at right. Trials showed they worked fine in iron-smelting furnaces.

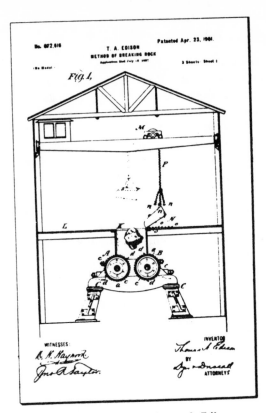

Unconventional ore crusher of Edison's design tore boulders to pieces with high-speed hobbed rolls. He later used it in making cement.

Edison, iron miner, superintends operation. It collapsed with discovery of vast Minnesota deposit of competing and cheaper iron ore.

With cement-making machinery salvaged from iron-ore mill, Edison tried producing concrete homes, poured in one day. Photo below shows one under construction at Union, New Jersey. Model of a finished all-concrete house is pictured in illustration at right.

ter to stick to one of his principal projects at a time:

One of the pioneers of motion pictures, Edison became a movie mogul. On the same day, July 31, 1891, he successfully applied for patents on a movie camera, which he called the Kinetographic Camera, and a viewer of the peephole type named the Kinetoscope. Having provided the equipment, Edison began producing movies himself.

At his West Orange laboratory, he built the world's first motion-picture studio. The wooden building admitted direct sunlight to its stage through a wide door in the roof, and turned on a pivot to follow the sun. A tar-paper covering and a black-painted interior, to eliminate reflections, gave it the nickname of the "Black Maria."

At first the studio produced short films—only a minute or so in length. Subjects included a dancer named Carmencita, performing bears, fencing matches, and feats of horsemanship, a *Popular Science* writer recalled. A few of the day's celebrities received the top fee of fifty dollars for appearing before the camera. (Among these was "Gentleman Jim" Corbett of contemporary boxing fame.)

Parlors lined with batteries of coin-operated peepshow-type viewers opened in cities, and attracted crowds to see the brief films.

For larger audiences, promoters urged Edison to develop a projector that could throw movies on a theater screen. Cool to the suggestion, he almost missed a great opportunity. In 1895 another inventor, Thomas Armat, came up with a theater-screen movie projector. Before anyone else could snap it up, an intermediary persuaded Edison and Armat to make a deal. Edison acquired the projector— and it was agreeable to both parties for him to make and market it under his famous name, rather than Armat's little-known one.

What resulted was the storied "nickelodeon," the five-cent theater. The Sears, Roebuck catalog of 1902 offered prospective operators the "Edison Projection Kinetoscope" (with either an electric arc lamp or a calcium burner) for $105; and a wide selection of films, some twenty minutes in length, "exclusively made in the Edison laboratory." Such was the popularity of the innovation that the 1908 Sears, Roebuck catalog declared, "THE FIVE-CENT THEATER IS HERE TO STAY. It fills a want that has existed in every community for a clean, up to date amusement . . . almost any vacant store room can be made into a five-cent theater by removing the glass front and replacing it with a regular theater front," complete with ticket booth, of which it printed an illustration.

A hit with audiences was a prototype of film dramas, *The Great Train Robbery,* released by Edison in 1904.

From the first, Edison experimented with synchronizing phonograph recordings with his pictures, anticipating the talkies; but they had to wait until much later to catch on with the public.

Patents controlled by Edison ruled the country's movie industry up to as late as 1917.

Edison the Iron Miner should have had a place in history alongside Edison the Moviemaker. His iron-mining venture of 1890–1900 was remarkable for the brilliantly original engineering that went into it—though today it is almost forgotten, because an unpredictable quirk of fortune cheated it of well-deserved success.

A prized ore of iron was black magnetite—popularly called lodestone—which attracts a compass needle and, conversely, is attracted by a magnet. Back in 1880 at Menlo Park, Edison had invented a magnetic separator that could extract this iron-bearing ore from powdered rock containing it. In 1889 he sent a crew with special magnetic needles on a survey from Canada to North Carolina, to look for the magnetic ore at 1,000-foot intervals and report what they found. They discovered a surprising number of promising deposits—most notably, a veritable mountain of magnetite ore overlooking Ogdensburg in the picturesque Sparta Mountains of northwestern New Jersey's Sussex County.

In 1890 Edison began construction there of a huge iron-mining and ore-concentrating plant, which became the center of a mountaintop community called Edison, New Jersey. The key to success, he figured, would be an economical way to recover the estimated 200 million tons of magnetite from three times as much barren rock with which it was intermingled.

Boldly Edison proposed to tear down the whole mountain of ore and reduce it to powder for his magnetic separator. Dynamite was an expensive source of energy, he reasoned, compared to steam power from coal. So he would use blasting only to knock loose great boulders of ore from the face of his open-pit workings. Out the window went the conventional next step of drilling and blasting each boulder into pieces small enough for an ordinary rock crusher to handle.

Instead, five-ton boulders were picked up bodily by the largest steam shovel yet built, and loaded into skips aboard narrow-gauge rail cars, to be hauled right to his mill. There, a traveling crane seized the loaded skips, and dumped the boulders into the most awesome mechanical rock-breaker the world had ever seen.

With a rending crash that could be heard from afar, a boulder as big as a piano was literally torn to pieces between a pair of six-foot-diameter "giant rolls" with projecting spikes, spun up to a surface speed of nearly a mile a minute by belts from a 700-horsepower steam engine. At the moment of impact, the belts could slip on the drive pulleys—an Edison innovation that averted damage to the driving machinery from the shock. The sheer momentum of the heavy,

Edison set out to produce a better storage battery than the conventional lead-acid kind. The result of his ten years' work was the nickel-iron-alkaline battery that he examines, left, in West Orange lab. It got test in thousand-mile run by Bailey electric car above. Ironically, Edison's new battery turned out to be better for other uses than in cars, the purpose he originally intended.

Battering-ram cart gave experimental new storage batteries a rugged test of stamina by jolting them against brick wall in background of photo. They were dropped from a height of three stories in other strenuous trials.

Mrs. Edison, at tiller, and her husband take a spin in a contemporary Baker Electric automobile that drew its power from Edison storage batteries. The date of the photograph is believed to be about 1903.

By test of time, Edison's alkaline storage battery has proved best suited for applications like those at top of this page, including electric tractor pictured in use above in an industrial plant.

A 1912 seven-cell Edison battery was still operating a crossing signal of the Delaware, Lackawanna and Western Railroad at Ackermanville, Pennsylvania, in 1959, when *Popular Science* printed this photo.

A family portrait shows the Edisons and some of their children in a Berlin hotel on a visit to Germany in 1911. Missing when picture was taken of group below was son Charles, by Edison's second wife, whose distinguished career included three years' service as governor of the state of New Jersey.

Storage batteries under seats powered this streetcar designed by Edison to run without trolley wire. Inset, lower view, shows him at its controls.

Edison was master of the art of cat-napping. Dozes of twenty to thirty minutes sufficed him during days on end of intensive laboratory work, and habit persisted in later years. Above, he snoozes on 1921 Maryland outing with friends, President Harding and Harvey Firestone.

Photographer caught another rare view of Edison asleep, on an outdoor camp cot, during a vacation in Canada. Camping trips with congenial companions to enjoy the surroundings of nature, far from the built-up scenes he left behind, had become one of Edison's favorite diversions.

speeding rolls sufficed to crack the boulder into pieces that would drop between them. Then the drive belts took hold again and brought the rolls back up to full speed for the next boulder.

Successively smaller rolls took turns in reducing the rock fragments' size—and ultimately they became a flourlike powder. It sifted in a thin stream past powerful magnets, which deflected the falling grains of magnetite into a bin to one side, while the barren rock dropped straight down into another bin.

The mill's final product was "briquettes" of the concentrated iron ore, made by mixing the black powder with a resinous binder and pressing it into round cakes, three inches in diameter and half as thick. The binder kept the briquettes from crumbling and made them weatherproof, so they could be shipped to market in open railway cars. They looked like plump, burnt-black hamburger patties—but if you picked one up, its telltale weight bespoke its heavy content of iron.

By 1897 the mill was ready for trial-scale production. Like a theatrical producer awaiting the critics' reviews of a play, Edison hung upon reports from the first users of the briquettes. They were enthusiastic. A typical report of a blast furnace trial by the Crane Iron Works at Catasauqua, Pennsylvania, showed the briquettes served better than standard iron ores—raising the furnace's output and reducing its fuel consumption at the same time.

As the word spread, orders rolled in. In 1898 and 1899, the mill was running at capacity. Then came the catastrophic blow:

Iron ore in fabulous quantities, easily mined, was discovered in the Mesabi Range of Minnesota, along the coast of Lake Superior. The new Sault Sainte Marie Canal gave it ready access to market—and the price of high-grade iron ore tumbled from $6.50 to $3.50 a ton.

At his mining headquarters in 1900, Edison studied his engineers' gloomy reports on the Mesabi development. Then he made the only possible decision: "Blow the whistle and pay the men off. We can't compete with this."

With abandonment of his iron works, two million dollars—largely Edison's own money—went down the great hole he had dug. A game loser, he remarked to a close associate, "Well, it's all gone, but we had a hell of a good time spending it."

He paid back every cent contributed by other backers. Then he plunged into new enterprises to recoup his own losses.

For the unique rock-breaking machinery he had devised, he found another use—and went into the business of making Portland cement. Edison cement plants of his own design introduced monster rotating kilns 150 feet long, compared to standard sixty-foot size. Contrary to skeptics' expectations, the plants were successful, and Edison became

Electrical geniuses got together when E[dis]son, left, inspected new apparatus sho[wn] him during visit with General Electric Co[.] Dr. Charles P. Steinmetz.

Milestone of a sort came when birthplace of Edison in Milan was first lit by electricity, as announced by *Popular Science* headline in 1924.

Fellow campers with Edison (center) 1923 were Henry Ford, at left of pictu[re] and Harvey S. Firestone at its right.

Now a grandfather, Edison poses proudly with daughter Madelaine's children—Ted, Jack, and Peter Sloane —for photograph taken in 1926.

To Frank Parker Stockbridge

Thos A Edison

Edison presented this autographed photo of himself to *Popular Science* interviewer Frank Parker Stockbridge in 1927, as age overtook him.

one of the country's largest producers of cement. His product went into New York City's Yankee Stadium, as well as a part of the Panama Canal, and countless buildings and bridges.

A pet idea he proposed in 1909, *Popular Science* noted, was to construct "instant houses" by pouring a free-flowing concrete mix he had developed into iron molds. He believed the houses could be erected in six hours, and ready to move into in three days. Actual poured-concrete houses demonstrated his idea a decade later.

In 1900 Edison embarked upon another major ten-year project—to develop a radical new kind of storage battery, which he thought would replace the standard lead-acid kind, and power electric automobiles of the future.

The result was his nickel-iron-alkaline battery—and the course of perfecting it was a struggle against "bugs" that plagued the first ones to be marketed. In the end the new storage battery was a success—though on a much more limited scale than Edison had optimistically pictured when he began.

What time showed the battery could and couldn't do was assessed by a *Popular Science* article about it in 1959:

> Edison had hoped, above all, that it would be adaptable for automotive traction. Automobile traction proved to be just what it was *not* suited for. Nor was it useful as a starter battery. Its voltage capacity tended to be lower than that of contemporary lead batteries, so that one needed more Edison cells for a given task—which offset their advantage of lighter weight.
>
> On the other hand, the beautifully constructed Edison battery was found particularly useful where dependability and long life were important, as for standby purposes at power plants, and for railway signaling; or to provide current for miners' lamps, train lights, and other railway and marine appliances. A remarkably wide field of usage was developed in industries such as mining and quarrying (for firing blasts), on merchant vessels, and on ships of war.

Contemporary accounts tell us what Edison looked like as a man. He was of chunky build, five foot ten in height and with a weight of about 185 pounds, which varied little for years. Gray eyes peered searchingly from beneath a high-domed forehead—in later years, "thatched as Pike's Peak in winter." Bluff and hearty in manner, he conversed informally in language well-laced with slang, with an oddly high-pitched voice that could become nasal at times.

His laboratory garb, original with him, bordered on the ridiculous. Instead of wearing a chemical worker's rubberized apron to protect his clothes from acids and such, Edison flapped about, one reporter noted, in "a long frock of checked gingham, which buttons close at the chin and reaches to his heels . . . a sight to laugh at, until you remember that it is Edison."

No teetotaler, Edison enjoyed a bottle of beer or a glass of champagne now and then. He smoked ten to twenty cigars daily—and kept a package of chewing tobacco in his pocket, too.

Rough-hewn Edison was a notorious practical joker. Neither his laboratory workers nor his social guests were spared. For a prize example, the tale is told that when he once invited friends to a steak dinner, he cut up slabs of half-inch-thick leather belting with his jackknife and had his cook heat them in an oven, cover them with gravy, and serve them to the unsuspecting diners. When he was sufficiently convulsed by watching their futile attempts to eat the mock "steaks," these were whisked away and the real ones brought in. The prelude could hardly have been much of an appetizer.

But as the years mellowed the boy in him, another brand of Edison humor appeared in his dry wit. Did he think, a *Popular Science* interviewer asked him, that mankind had progressed mentally in recent decades or millennia? He replied he definitely believed the proportion of honest, humane, and highly intelligent men was increasing; but, he added with a twinkle, "The Lord appears to be in no hurry."

Besides new projects, Edison worked at West Orange on unfinished business left over from his Menlo Park days.

His lamp filaments had been made for the past ten years from bamboo, the best material tried at Menlo Park, but he was still looking for a better one. He found it in "squirted cellulose," a synthetic product he made by forcing a cellulose material through a die. This gave a filament of perfectly uniform thickness, avoiding hot spots that would shorten its life when it was lit.

Edison returned to his long-neglected phonograph. His work on it had been pushed aside by his preoccupation with electric light. Now its improvement became urgent to meet the competition of rival phonographs like the Graphophone, introduced in 1887 by Alexander Graham Bell and associates, which used cylinder records of wax-coated cardboard. Edison countered with an all-wax cylinder record, and by intensive effort developed a new phonograph to play it.

Disc records, pioneered by Émile Berliner and adopted by leading companies like Victor and Columbia, came into vogue in the early 1900s. Edison held out until 1910, when he and his "insomnia squad" worked day and night for weeks, without leaving his laboratory, to perfect his "diamond-disc" records and a phonograph to go with them.

Edison had ideas all his own of what a disc record should be. His discs, nearly a quarter inch thick and weighing almost a pound apiece, looked like millstones compared to other makers' wafer-thin ones—and would fill a shelf or record cabinet in short order. Until the late 1920s they were "hill-and-dale" recordings, rather than the "lat-

At desk, Edison scans day's pile of mail, and jots down penciled directions for answers by his secretaries or his right-hand man, William H. Meadowcroft (in oval, top left). Balcony of West Orange laboratory, above, holds Edison's reference library.

Edison poses for a friend and noted fellow inventor—George Eastman, holding a 1928 Eastman home-movie camera. Eastman had just introduced pioneer home movies in color, using ribbed film and a three-color filter on the camera lens.

One of the last of Edison's record total of inventions was this improved miner's lamp, which he displays in a 1928 picture. Its current comes from case containing a compact version of his now widely used alkaline storage battery.

eral" ones that dominated the market long before then. Edison's own studio recorded the many famed artists they featured.

A striking phonograph innovation was a forty-minute Edison disc record, described and illustrated in *Popular Science* in early 1927. The invention of the modern long-play record in 1948 is credited to Peter Goldmark, but Edison must be rated as a pioneer.

Legends and myths grow up around famous men, and Edison was no exception. His mail, his confidential secretary William H. Meadowcroft recalled, long included inquiries about the "Edison star" that the inventor was supposed to launch daily in the evening sky. Actually it was just a yarn, concocted by a reporter at the time of the incandescent lamp's debut, and not intended to be taken seriously.

Once an interviewer reported Edison was working on a loudspeaker for receiving spirit messages. Edison long evaded other reporters' questions about it, but finally confessed sponsoring the myth himself, and a *Popular Science* writer told how the tale was born:

"That man," Edison said of the interviewer, "came to see me on one of the coldest days of the year. His nose was blue and his teeth were chattering. I really had nothing to tell him, but I hated to disappoint him—so I made up the story about communicating with the spirits. . . . It was all a joke." Not knowing it, the reporter happily bore away a "scoop" of a sort.

In 1916, Edison at sixty-nine was introduced to the pleasures of camping out, close to nature, by his good friends Henry Ford, Harvey Firestone, and the naturalist John Burroughs. Thereafter they took an annual camping vacation together, traveling by car to peaceful spots remote from the workaday world for an outing of ten days or so. When Burroughs died in 1921, President Harding accepted their invitation to take his place. They were dude campers, taking along a chef, and tents lit by Edison's storage batteries. Edison brought books to read, often dozed, and joined the others in swapping yarns late into the night.

With the outbreak of World War I, Edison relieved U.S. shortages of imported chemicals by designing a factory that produced a ton a day of synthetic carbolic acid, and plants making coal-tar derivatives that are said to have led the way in development of the American coal-tar chemical industry.

In 1915 the Secretary of the Navy asked Edison to head a board to devise new military weapons for national defense. It was a task abhorrent to him, for he hated war; but he considered it his patriotic duty to accept, and contributed many original ideas of his own. Perhaps to his relief, the conservative Navy brass never got around to adopting any of them.

Final major project of Edison aimed to end U.S. dependence on foreign rubber by discovering native source. He tested fourteen thousand plants, and notes some results, top left. Harvey Firestone, at far right above, shows him how rubber trees are tapped.

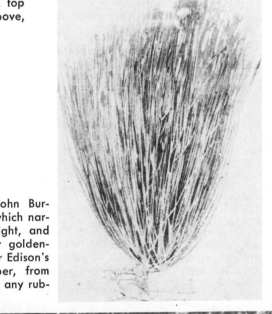

Henry Ford (holding saw) and naturalist John Burroughs view Florida site of Edison's tests—which narrowed choice to desert milkweed, upper right, and goldenrod. Net result of entire project: four goldenrod rubber tires made by Harvey Firestone for Edison's Model A Ford touring car. Synthetic rubber, from chemicals, would ultimately prove better than any rubber extracted from domestic plants.

In 1927, at Edison's age of eighty, his great lifework was nearly done—though he would have refused to admit it. That year he began his last major project, a four-year search for a domestic rubber-yielding plant that could make the nation independent of foreign rubber.

His long robust health was finally failing. His loyal associates knew it, and made allowances for his uncharacteristic testiness in the laboratory. Knowing he would go on working regardless, his wife encouraged him to undertake the rubber project, primarily because it would spare him the rigors of northern winters. The work of growing and testing semitropical plants could best be done at an experimental plantation in Fort Myers, Florida, where he had earlier acquired a winter home that could be his headquarters.

In all, Edison tested more than 17,000 different plants—and found as many as forty domestic species that would yield appreciable quantities of rubber. One promising candidate was desert milkweed, a leafless shrub, reported a *Popular Science* interviewer, Frank Parker Stockbridge, in December 1927. But, surprisingly, the best turned out to be goldenrod, which could be grown anywhere in the country and harvested by machinery. Toward that end, Edison bred a strain of goldenrod more than ten feet tall.

For once, though, Edison's trial-and-error technique was unequal to an impossible task. Not even the most promising plants that he tested proved able to yield rubber at a cost competitive with the imported kind. The net result of the whole project was a set of goldenrod-rubber tires that his friend Harvey Firestone had custom-made for Edison's Ford car. Long after, by the time of World War II, the answer that Edison had vainly sought in nature was found in synthetic rubber made from chemicals.

The highlights of Edison's final years were honors he had so richly earned by his past achievements.

In 1927 the prestigious National Academy of Sciences elected him to membership. It was a fitting put-down for some of his learned critics of the past, who had looked down their noses at his comparative lack of formal academic qualifications for the ambitious projects he undertook.

A Congressional medal awarded to Edison in 1928 was a curtain raiser for the following year's national celebration of the fiftieth anniversary of his incandescent lamp—the "golden jubilee of light."

The scene of the golden jubilee's climax, attended by President Hoover, was a unique tribute to Edison—a reconstruction of Edison's Menlo Park laboratory, at Dearborn, Michigan, by his friend Henry Ford.

Ford had spared no expense or effort to reproduce it meticulously in every detail. Having bought the Menlo Park site, Ford scoured it

for all the remains that could still be found. The abandoned building
—successively used as a church, a dance hall, and a chicken shed—
had finally been torn to pieces by nearby farmers for lumber
to mend homes and barns. Ford bought every scrap of the authentic
lumber he could find around the countryside.

Like an archaeologist, Ford recovered and restored relics buried in
the ground—among them, Edison's broken laboratory mortar and
pestle. Ford tracked down, and bought up, genuine pieces of Edison's
Menlo Park equipment that had become scattered all over the
country.

To put it all together, just as it once had been, Ford needed expert
help—and found it when he located the only survivor of Edison's
Menlo Park team, Francis Jehl, in Europe and brought him to
America for the task.

Carloads of Menlo Park soil, brought to Dearborn and spread on
the ground around the rebuilt laboratory of half a century before,
were the finishing touch.

When Edison and his wife arrived in Dearborn two days ahead of
the great October 21 celebration, Ford gave him a preview of the big
surprise for him. As Edison approached the faithfully reconstructed
laboratory, he could hardly believe his eyes, The surprise was capped
when the door opened and he was greeted with open arms by Francis
Jehl, whom he hadn't seen for forty years. With tears in his eyes,
Edison embraced his old assistant.

What Edison saw inside completed his sensation of being
transported backward in time to fifty years before. There were his
Sprengel vacuum pump, his potbellied stove, the pipe organ at the
back wall, and all his Menlo Park laboratory furnishings arranged exactly as they once had been. Library shelves were stocked with
precisely the same books, including bound volumes of *Popular
Science,* that Edison had kept at hand.

Almost overcome with emotion, the frail old man passed it off with
a quip. "Well," he told Ford, "you've got this just about ninety-nine
and one-half per cent perfect." When Ford anxiously inquired what
was wrong with the other half per cent, Edison laughingly replied,
"We never kept it as clean as this!"

Two days later the climactic event of the golden jubilee took place
when, in the presence of the President and other onlookers, Edison
and Jehl re-enacted the making of the first successful incandescent
lamp—and a radio announcer's description of the ceremony ended
triumphantly with, "It lights!"

A banquet followed and Edison was escorted to his place of honor
at the head table. Exhausted by the gala program and the emotional
impact of his Dearborn visit, he was unable to eat and his deafness

Mina Miller Edison, who survived her older and ailing husband, tenderly cared for him to the end —and saw honors heaped upon him in the final days of his eighty-four-year-long life. Photo of her at left was made in 1947, long after the death of Edison in 1931.

Edison lived long enough to see the fiftieth anniversary of his electric light—commemorated by this medal—and to attend ceremony observing it led by President Hoover.

Portrait drawn especially for *Popular Science* of March 1929, by artist B. J. Rosenmeyer, depicts a gaunt though still active Edison at his desk at eighty-two. His health was failing, and the memorable story of his phenomenal career was now approaching its end.

Faithful restoration of Edison's famous Menlo Park laboratory, pictured inside and out, was built at Dearborn, Michigan, by his friend Henry Ford, who had scoured the country for authentic remnants of its original fittings.

kept him from hearing a word of the speeches of praise by the President and other notables. At last all eyes turned to him. Unsteadily he arose, managed a few graceful words of acknowledgment—and then, his duty done, collapsed into his chair.

He was a sicker man than anyone had known. A medical examination found him suffering from what proved to be a hopeless combination of gastric ulcers, diabetes, and Bright's disease. Back home in West Orange, his visits to his laboratory dwindled and ended.

Tenderly Mina Edison nursed him as he waited for what could only be the end. His last words were, "It is very beautiful over there," and then he lapsed into a coma. Early the next morning, on October 18, 1931, he peacefully stopped breathing. At the age of eighty-four, the human dynamo had run down.

Posthumously Edison was granted the last four of his astounding total of 1,093 patents.

In retrospect, Edison's fantastic total of inventions was extraordinary for their quality as well as their quantity.

There were rare exceptions; anyone of his stature was entitled to indulge a strange whimsy now and then, and a *Popular Science* article, "Flops of Famous Inventors," recalled a dilly: Edison actually patented a "Vocal Engine," to be powered by speaking into a telephone mouthpiece! (Forty brass bands playing at once, the article opined, could barely yield power enough to light an ordinary lamp bulb.) Ironically Edison tossed off both this brainstorm and an anachronistic scheme for non-electric "telephoning" over a building's gas pipes at just about the time his carbon-button transmitter made a revolutionary improvement in Bell's telephone.

Not even in Edison's round-the-clock life was there time enough for any one man to carry all his great inventions to final perfection. That may help to explain his readiness to stick stubbornly, in many cases, to the original version that worked.

His first successful carbon-button telephone transmitter, as has been told, was of lampblack from a kerosene-lamp chimney—and so the raw material for his succeeding ones came from an inelegant "lampblack factory" consisting of row upon row of smoking kerosene lamps. Only later did telephone makers switch to carbon granules from "telephone coal," a high grade of anthracite.

The first phonographs Edison marketed, like his original one, played primitive tinfoil records. How he was forced by competition to go to wax-cylinder records and finally to disc records (of his unconventional thick design) has been told. Only in the late 1920s did thin Edison discs like everyone else's appear, just before radio's competition and the period's Great Depression wiped out the Edison record business.

In the fashion of his time, Edison favored direct current, and used it in his electric-lighting plants. He took a dim view of alternating-current systems developed not long afterward by the Tesla-Westinghouse team. By hindsight that was a mistake. Because New York City pioneered in adopting Edison's electric lighting, dwellers in some areas of the city were still stuck with direct current, and unable to use the alternating-current appliances that ultimately prevailed, as late as the middle of the twentieth century.

Edison's movie camera and his peepshow-type viewer seemed to him a complete motion-picture system. Until he was reluctantly persuaded to acquire another inventor's movie-screen projector, his vision seems to have had a blind spot for the infinitely greater possibilities of movies for theater audiences. Recovery of his fumble gave him a rich new source of income, especially welcome after his staggering financial loss in his ill-starred iron-mining enterprise.

All in all, it took generations to finish everything Edison had started. But the credit rightfully goes to him for starting it.

CHAPTER **6**

The Man Who Invented the Twentieth Century— Nikola Tesla

Hᴇ ɪɴᴠᴇɴᴛᴇᴅ the electrical system that today powers the world. He devised the electric motor that turns everything from your kitchen refrigerator to the machines of industry. He dared call the legendary Thomas Edison wrong at the height of Edison's career, then proceeded to demolish Edison's electrical system and substitute his own.

In an absolutely incredible two-decade frenzy of discovery and development, he laid the basis for radio, remote control as now used on missiles and drone airplanes, medical diathermy, X-ray equipment, and many other devices. He was the owner of 700 patents that have shaped the world as it exists today.

He was frequently an impractical dreamer, too—a supreme egoist who was wrong as often as he was right. In old age he became a genuine eccentric, a hermit who spent most of his time feeding pigeons and dreaming of glories that would never be.

He was Nikola Tesla, a name most people living today have never heard. While unknown to the general public over the last fifty years, Tesla has inspired fantastic loyalty among a small band of admirers. Biographers have sometimes found themselves changed from objective reporters to fanatical supporters. Thus the truth about this amazing man cannot always be sorted out from the legend.

But the basic facts of his remarkable life are clear. Nikola Tesla was born on the stroke of midnight between July 9 and 10 in 1856 in the town of Smiljan in the Austro-Hungarian border province of Lika, now a part of Yugoslavia. His father was a pastor, his mother could not read or write but was a brilliant woman who invented improvements for household implements. Tesla's parents wanted him to follow in his father's footsteps and become a minister. But the boy was full of curiosity about the then developing scientific world, and finally persuaded his parents to let him study physics and electricity.

He started on the road to his first important invention in 1878 while a student at the Polytechnic Institute at Graz, Austria. One day a Professor Poeschl demonstrated to the class a Gramme direct current machine that could run as either a motor or a generator. Tesla, like the rest of the class, was impressed. But he was disturbed by the large amount of sparking at the brushes contacting the commutators. He mentioned his objection, and suggested that perhaps a motor could be designed to run without brushes and thus eliminate the obviously inefficient arcing.

Professor Poeschl was annoyed, delivered a long lecture on the impracticality of such a scheme, and temporarily silenced Tesla. But the student was not convinced, and continued to dream of a brushless motor. In 1880, he transferred to the University of Prague, and a year later took a job as chief electrician with the newly formed telephone company in Budapest. But he could not forget the idea of a brushless motor.

According to Tesla himself, in an article he wrote for *Scientific American* in 1915, the answer came in a blinding flash one afternoon in February 1882. As told in Chapter 1, he was walking through a Budapest park with a friend, reciting stanzas from Goethe's *Faust,* which he had memorized. Suddenly, Tesla stopped. In his mind he saw the solution he had been seeking: an iron rotor spinning in a rotating magnetic field. Tesla began drawing diagrams in the sand, explaining to his friend the details of the idea.

As he visualized it, two sets of windings would be placed at right angles to each other so that an iron rotor could turn inside them. Then, if two alternating currents, ninety degrees out of phase (with the peaks of one following peaks of the other) were fed to the two sets of coils, one set would be producing its maximum magnetic field while the other was minimum and vice versa. Further, as the magnetism began to wane in one and build in the other, the resultant field would move smoothly from one to the other. Thus the magnetic field would rotate, locking the armature in and carrying it around at precisely the speed of the generator back at the power plant.

This was Tesla's polyphase synchronous motor. He then went on to develop a variation on the same theme by replacing the iron rotor with closed coils of wire. A magnetic field induced in the coils locked into the rotating magnetic field of the stator windings, producing high starting torque and good speed regulation under a wide variety of load conditions. This was known as the polyphase "induction motor." This and a variation called the split-phase induction motor are still today the workhorses of the industrial world.

But this ingenious development, Tesla's first and probably greatest invention, was far more than just a new kind of motor. It was the ingredient, missing until then, that made possible the vast electrical generating and transmission system that supplies power to run the industrial world today.

Until Tesla, the world's rudimentary electrical systems operated on direct current. Engineers of the day knew that electric lights would work equally well on AC or DC. But there were no successful AC motors and no one could figure out how to make a current that was constantly changing direction drive a motor in only one direction. Thus, to take advantage of available DC motors, all systems were DC. But that created another problem. DC generators used carbon brushes resting on a rotating commutator to extract the power being generated. A certain amount of arcing occurred at this sliding contact. The higher the voltage being generated, the greater this arcing, so generator voltages had to be held to relatively low values to keep arcing within acceptable limits.

When electrical current flows through a conductor, some of it is lost in the form of heat. The higher the current, the greater the heating loss; in fact, double the current and heating loss is squared. To minimize such losses, power line designers use a transformer to boost line voltages to very high values—commonly hundreds of thousands of volts. For a given amount of power, as voltage goes up, current goes down, and losses are minimized. At the receiving end, another transformer lowers voltage to a usable level, and current comes back up to almost its original value. This is the principle that has made possible the economical long-distance transmission of electrical power and thus made possible the age of electricity.

When Thomas Edison set up his generating plants in New York in the last half of the nineteenth century, they could furnish power only to those customers within a few blocks of the station. Beyond that, the loss was too high. There was no way to raise the DC voltage for efficient transmission, because of the commutator arcing that Tesla had objected to in his student days at Graz. Yet no one could switch to AC because, as reported in an October 1893 article in *Popular Science*, "it has lacked the prime requisite for such a use—a satisfactory motor. This missing link in the chain of appliances necessary to render the system complete," the magazine went on to report, "has in recent years been supplied by the discoveries and inventions of Mr. Nikola Tesla, whose remarkable experiments with alternating currents of great tension and enormous frequencies have excited such widespread interest among scientific men."

As has happened so often in the past, the importance of the startling new development was not recognized and the industry stuck tenaciously to its old ways. Shortly after the invention of the polyphase electric motor, Tesla left Budapest to take a job with the

On the one hundredth anniversary of Tesla's birth, in 1956, *Popular Science* printed this picture story of his career. Its captions for the eighteen pictures, slightly abbreviated, are reproduced here.

1856 Nikola Tesla was born at midnight, July 9–10, in Smiljan, Croatia (now part of Yugoslavia). Little is known of his father. His mother could not read or write. But she could use her mind: She recited dozens of long poems and mechanically improved such household items as churns . . .

1857–60 In a world where 25 men scrounged a living with their muscles for every one who made a living any other way, Nikola, before he was five, played with another source of power. The use of wheels to harness water power was as old as history. From the disk of a tree trunk he made one and set it up as shown . . .

1850s–60s In America, some men hauled carts by hand from the Missouri River to Salt Lake. Horses worked just as hard: The Pony Express raced mail from St. Joseph, Mo., to San Francisco in 10 days. In Croatia, Nikola, seven, saw a fire engine that wouldn't pump water . . . He dived into the river and unkinked the hose.

1865 The world struggled with a new power—inefficient, dirty, hissing steam. In four years men would complete (by hand) a track across the U.S. Tesla, nine, struggled with another power: He made a tiny windmill, glued four June bugs to the blades. Their beating wings turned the blades, and a spindle . . .

1866—80 Steam power spread. An engine reached Croatia. Nikola, about 14, saw it —the first man-made source of power he had ever seen. He also saw a snowball, rolling downhill, become an avalanche. He noted . . . snow had turned into . . . power. He saw a picture of Niagara Falls, and said, "Some day I'll harness that."

1882—83 After Thomas Edison opened his first plant—DC—to light lamps of his 59 nearby customers, the world grew dimly aware of the wonders of electricity. In Europe, Tesla, 25, thought that electricity could also provide power. Needed: an AC motor, thought to be impossible . . . He dreamed up the plans . . . It ran.

1888 Suddenly Tesla hit the jackpot. He got patents on his AC motor and impressed the American Institute of Electrical Engineers (this month celebrating his 100th birthday) with a lecture which explained his idea. George Westinghouse . . . gave Tesla, the recent ditchdigger, a million dollars for the patent rights to his motor.

1889—90 Working together, Westinghouse and Tesla soon evolved AC motors and dynamos of many sizes. Tesla built a high-voltage coil—the Tesla coil—that with one end inert, the other spouting thousands of volts, would light lamps . . . without using wires. This was the beginning of his attempts to broadcast power.

1884 "No more will men be slaves to hard tasks," Tesla said. "My motor will set them free." But no one would give him financial backing. He sailed to the U.S., lost his baggage, his model—all but four cents. But of all the 518,592 immigrants who arrived in '84, he would change the country most. His mind carried all the plans . . .

1885–87 Tesla met and worked for Edison. But Edison was no readier for AC than Europe had been. The arguments were vigorous. Tesla and Edison described each other's mentality as low. Tesla quit his job with the inventor. Soon he was reduced to the drudgery that the world was full of. He became a day laborer . . . a ditchdigger.

1892 To concentrate on work, Tesla ruled out romance. If his discoveries looked impossible in those days of . . . horsecar commuting, he did something—for a man —which was considered more impossible. The "divine" actress, Sarah Bernhardt, dropped her handkerchief before him. He returned it—without saying a word.

1893 The big shows were the late P. T. Barnum's, Buffalo Bill's, Sarah Bernhardt's and the World's Columbian Exposition . . . Westinghouse and Tesla lighted and powered the Exposition, an accomplishment that finally sold the doubting U.S. on AC. Tesla himself lighted glass tubes without using any wires.

1895–96 Westinghouse and Tesla put on their biggest show. They built a powerhouse at Niagara Falls. General Electric, with Tesla methods, built a 22-mile transmission line to Buffalo. This was a significant advance; Edison had delivered power about a mile. . . . The age of sending power far and wide had dawned.

1898 The U.S.'s Admiral George Dewey licked the Spaniards in Manila Bay. Tesla, at Madison Square Garden, put a boat equipped with radio in a tank of water. From afar, he started, steered, and lighted the vessel—by radio. It was, he said, the first of a race of robots that would fight . . . the future wars of the world.

1920s–30s Growing old, Tesla withdrew even more into himself. This man, who was responsible for every AC motor (162 million horsepower when he died), and every transmission tower and line, kept his blinds closed—except during storms. Then he would throw open his windows, lie down on a couch and watch the lightning . . .

1930s–40s The world last saw Tesla on the steps of the New York Public Library. He had found a love: Daily he fed the pigeons. The man who had made work easier for millions all over the world was the old man whom unknowing thousands saw feeding the pigeons. . . . At 86, Nikola Tesla died alone in a New York hotel room.

1899–1900 Tesla thought that the earth was electrically charged. (It is.) At Colorado Springs, he set up a plant that would add to the earth's charge so you could plug in anywhere and get electricity. He pumped power in, claimed to draw it back—creating lightning. Unfortunately, he never wrote down the details of his experiments . . .

1901–16 At a time when radio consisted only of dot-dash messages, Tesla set out to build, on Long Island, N.Y., a radio city that would broadcast both power and all the kinds of programs that are known to such widespread audiences today. Tesla never got around to broadcasting . . . He went broke.

Tesla's appearance was striking; people who wrote about him after meeting him almost always commented on the intensity of his expression; his pointed chin; his piercing eyes; his large hands. The two pictures at top left show Tesla around the age of forty; below he is nearing eighty. In the photo above, he is experimenting with electrical equipment.

Continental Edison Company in Paris, where he designed dynamos and did troubleshooting of power plants all over France and Germany. But he had no luck in convincing his bosses of the superiority of his system, and in 1884 quit his job and left for the United States.

In the tradition of soon-to-be-great immigrants, he landed broke. "Tesla arrived in New York in June, 1884, with four cents in his pocket, a book of poetry, designs for a flying machine, and a headful of ideas," reported his longtime friend Kenneth M. Swezey in a 1958 article in the journal *Science*.

The man whose ideas would transform society looked the part as he arrived in the new world. He was more than six feet tall, and thin (142 pounds). "He had strikingly unusual angular features," recalls *Popular Science* reporter Alden P. Armagnac, who, as a young reporter in the 1920s, interviewed the then aging Tesla more than once. "I'd have called him hawklike, except for the unflattering connotation, since I thought him distinguished looking. His gracious, old-worldly manner—'continental' was the word for him—instantly put me at ease."

"So far as personal appearance goes no one can look upon him without a feeling of force," wrote a reporter named Franklin Chester in a newspaper article on August 22, 1897. "His hands are large, his thumbs abnormally long, and this is a sign of great intelligence. His hair is black and straight, a deep shining black. He brushes it sharply over his ears, so that it makes a ridge with serrated edges."

"He has eyes set very far back in his head," wrote famed editor Arthur Brisbane in *The World* on August 22, 1894. "They are rather light. I asked him how he could have such light eyes and be a Slav. He told me that his eyes were once much darker, but that using his mind a great deal had made them many shades lighter.

"His head is shaped like a wedge. His chin is as pointed as an ice pick. His mouth is too small. His chin, though not weak, is not strong enough. His face cannot be studied and judged like the faces of other men, for he is not a worker in practical fields. He lives his life up in the top of his head, where ideas are born, and up there he has plenty of room."

Tesla's first job in the new country was as a dynamo designer with the Edison Machine Works. And although he tried to get the great man himself to understand the benefits of his AC polyphase system, Edison was not interested. He was soundly wedded to the DC approach, Tesla to AC. "The electricians of that day could, and did, become highly emotional over their differences of opinion on this subject," wrote John J. O'Neill, a friend of Tesla's, in a 1944 biography of the inventor. Edison constantly claimed that AC was too dangerous, a charge Tesla hotly denied.

"Edison was no readier for AC than Europe had been," wrote Gardner Soule in a 1956 *Popular Science* article on the hundredth anniversary of Tesla's birth. "The arguments were vigorous. Tesla and Edison described each other's mentality as low. Tesla quit his job with the inventor. Soon he was reduced to the drudgery that the world was full of. He became a day laborer and went to work as a ditchdigger."

Tesla remained bitter about Edison the rest of his life. In fact, when New York State prison authorities began using AC power to electrocute prisoners, Tesla was convinced that Edison had put them up to it to back his claim that AC was a "killer current."

But by April 1887, Tesla had found financial backing and opened a laboratory of his own at 33 South Fifth Street (now West Broadway) in New York, just a few blocks from his competitor and former boss, Tom Edison. There he began producing dynamos and motors built on his ideas, showing not only the practicality of his approach, but a wide variety of ways in which the principles could be put into operation.

Despite the fact that few people realized it, the world was now ripe for Tesla's invention. There were several thousand central stations throughout the United States, operating on more than twenty completely different systems. For example, Edison's DC system was used almost entirely for lighting in densely populated cities, serving customers within a few blocks of the station. A man named Charles Brush had a higher voltage DC system for arc lights, but it could not run motors or incandescent bulbs. George Westinghouse, who had just gone into business, was using an AC system with step-up and step-down transformers to improve transmission efficiency, but his system could not run motors. And so on.

Westinghouse saw in Tesla's work the key to making the AC system to which he was committed practical. The story has been repeated endlessly that Westinghouse paid Tesla a flat sum of a million dollars for the use of his patents, plus a royalty of one dollar per horsepower for equipment built. But despite the fact that Tesla himself is reported to have made such a claim, evidence now indicates that the sum was closer to $200,000. And that it was made not to Tesla personally, but to his company, of which he owned only a one-third share.

Whatever the truth, it was Tesla's first big break. With enough money to operate his laboratory the way he wanted to, he jumped into a frenzy of creative efforts. And almost immediately Tesla and Westinghouse saw a great opportunity. The Columbian Exposition, a giant World's Fair, was scheduled to be held in Chicago in 1893. It was the first such event to be lighted and powered by electrical energy, and the two underbid Edison, who was also trying to get the job, so that they could show off the multiphase AC system.

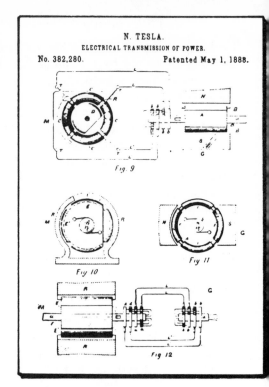

N. TESLA.
ELECTRICAL TRANSMISSION OF POWER.
No. 382,280.   Patented May 1, 1888.

Fig. 9

Fig 10

Fig 11

Fig 12

Tesla's first and most important invention was the polyphase induction motor, still the basic machine that drives the world's industry. Above, a 1920s version. At right, is one page of diagrams from Tesla's monumental 1888 induction motor patent—one of some seven hundred he received. It shows the heart of the invention that ushered in the modern age of electrical power—the rotating electrical field that made the alternating-current motor work.

The first fractional-horsepower electrical motor for a household appliance appeared in the fan above. It was built in 1889 by Westinghouse. Weight and size of such AC motors decreased from 69 pounds for a ¼ hp version in 1903 (center) to 16 pounds by 1955.

Nikola Tesla and George Westinghouse were certain that Tesla's alternating-current system would change the world. But the world was hard to convince. This huge machine, which supplied electrical power for the 1893 Columbian Exposition in Chicago, helped do it. Niagara Falls powerhouse, below, is pictured during construction.

It was a spectacular triumph. As reported in *Popular Science* in October 1893, "The power and machinery which give vitality to this vast array of lights are to be found in Machinery Hall, and constitute one of the chief electrical exhibits. The most striking feature of this exhibit is the great Westinghouse alternating plant . . . It consists of twelve enormous alternating-current generators, each having a capacity of ten thousand sixteen candle-power lamps and requiring a thousand horsepower apiece to drive them . . . The exhibition is, therefore, an illustration of the electric transmission of power upon a large scale, and should furnish a basis for the collection of instructive data."

For the first time, the world saw the Tesla system and what it could do. And the event was undoubtedly responsible for the next Tesla-Westinghouse triumph: the winning of the contract to harness Niagara Falls.

As far back as 1886, a charter had been obtained to set up an organization to tap about 120,000 horsepower from the falling waters of Niagara. But the original scheme, based on 238 waterwheels and miles of turning shafts, was totally impractical and never built. In 1890, the International Niagara Commission, headed by Lord Kelvin, one of the world's most famous scientists, announced a $22,000 prize for anyone able to come up with a practical scheme.

Only two of the seventeen schemes submitted were based on alternating current; both Lord Kelvin and Edison (who did not compete) favored DC. But in 1891, the commission found that no plan merited the prize and disbanded. In 1893 came the Columbian Exposition, and in October, Westinghouse signed a contract to build the first two Niagara generators of 5,000 horsepower each.

Early in 1895, the first generator began to turn out AC kilowatts. First customer was the Pittsburgh Reduction Company (later the Aluminum Company of America). Less than two years later, a twenty-two-mile transmission line piped Niagara power into Buffalo. "Almost overnight, the Niagara plant became the electrical wonder of the world," wrote Swezey in his *Science* article. More generators were ordered and installed. Then, "in 1896, the New York Edison Company began to expand the range and usefulness of its direct current system by means of polyphase transmission between stations, and several years later it adopted the Tesla system for all new stations. By the time the Niagara plant was completed, in 1903, all new generating stations in the United States were being founded around the Tesla inventions. The age of modern electric power had begun." Today, virtually all of the electrical energy in the world is generated, transmitted, and used with equipment based on Tesla's patents.

The Niagara plant was a turning point in human history. It proved "that the Tesla polyphase system itself was even more important than the motor it ran," wrote Swezey. "It constituted the first practical means by which electricity of a single kind could be generated in great blocks in one place, transmitted economically over long distances, and used, for any purpose whatever, at another place. So far it has been the last practical means of accomplishing these results, for no substitute that can even approach it in economy and versatility has ever been found."

Even before his polyphase system triumphed, though, Tesla was involved in scores of other projects. Most spectacular of these were his experiments in high-voltage, high-frequency phenomena. The inventor wanted to develop a light more efficient than the incandescent lamp of Edison. Earlier experimenters—Hertz and Crookes—had demonstrated that a discharging condenser would produce high-frequency oscillations and various mixtures of gases in glass tubes could be made to glow by passing these high voltages through them. Tesla thought such effects might be used to develop better lighting.

The first problem he turned to was developing a better source of high-frequency, high-voltage current. The result of this work was the famous Tesla coil—perhaps the item for which the inventor is most widely known. The Tesla coil is an air-core transformer having the primary and secondary tuned to resonance. With this device, he was able to generate currents of almost any frequency and magnitude. And with his Tesla coils and collection of glowing tubes, he put on the spectacular shows that made his name a household word during the closing years of the nineteenth century. For example, on May 20, 1891, Tesla spoke at Columbia University in New York before the American Institute of Electrical Engineers. He was a born showman. He rose before his audience, picked up two apparently empty but actually gas-filled tubes, and held them in the air. When a nearby Tesla coil was energized, the high-frequency current ran through his body and the tubes glowed brilliantly. Tesla always referred to them as "flaming swords."

He also showed how a variety of other gas tubes could be made to glow in various colors; coated some of them inside with phosphors to increase their brilliance (this was the principle of the fluorescent light, developed a half-century later); demonstrated forerunners of neon lamps; showed the importance of capacitance in high-frequency circuits by running motors and lighting lights with only one wire attached, the return path being through a capacitive link back to the generator.

Tesla also pointed out that high-frequency currents could be used to heat metals—a technique that can be used for certain types of metal melting jobs—and how heat can be induced in body tissues, the

The original Tesla coil, a high-frequency transformer, produces spectacular electrical effects.

Charge density on a point creates electrical "wind" that distorts a candle flame. Below, other weird Tesla effects.

JACOB'S LADDER. Electric flames snarl up two diverging wires just as they do in horror movies. One wire can be handheld, but don't touch the sparking part, which gets hot. In this time exposure, one spark looks like a series; the eye sees a single one moving up.

ELECTRIC PINWHEEL. An S-shaped piece of wire pivoted on the terminal so that it can spin freely forms a circle of sparks. The pinwheel is driven by an "electric wind."

WILD VOLTAGE. Tearing at its barriers, high-frequency voltage provides fireworks as it leaps out from a ball of steel wool.

basis of modern diathermy. And finally, he said that such high-frequency currents could be used for communications and showed radio circuits and apparatus very much like those adapted later by other inventors.

Tesla's striking discoveries and flamboyant platform manner put him much in demand. In 1892 he was invited to lecture before the most prestigious British and French scientific groups, and the following year appeared again before several American societies.

But perhaps his most startling public performances were at the Chicago World's Fair in 1893. In addition to the Tesla-designed polyphase generating and power transmission systems, the inventor had a personal exhibition of his own. Among other things he had made a metal egg. When he placed it on a velvet-covered table and closed a switch, the egg stood on its small end and rotated at high speed to the amazement of the crowd. Of course, it was simply acting as the rotor for a Tesla induction motor, spinning in the rotating magnetic field from coils hidden beneath the table. But it seemed like magic to the crowd. Tesla also waved his magic "flaming swords" and held up all kinds of glowing tubes, bulbs, and spheres. And his spectacular climax was to pass a million volts of high-frequency current harmlessly through his body, never failing to point out that Mr. Edison could not do the same thing with his supposedly safer direct current.

While the inventor's work with the coil that bears his name started in the attempt to build better lights, it quickly progressed into fields he thought far more important. Tesla became convinced that he could devise a way to transmit power wirelessly and efficiently through the earth to every part of the globe, and, in fact, frequently claimed that he had done so.

The work certainly led to some of the most spectacular electrical displays ever seen on earth. In 1899, with backing from the famous financier J. P. Morgan, Tesla began construction of the world's biggest Tesla coil at a site near Colorado Springs, Colorado. The primary coil was eighty feet in diameter. Centered within this was a coil about ten feet tall and ten feet in diameter, connected to a huge metal ball on a 200-foot tower above the building.

Tesla's theory was intriguing. He believed that the earth was electrified (which it is, in the sense that currents constantly flow through it). He envisioned electricity as something like an incompressible fluid that could be jammed into this electrical pool, which would upset its balance. Then anyone, anywhere on earth, could tap the pool and draw out electrical energy. *Popular Science* printed this Tesla prediction in 1928: "Houses will be lighted and powered by wireless, as will airplanes and other vehicles on land and sea. You will be able to go anywhere, desert or mountain top, valley or farm, and set up a compact equipment, small enough to be carried in a suitcase, that will give you heat to cook with and light to read by."

Tesla proposed to get this energy into the ground with his Colorado Springs machine. He planned to build up a potential of 100,000,000 volts at frequencies of 300,000 cycles. As the current surged alternatively up and down through the coil it would be slammed into the earth, thereby increasing the planet's electrical potential. Then it would rush upward, hit the ball on top, and explode into lightning bolts.

Pictures of the experiments in progress give only a dim idea of what it must have been like. Huge flashes of lightning more than a hundred feet long sprang from the ball, and the air inside the building was shot through with thousands of brilliantly blinding streamers of electric fire. The crashing thunder of the lightning strokes could be heard for thirteen miles according to some reports. And at least once, Tesla put the entire city of Colorado Springs in the dark by drawing too much power from the local generating station and causing the entire municipal system to collapse.

The effectiveness of the scheme as a wireless power transmission system is certainly in doubt, despite Tesla's claims to the contrary. He wrote many times and told audiences from the platform that he had transmitted power over great distances and "the practicality of the system is thoroughly demonstrated." Yet though he continued to work on it for years, nobody is really sure what happened, for he carried the whole thing in his head. He never published in a paper, or wrote down, precisely what he did, how he did it, or the results he obtained.

In 1902, Tesla raised enough money to begin construction of a gigantic tower to be topped by a huge copper ball at Shoreham, Long Island, which was to be the first part of a worldwide wireless power transmission scheme. But he ran out of money before it was completed. Then, in the early days of World War I, the tower was mysteriously destroyed by dynamite. Nobody ever knew why for sure; speculatively, perhaps it may have been bombed by self-appointed vigilantes who mistakenly suspected it of being used as a spy radio station, in the wave of anti-German hysteria at the time. Tesla wanted a build a similar plant at Niagara Falls but was never able to raise the money. Still, he never stopped making optimistic predictions about his system. "Within three years," he told *Popular Science* in 1928, his world system for transmission of wireless power through the earth should be in commercial operation.

Tesla's genuinely revolutionary discoveries, incredible claims, flamboyant manner, and eccentric personal habits combined to make him an object of intense interest, a highly visible celebrity in the heady atmosphere of New York society in the years around the turn of the century. He was a meticulous dresser, and once told his secretary that he was the best dressed man on Fifth Avenue. He usually wore a waisted coat, a black derby, gray suede gloves, and carried a cane. John O'Neill, a friend and biographer of the inventor, remembers these details: "Tesla paid $2.50 a pair for his gloves, wore them for a week, and then discarded them even though they still appeared as fresh as when they came from the maker . . . He purchased a new tie every week, paying always one dollar . . . Silk shirts, plain white, were the only kind Tesla would wear. As with other articles of his clothing, such as pajamas, his initials were always embroidered on the left chest . . . Handerchiefs he purchased in large numbers because he never sent them to the laundry. After their first use, they were discarded. His collars were never laundered either. He never wore one more than once."

Tesla avoided social engagements and apparently had few intimate friends. Still, he was very much in evidence around the city. For years, he dined nightly at Delmonico's, the city's smartest restaurant and a gathering place for the socially prominent. Then he switched suddenly to the Waldorf Astoria.

The routine was always the same. He invariably dined alone, always at a special table reserved for him. After dinner, he returned to his laboratory for more work. Tesla liked thick steaks, and it was not unusual for him to eat several at one meal. In later years, though, he gradually shifted from a meat diet and beame a vegetarian. He believed that coffee and tea were injurious and never drank them. But whiskey and wine he enjoyed in moderation.

Tesla had a germ phobia. He demanded that no one else be allowed to use his table, even when he was not there. He required a fresh tablecloth at each meal and a stack of freshly laundered napkins, which he used carefully to wipe each item of silverware and each dish set before him. He dropped each napkin to the floor as he finished using it. At the office he washed his hands constantly in a washroom that no one but himself was allowed to use. His secretary handed him a fresh towel after each hand washing.

Tesla never married; apparently he had no relationship with women at all. "I have planned to devote my whole life to my work and for that reason I am denied the love and companionship of a good woman . . ." he wrote in reply to a newspaper question. ". . . an inventor has so intense a nature, with so much in it of wild, passionate quality that, in giving himself to a woman, he would give up everything and so take everything from his chosen field. It is a pity, too; sometimes we feel so lonely."

Electrical power transmitted through the earth was a lifelong dream of Tesla's. In the early years of the century he built this 200-foot tower at Shoreham, Long Island, to perform experiments. In 1914 it was mysteriously dynamited.

"Automatons" such as this one, Tesla believed, could be remotely controlled to do much of man's work. This radio-controlled ship astonished the world, convinced many that Tesla could work magic. Unmanned space vehicles and other remotely controlled machines today are based on ideas first explored by Tesla.

Man-made lightning crackling from his apparatus in Colorado Springs, Colorado, inspired Tesla to try to perfect a system of transmitting power through the earth without wires. He left no records for future reference.

Tesla apparently had less than the normal need for sleep. He claimed that he never slept more than two hours a night, except for once a year, when he slept five hours to build up a reserve of energy.

Over the years, Tesla became not only a well-known figure on the streets of New York, but a widely respected scientist among his peers. Yet he could be terribly wrong. And stubborn. He never gave up on his concept of a wireless power transmission scheme, for example, and continued to claim that it was entirely practical. He maintained until his death that atomic energy was illusory. "The scheme is worse than that of a perpetual-motion machine," he is quoted as saying in a 1928 *Popular Science* article. "A motor driven by atomic power is irrational because it would take far more energy to break up an atom's structure than can be recovered in more useful work." (So it seemed to other prominent scientists, too, before discovery of atomic fission provided the key.) He also didn't believe in the existence of electrons, and continually attacked the validity of Einstein's theory of relativity.

In 1894, Tesla told an audience of engineers at a lecture in London that his worldwide wireless power transmission system would supersede transatlantic cables: ". . . ere long, intelligence—transmitted without wires—will throb through the Earth like a pulse through a living organism."

Tesla's thoughts spanned almost the entire range of human enterprise. In a remarkable thirty-six-page article that appeared in *Century* magazine in June 1900, Tesla lectured the world on the end of the solar system, religion, exercise, wine and whiskey, pure water, gambling, preventive medicine, personal cleanliness, morality, the evils of women who wanted to do things other than keep house and have babies, vegetarianism, ignorance, and how to end war for all times. (His solution to this problem was to develop "telautomatons," robotlike machines that would fight wars so that human beings would not have to be involved.)

But while much in the article was flayed by *Popular Science* and technical journals as arrant nonsense, other parts contained strikingly original thoughts that are just now beginning to be appreciated. He said, for example, that men should begin using the sun as a source of heat for smelting iron, since coal was a non-renewable resource and would eventually run out. He also suggested that we could harvest geothermal energy—the heat within the earth—as a source of power. His may have been the first such suggestion.

He correctly predicted that aluminum, then a rare, expensive curiosity, would become an extremely important material used in countless ways. But he also said that it would replace copper and put that industry entirely out of business. He said he had developed a system of communicating with inhabitants of other planets.

But such excesses pale before Tesla's genuine and almost endless accomplishments. He developed the basic circuits of radio before Marconi; it was not until after Tesla's death that the Supreme Court finally ruled that Tesla's patents invalidated those of the Italian inventor. He correctly predicted the ultimate electronic form of television and its basic operating principles in the 1920s—when experimental systems still used spinning disks for scanning. He described radar, synchronous clocks, and much else when these concepts were new to the world.

Tesla's golden years were the two decades between 1880 and 1900. For the last forty years of his long life—he died in the early 1940s—he became increasingly eccentric; in addition he was an extremely poor money manager and was constantly beset by financial problems. Despite the fact that his inventions had made billions for others, he himself profited relatively little from them. These were the years of constantly more spectacular claims, and constantly diminishing results. There was no money for a laboratory and experimentation.

But Tesla never stopped telling the world of his new developments, almost always with the claim that he had worked out the problems and the device was entirely practical. He described such things as his machine to extract energy from the ambient medium—the air around us—his rocket cars, jet flight. In 1928, *Popular Science* reported, "Besides his world power scheme, Dr. Tesla says he is devoting his time chiefly to his vertically rising flying machine. This aerial flivver is to weigh less than 200 pounds, and to occupy no more space than a seven-foot cube. It is to rise to a great height at the rate of from one to two miles a minute, and may attain a horizontal speed as high as 400 miles an hour, power being supplied by an exceedingly light oil-burning motor, a modification of a steam turbine Tesla invented. An all-metal framework and the absence of gasoline guard against fire hazard. Additional safety is to be attained by a parachute of new construction."

As Tesla aged, he withdrew increasingly into the private world of his dreams. He often called reporters in on his birthday to make predictions and tell of the wonderful things he was developing. The reporters he saw annually began to regard him less as an eminent scientist and more as a harmless but nutty old eccentric.

As his life moved toward its close, Tesla's attentions and energies turned more and more to an activity with which he became obsessed: feeding pigeons in public places. He became a familiar figure on the plazas in front of the New York Public Library and St. Patrick's Cathedral. When he was ill, he would hire a messenger to feed pigeons at his regular times and places. He also kept pigeons in his hotel room, sometimes staying home to care for them if he suspected they were ill.

In the last years of his life, Tesla was increasingly strapped for money. The Yugoslavian Government began granting its distinguished son an annual stipend of $7,000, but gradually, as all other income ceased, Tesla was forced to let his staff go one by one.

He lived in a series of New York hotels—the St. Regis, the Pennsylvania, the Governor Clinton, and the New Yorker. In each case but the last, he was eventually forced to move because of unpaid bills and trouble over the pigeons.

One day in 1937, while taking one of his daily long walks around the city, he was hit by a taxi. But he refused medical treatment and kept walking "on the theory that this would keep his blood from clotting," remembers his friend Kenneth Swezey. Tesla never fully recovered, and in the years that followed became almost a total recluse. He seldom saw old friends or even talked to them over the phone.

Swezey continues: "On the morning of 8 January 1943, a maid, knocking on the door of his room, got no response . . . Hidden from the flashing neon signs, rumbling subways, blaring radios, and light and power in a million homes of the city which had become the symbol for the world, of the modern age of electricity which he had so largely helped to create, Tesla had died in the night, as quietly as he had been born."

If Orville, left, and Wilbur, right, are the heroes of this chapter, their sister, Katharine, is certainly the heroine. She nursed them in illness, encouraged them, helped them financially, and acted as their social manager during their trying but exciting European adventure.

CHAPTER 7

The Wright Brothers— Fathers of Flight

"OUR FIRST interest in the problems of flight," wrote Orville Wright in his little book *How We Invented the Airplane,* "began when we were children. Father brought home to us a small toy activated by a rubber string which would lift itself into the air. We built a number of copies of this toy, which flew successfully."

Wilbur was eleven, Orville, seven, when their father, Bishop Wright, came home that evening in 1878 and called them into the modest living room. "I have a surprise for you," he said, cupping his hands over the tiny object. "Now, watch carefully." He stepped back, opened his hands with a flourish, and the shiny thing leaped into the air. It rose to the ceiling, whirled crazily for a moment, then sank slowly to the floor.

The boys were wide-eyed, demanding to know what it was and how it worked. Was it a bird or a bat? Neither, Milton Wright told them; it was not a live thing but a machine, a scientific toy with two little fans that whirled around because of the torsion of a twisted string of rubber. Its frame was cork and bamboo, its wings were paper. "I guess," explained their father, "these fans push against the air just as a ship propeller pushes against water."

The toy, known as a helicopter, was the invention of Alphonse Pénaud, an early aeronautical experimenter and the first to use rubber bands to power a model flier.

Perhaps the first machine tool the Wright brothers saw was their grandfather's turning lathe, operated by foot power. John Gottlieb Koerner—father of the boys' mother—was a German who fled his country in 1818 to avoid the military conscription of the Napoleonic era. He came to Hillsboro, Virginia, and there became a builder of fine farm wagons and carriages.

Orville recalled Grandpa Koerner taking him as a tiny boy between his knees and muttering: "Ja, ja, I could make you a good wagon-builder, ja!" His daughter, the boys' mother, Susan Koerner Wright, was born in Hillsboro. In addition to cooking, housekeeping, making clothes for her husband and children, mending, darning, sweeping, washing, she had an original mind and a knack for invention. It was she, not her dreamer husband busy with his writing, his sermons, and other church affairs, who was handy with tools. Once she constructed a sled for her oldest sons (oddly named Reuchlin and Lorin).

· She was also, incidentally, an early advocate of woman suffrage. Years after her death, her husband, then eighty-six, marched with Orville a mile and a half in a suffrage parade in Dayton, Ohio.

The boys' father was born in a log cabin on a farm in Rush County, Indiana. Descended from deacon and lay preacher Samuel Wright, who settled at Springfield, Massachusetts, in 1636, Milton Wright studied for the ministry at Hartsville, a little college in the town of the same name in Indiana. It was here he met and married Susan, who was a fellow student. After their marriage they moved often, Milton combining schoolteaching with farming and circuit riding. They spent two years on a farm near Fairmont, Indiana, where their first son, Reuchlin (named after a German theologian), arrived; then a winter with Milton's widowed mother in Fayette County, Indiana, where second son Lorin (a name picked offhand from a map) was born. Then to Dublin, Indiana, for two years, and Millville, Indiana, for three— and there, within a frame house of five rooms, the co-inventor of the airplane was born (April 16, 1867), named after Wilbur Fiske, of the Methodist Episcopal Church.

Milton Wright, always a dreamer, went through a succession of jobs, ranging from the minister of the local church in Hartsville (where he met and married Susan) to teacher of theology at the college there and finally to editor of the *Religious Telescope,* a weekly church organ, published in Dayton, Ohio. With the exception of a few brief stays in other towns, a small house at 7 Hawthorn Street, a mile and a half from the town of Dayton, became their home for most of forty years. It was there on August 19, 1871, that Orville Dewey Wright (named after a Unitarian minister) entered the world. It was in this house that the brothers did much of the preparatory work for the gliders and airplanes they began testing in 1900. It was a small frame structure with wood shingles on its peak roof, wide clapboards painted white, and green shutters at the windows. It had a porch at the kitchen end, a partial cellar under the living room, and the back roof was raised by the new owner to provide four bedrooms upstairs. There was no plumbing or bath. The water supply consisted of an open well with a wooden pump at the back door. Light: oil lamps. Heat: coal stoves. Cooking: on the kitchen range with firewood. Value: about $1,500.

The last child born to Milton and Susan was a girl, Katharine, who was to play an important part in the lives of her to-be-famous brothers. Her birthday was August 19, the same as Orville's—but she was born three years later, in 1874. The German influence appears in her nickname, *Schwesterchen,* meaning "little sister," but the boys soon shortened that mouthful into "Swes" or "Sterchens."

·When Susan Wright died on July 4, 1889, Katharine was fifteen, Wilbur, twenty-two, and Orville, eighteen. The three became inseparable; no one was as close to the brothers as "Sterchens," who was their confidante, their adviser, and, from that time on, their "little mother."

Although shy and sufficient unto themselves in most of their early lives, Wilbur and Orville managed to get themselves involved in myriad activities. They were not too concerned with being formally educated (the imperative of a college education was still to come). One biographer, Fred C. Kelly, put it this way: "Both Wilbur and Orville gave up the idea of going to college, and neither even received a diploma from high school." Wilbur, says Kelly, went to school in Richmond, Indiana; then, when the family moved to Dayton, he decided not to return for commencement. As for Orville, he took studies instead of regular courses, in order to prepare for college in his last year at high school. As a result he did not earn his diploma. Then he abandoned the plan to go to college.

At seventeen, however, Wilbur did take a year's course at the Dayton high school to supplement his Richmond schooling. He studied science, mathematics, and history. He also liked sports. Once, in a game of ice hockey, he was hit in the mouth by another player's stick, and he lost all his upper front teeth. Although he walked home from the accident—so as not to frighten his mother—the accident brought on heart and stomach trouble that resulted in a long period of semi-invalidism. Somehow, his ill health brought him closer to Orville, who, although four years his junior, caught up to his ailing older brother. Yet it seemed to be the function of the older, wiser Wilbur to encourage the enterprising Orville and to improve his various projects.

At fourteen, Orville with his friend Ed Sines started a print shop in the Sines basement. A toy press, a hellbox of type, and some wood engravings of Orville's enabled them actually to print and decorate a catalog. Milton Wright encouraged them with twenty-five pounds of secondhand brevier type. For a "Model" press (three inches by five inches), Wilbur traded a boat he had built. Then Ed Sines and Orville started a school paper called *Midget.* When he was sixteen, Orville built a printing press, which Wilbur improved with a lever to shoot its roller back and forth (instead of the operator running up and down

Parents of the inventors were Susan Catherine Koerner Wright and Bishop Milton Wright. A small toy helicopter that Bishop Wright brought home to his boys aroused their first interest in problems of heavier-than-air flight.

Sister Katharine, shown here between her brothers, was the youngest in the family. Orville, left, was four years younger than Wilbur but the pictures show them at the age of five. They were shy and sufficient unto themselves. Their heritage was English, Dutch, and German-Swiss. The German influence appears in Katharine's nickname, *Schwesterchen*, meaning "little sister," and her nickname became abbreviated to Swes or Sterchens.

The Wright family moved many times because of the changing fortunes of Milton, the father. In this house, at 7 Hawthorn Street in Dayton, Ohio, they settled for forty years. It was here Orville was born in 1871 and Wilbur died in 1912.

Grandfather, John Gottlieb Koerner, right, was born in Germany, came to America in 1818. He became a builder of fine farm wagons and carriages. The foot-driven lathe in his shop in Hillsboro, Virginia, was perhaps the first machine tool the little Wright boys saw.

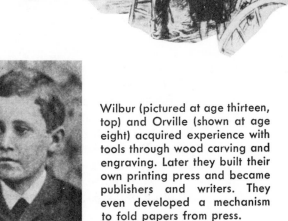

Wilbur (pictured at age thirteen, top) and Orville (shown at age eight) acquired experience with tools through wood carving and engraving. Later they built their own printing press and became publishers and writers. They even developed a mechanism to fold papers from press.

with it). Other improvements followed—finally including a mechanism that folded printed papers coming off the press—and they were able to produce an eight-page church paper.

They built yet another press (a secondhand tombstone served as the flat bed) and published the *West Side News,* which Wilbur edited and to which he also contributed some humorous pieces. Orville was business manager and publisher: he managed to get seventeen advertisements for the first weekly issue. History does not record the number of advertisements in later issues, but the *News* was made into a daily, *The Evening Item,* which lasted only a few months. After the demise of the *Item,* the team of Wright and Wright, Job Printers, was born. They printed pamphlets, such as the minutes of the United Brethren Church, as well as *The Tatler,* a paper for black readers published by their black friend Paul Laurence Dunbar, a classmate of Orville's who became a famous poet.

On Third Street in Dayton there appeared in 1892 the Wright Cycle Co., a bicycle repair shop. Here, they acquired the craftsmanship for the experiments that were to usher in the Aviation Age. (One of their first efforts to produce an all-important machine to record and analyze wind pressure on surfaces was a whirligig on a bicycle seen cruising along the Dayton streets.) The boys were now twenty-five and twenty-two (Wilbur would be twenty-six on April 16). They went into the manufacturing business—bicycles, of course. They assembled them from parts they bought; an assembling shop was set up on William Street, which included an oven for enameling. Their product was first-class and modern, and was offered to the public as the Van Cleve bicycle, named after Wright ancestors, Benjamin and Margaret Van Cleve; Ben helped found Dayton, Maggie was the first white woman there.

Other models followed: the St. Clair and the Wright Special. (The shop can still be seen in Ford's Greenfield Village museum in Dearborn.)

Rounding out their inventive activities before their concentration on gliders and a motorized flier, they worked not only to improve bicycle pedals, which to the chagrin of other manufacturers came unscrewed, but also on bicycle tires of the "balloon" type; a calculating machine for multiplying and adding; and a simplified typewriter. Fred Kelly reports that when a friend of theirs built the first "horseless" buggy in Dayton, in 1896, Orville, always the innovator, proposed that they go into *that* business. What happened is recorded in the issue of *Popular Science,* which celebrated the sixtieth anniversary of their famous flight on December 17, 1903 (December 1963):

> Should the two young bicycle-makers give up their business and instead manufacture newfangled horseless carriages?

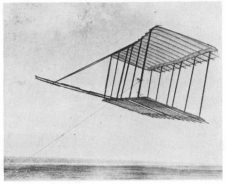

Their first experiments with the 1900 glider were to fly it like a kite, a rope tied to its nose. It weighed only 52 pounds and cost them all of $15 to build.

On Third Street in Dayton there appeared in 1892 the Wright Cycle Co. It was a few blocks from their home and here the Wrights learned mechanics by repairing and making bikes.

Wrights took up flying in 1900 at Kitty Hawk, North Carolina. Orville, the cook, can be seen scouring a frying pan in front of their tent camp.

The following year, 1901, "We erected a cheap frame building," wrote Wilbur. It was their home but since the entrance was the full width of the building the shed also became the first airplane hangar.

With Orville and a friend at the corner struts, Wilbur launched their second glider from Kill Devil Hill on July 27, 1901. At first the craft nose-dived to earth in the thirteen mile wind but then Wilbur moved his weight about a foot to the rear and the glider sailed off above the dunes for more than 300 feet.

Before construction of their wind tunnel, they had tried unsuccessfully to revise existing air-pressure tables with this makeshift gadget mounted on a bicycle's handlebars.

The Wrights found they needed to correct other experimenters' faulty air-pressure tables. When they returned to Dayton in August 1901, they decided the way to do it was with a wind tunnel, which they proceeded to build for $15. The wooden apparatus (now at the Smithsonian) was 16 inches square and 8 feet long. It gave them true figures for the center of pressure on plane and curved surfaces at various angles.

Wilbur (portrait at left) was invited to address scientists in 1901. Reluctantly he put on his good suit and appeared. Years later he declared, "I know of only one bird, the parrot, that talks and it can't fly very high."

The Wrights built their wind tunnel in their Dayton bicycle shop. A homemade metal fan mounted on an emery-wheel shaft was driven by a two-cylinder gas engine. More than two hundred little wings from 3 to 9 inches long were tested to record the angles according to the velocity of the air.

"No," insisted Wilbur, horseless vehicles would never be practical. "To try to build one of any account would be tackling the impossible. Why, it would be easier to build a flying machine."

So they went on making bicycles. But soon they set out to do the task "easier" than building automobiles—to build a flying machine.

In 1896 Orville developed typhoid fever. He was looked after jointly by a trained nurse, Wilbur, and Katharine, home on summer vacation from Oberlin College. It was during the period of Orville's long convalescence that the two men began to delve into material dealing with flight. Their idol, Otto Lilienthal, had been killed in a gliding accident in his native Germany. Although gliding at the time was viewed only as a sport, Lilienthal was regarded quite seriously as "The father of gliding flight." The Wrights had read about his experiments and Wilbur now proposed that they study the subject. He would go to the public library and they would also delve into the book on bird flight in their father's library, *Animal Mechanism* by Marey, a Frenchman. Now the meager literature was read aloud to Orville by Wilbur. There was much arguing between them about ideas that occurred to them. It was the agreed duty of each brother, wrote John R. McMahon in a six-installment biography (1929) in *Popular Science,* to attack, punch, and smash with all vigor the other's concept. Their housekeeper, Carrie, would listen to their arguments and would be fearful that they were getting angry. They were not. They often fought each other to a mental standstill but did not lose their tempers. After a fair fight the loser was quick to concede victory, and often even adopt his opponent's viewpoint. Orville recalled his brother saying, "I like to scrap with Orv because I like to scrap with a good scrapper."

On May 30, 1899, Wilbur wrote the Smithsonian Institution requesting literature about efforts to fly. "We then studied with great interest," they wrote later, "Chanute's *Progress in Flying Machines,* Langley's *Experiments in Aerodynamics,* the *Aeronautical Annuals* of 1895, 1896 and 1897, and several pamphlets published by the Smithsonian Institution, especially articles by Lilienthal and extracts from Mouillard's *Empire of the Air.*" These pioneers, they wrote, "infected us with their own unquenchable enthusiasm, and transformed idle curiosity into the active zeal of workers."

The real battle had begun. Lilienthal had been their hero, Langley was to become their unwitting rival and adversary, Chanute was to become a great friend and supporter, and a later secretary of the Smithsonian Institution was to become their cruel and unheeding antagonist.

"While the Wrights were just beginning their study of flight as the merest novices," said *Popular Science* in February 1929, "it seemed that men like Clément Ader in France, Sir Hiram Maxim in England, Octave Chanute, and Professor S. P. Langley in America, were past masters in the study of aviation. They had built gliders, written learned books, made model gliders fly, and some of them were at work on ponderous powered machines. They had prestige, money, and apparent science. Maxim was the famous inventor of the Maxim gun. Chanute was a leading engineer. Langley was secretary of the Smithsonian Institution, a government museum and scientific laboratory."

Despite the experiments of these zealots in the United States and abroad, the intellectual climate was unfavorable to the ambitious young Wrights. Outstanding in creating this unfavorable climate was Professor Simon Newcomb, leading scientist and mathematician, who wrote a treatise to prove that it would be scientifically impossible to build a flying machine that would carry a man.

And later, while the Wrights were experimenting with gliders at Kitty Hawk, the chief engineer in the U. S. Navy, Admiral Melville, published an article about the difficulties of building a flying machine which could carry a man. The first flying machine, he declared, would be more expensive than the most costly battleship.

Yet, years later, when the Wrights were asked whether they would have sold their patent if anyone had offered to buy it, they replied in the affirmative, naming the figure of $10,000, on the grounds that the planes had cost them $1,500 and the balance would cover their labor. (In later years they offered their whole company for $100,000 but found no buyer at that time.)

The essence of the problem of flight was equilibrium—fore-and-aft and lateral control. Lilienthal and Chanute relied on the rider shifting his weight again and again but a minute in the air was considered the limit for that acrobatic stunt. The gliding record before the Wrights was thirty seconds, and no one had flown a split second in a power machine.

For their planned experiments in gliding, the Wrights decided the birds could teach them. "If the bird's wings would sustain it in the air without the use of any muscular effort," wrote Orville later, "we did not see why man could not be sustained by the same means." They discussed the idea of using hinges on the wings of a plane but decided it was impractical. They spent Sundays lying on their backs beside the Miami River near Dayton studying the hawks and buzzards flying overhead. At home they observed swallows and other small birds.

In July 1899, Wilbur was on duty in their bicycle shop. John McMahon reports (*Popular Science,* September 1925): "A customer came in. If he had asked for tire tape, a wrench, or a pump, the course of history might have been changed. But this customer asked for an inner tube for his bicycle tire. That tube was packed in a rectangular pasteboard box. Wilbur held the empty box by its ends while the customer examined the contents. Wilbur's hands were inclined to be nervously active. He looked down and suddenly realized what he was doing with an empty box—twisting it—warping it. Can't hinge wings? Never. But you can warp them! Eureka!"

Wilbur closed the shop and hurried home to tell Orville. Part of the problem of lateral balance had been solved for all time. They could warp the wing tips of a plane so the operator could vary their inclination to restore balance from the difference in the lifts of the two opposite wing tips. The warped wing (and its successor, the aileron) had been born.

They decided to test this idea for lateral control with a box kite, a five-foot biplane. Early in August 1899, Wilbur lugged it to Seminary Hill, about a mile from their Dayton home. By twisting a stick in each hand, with two cords attached to the frame, he could warp the corners of the soaring kite from the ground and thus guide it through the air. A group of youngsters watched this grown man (then aged thirty-two) playing with his kite and laughed at the crazy antics of the toy biplane. But Wilbur grinned at them as they taunted him. How could they know that the experiment was a success?

The next step was to adapt the warping principle to a man-carrying glider. They based its design on a biplane as originated by an earlier experimenter, Wenham, and developed by Stringfellow and Chanute.

First, they faced years of experimenting with this and improved models. In December 1899, they wrote to the Weather Bureau in Washington to find out about wind velocity in various places around the country. What they needed was a place where the weather would be good, where winds would be about fifteen miles per hour in a sandy area, without trees or shrubs for safe landings. The best prospect, came the reply, was Kitty Hawk, North Carolina, a fishing town on a strip of sand, separated from the mainland by Albemarle and Pamlico sounds. In early September of 1900, Wilbur made the 600-mile trip there. Through correspondence he had been offered room and board by the postmaster, William J. Tate. Nearly shipwrecked on his way, by boat, Wilbur finally arrived at the Tates', not having eaten for two days.

The next day Mrs. Tate loaned him her sewing machine so he could stitch up cream-colored sateen for the wings.

On September 25 of that first year at Kitty Hawk, Orville joined his brother. They lived in a wall tent, twelve by twenty feet, which housed them, a small workbench—and the glider. They had tools but, most important, a panacea for mechanical ills of all sorts, from slippage to fracture: bicycle cement from their shop.

Wilbur flew the Wrights' third glider at Kitty Hawk in 1902. Its span was 32 feet; it had an area of more than 300 square feet.

The 1902 glider, here flown as a kite, had a vertical tail and an elevator in front. The wing tips of the craft could be warped.

In front of the 1902 glider, left to right, are Octave Chanute, Orville, Wilbur, A. M. Herring, Dr. George A. Spratt, and Dan Tate. All that this model lacked was a motor—the Wrights would add that for their 1903 experiments.

The success of this glider—they made over one thousand glides to test it—led the Wrights to build a powered machine. Here Orville is pilot, Wilbur at right wing tip.

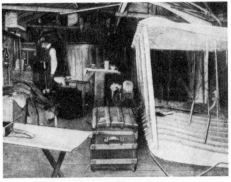

Orville boasted this model kitchen at Kitty Hawk by 1903. He even invented a French drip coffee pot!

This is the interior of the 1902 camp which housed them and their glider. Here Wilbur is at work on the machine.

Another Kitty Hawk picture shows Orville and Wilbur at work on one of their numerous experimental glider models. A small boy is an eager spectator.

The first glider weighed only fifty-two pounds—it cost them all of fifteen dollars to build! There was a space for an operator to lie on his stomach but the first experiments were to fly it like a kite, a rope tied to its nose. But finally Wilbur stretched himself on it, face downward between the wings. Gradually Orville let out the rope and the super-kite rose just as it had with no man aboard. Orville was ecstatic and let out more rope. It was a wobbly and skittish air horse Wilbur rode that day and as he looked down at the ground eight feet below he began to shout to be let down. Orville thought he was cheering and wanted to go higher. But he finally understood and pulled the glider down.

Orville tried it next with a little more success. They took turns as jockeys, having innovated the lying-down position of the pilot. Previous experimenters had used a sitting position.

Later they moved for further tests of the glider to Kill Devil Hill, where there was a sand strip of a mile between ocean and sound. By means of strings from the ground to the steering apparatus they flew the glider against the wind at ten to fifteen miles per hour, or twenty-five to thirty mph with allowance for speed of the wind.

In the course of that year's experiments they discovered that the "lift and drift" measurements varied greatly from those of Lilienthal and Chanute.

"The most discouraging features of our experiments so far," wrote Wilbur in his diary on July 30, 1901, "are these: The lift is not much over one-third that indicated by the Lilienthal tables . . . we find that our hopes of attaining actual practice in the air are decreased to about one-fiftieth of what we had hoped. Five minutes' practice in free flight is a good day's record."

Although they had a fine vacation, they left their battered glider on the dunes at Kill Devil Hill. They were thoroughly discouraged about the prospects for a man-carrying machine.

A week after their return to Dayton, they wrote to Octave Chanute, telling about their experience at Kitty Hawk and noting that they had found some possible errors in his and Lilienthal's tables. A friendly correspondence ensued in which Chanute encouraged them to continue their work with gliders. They decided to try another vacation at Kitty Hawk the next summer and meanwhile to check up on those tables of air pressure. It was then that they built a wind vane on the handlebars of one of their bicycles, hoping while riding the bicycle to get information about the air pressure at ten to thirty miles per hour. But it shed little light on the problem.

They now decided they would have to build a new and bigger glider. They planned an increase in the wing curve, a greater overall area (from 165 square feet to 308), a weight almost double their last

The Wrights built their own motor with four horizontal cylinders. It weighed 170 pounds.

Charley Taylor not only helped the Wrights build their first airplane motor but he also took care of their bicycle trade while the brothers were away at Kitty Hawk, experimenting.

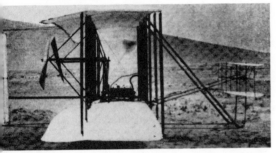

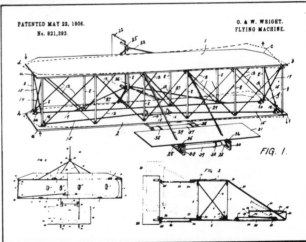

Wrights' airplane added engine and two propellers to the 1902 glider. Twin propellers were 8½ feet long, and whirled in opposite directions. Sled runners put on in front prevented nose-over in landing.

Right, patent for the "flying machine," May 22, 1906. Below, one of the most prized photographs in the world, showing Wilbur at the side as Orville piloted the historic first airplane ever to fly under its own power.

PATENTED MAY 22, 1906.
No. 821,393.

O. & W. WRIGHT.
FLYING MACHINE.

FIG. 1.

year's glider, a height of about 6 feet, a wingspan increase to 22 feet, and a 14-foot front rudder. And, instead of preparing sateen for the wings, Wilbur stitched muslin in the backyard of their Hawthorn Street home. (The sateen from their abandoned glider, they found on their return to Kitty Hawk, had been turned into colorful dresses for the Tates' daughters.)

The second year (1901) they built a shed near Kill Devil Hill at Kitty Hawk—more comfortable than a tent. When Octave Chanute had visited them in Dayton, he proposed they invite E. C. Huffaker to camp because he was building a glider for Chanute in Tennessee—which they did. They also invited Dr. George A. Spratt of Coatesville, Pennsylvania, because prudent Chanute thought a medical man might be useful. The shed served as a hangar, workshop, and home for the four men. Orville was chief cook, tended a gasoline stove, and laid out a model kitchen, stocked mostly with canned goods. That year they were plagued with mosquitoes. Chanute came for a week to observe the new Wright glider and Postmaster Tate and his brother Dan helped them with the launchings.

The first flight, with Wilbur aboard, was made on July 27 in a thirteen-mile wind down Kill Devil Hill. Orville and Spratt were at the corner struts. After a quick nose dive to earth, Wilbur moved his weight about a foot to the rear of the position and the glider sailed off for more than 300 feet.

But that tendency to nose-dive and to stall backward worried them. The air tables, as they suspected last year, were wrong—the wing curve was too great. So they decided to truss the ribs to make the curve less.

Now the glider flew 389 feet against a twenty-seven-mile wind, but it was still too wild and inefficient to suit the Wrights. In their diary entry for July 30, 1901, they wrote some 600 words recording the results and their discouragement.

Although they had broken the record for distance in gliding, they were disappointed, returning to Dayton on August 17. Wilbur declared to Orville: "Man won't be flying for 1000 years!" And in the September issue of *McClure's Magazine* that year appeared an article by Professor Simon Newcomb stating: ". . . the construction of an aerial vehicle which would carry even a single man from place to place at pleasure, requires the discovery of some new metal, or some new force."

The classic air tables were wrong, without a doubt, so now Orville began to rig up a new device to measure air pressure on plane and curved surfaces. They had fumbled the problem with their whirligig projecting from a bicycle. Now they realized they needed a wind tunnel, and built it in their Dayton bicycle shop for less than fifteen dollars. More than 200 little scale-model wings from three to nine inches in length were tested in the wooden apparatus, sixteen inches square and eight feet long. A homemade metal fan mounted on an emery-wheel shaft was driven by a two-cylinder gas engine which the Wrights had previously built for their bicycle shop. A gauge pointer automatically recorded the angles of objects suspended in the air blast according to the velocity of the air.

The Wrights were now able to find the true figures for the center of pressure on plane and curved surfaces at various angles. They also were able to find the ratio between lift and drift. Lift is the weight-carrying ability of a wing at a given speed, while drift is its travel in the line of motion. As *Popular Science* put it, "The Wrights recognized lift and drift as Siamese twins, which Nature itself had bonded together in a permanent union."

Beyond a certain speed, it was now clear, power must be greatly multiplied to increase speed. The Wrights completed their tabulations by February 1902, and sent the new air tables to Octave Chanute.

The brothers arrived again in Kitty Hawk on August 28, 1902, where they had to lift their old shed, which had settled in its sandy foundations. Their diary of this experience has some homelike entries: "Kitchen fixed up and 16-foot well driven . . . Raised building, made bets to last half a year . . . Began work on glider after shooing away native razor back pigs . . . Devised a deadly trap for unfortunate but very annoying mouse . . . Orville roused from sleep by mouse walking across his face . . . Collected shells and starfishes at the beach for brother Lorin's children . . ."

They remembered that Lilienthal had been killed in a glider by a drop of fifty feet and Pilcher, an English experimenter, from forty feet. So they proceeded with caution. Their 1902 glider had a span of thirty-two feet (compared with twenty-two of the year before), with chord (wing width) of five feet, and an area of 305 square feet. But the tests that year, though dangerous, were essential to progress in perfecting a safe flier. They were encouraged by the machine's good response to controls and ability to soar at low angles. But a crash from a height of thirty feet—with Wilbur aboard but unhurt—damaged their plane.

To aid lateral stability they added a vertical tail; it was supposed to counter the machine's tendency to pivot or turn on its axis when the wings were warped. But sometimes this failed and the craft yawed dangerously. Then Orville had the inspiration to make the tail movable. A movable rudder, he realized, turned toward the high or fast wing, would both check its speed and reduce its undue lift, thereby restoring lateral balance. Turning the rudder right or left would keep both wings even and the craft level in the lateral plane. Rudders on ships had long been used, but only for the purpose of steering. The object of the aerial rudder was totally different: to maintain sidewise equilibrium in conjunction with warpable or movable wings.

First, the twisted pasteboard box that inspired the warped wing! Now, the fire of genius brought forth the movable rudder.

Then Wilbur added the notion to let the rudder and wings be connected with wires so as to operate together. One lever to control lateral balance, another to take care of fore-and-aft equilibrium. It was this system of effecting straight flight and balance for which they decided to apply for a patent, granted in 1906. (The diaries indicate they had no expectation of money return but felt they should establish a record of priority for the sake of scientific credit.)

The ensuing 700 flights during the next 10 days were wonderfully successful—against a 35-mph wind they repeatedly covered distances of over 600 feet.

That crucial year, 1902, Octave Chanute repeated his visit to the Wrights' camp; he also brought along an employee, A. M. Herring, to test two of Chanute's gliders. Herring had formerly worked for Professor Langley. Later he was to be associated with Glenn Curtiss, a rival of the Wrights.

After Chanute saw the successful glider flights at Kitty Hawk (his own had failed utterly) he went to Washington and talked with Langley. On October 17 Langley wrote Chanute asking for more information about the Wrights' glider flights and two days later he addressed a wire to "Mr. Wright, Kitty Hawk, North Carolina." It read: "Mr. Chanute has interested me in your experiments. Is there time to see them? Kindly write me."

They replied that they'd broken camp and ended their experiments. On December 7 Langley persevered with a letter to Chanute in which he asked "to hear more of what the Wright brothers have done, and especially of their means of control." In the letter he mentioned his own machine, which he said was nearing completion. He stated: "I have been spending a great deal of time and money on an apparatus to accurately measure the lift and drift of the wind."

In the light of subsequent events, this correspondence is significant and ironic. What Langley had failed to discover, the Wrights had learned with a fifteen-dollar wind tunnel. The later allegations that Langley was the teacher and the Wrights his pupils were obviously false. Langley had wanted to learn from them but the Wrights had been unable to give him the opportunity.

The time had come to add a motor to their glider. Back in Dayton, they tried in vain to buy a suitable gasoline engine from several manufacturers. So, with the help of their mechanic, Charley Taylor, they built their own. It was Charley who looked after the bicycle trade while the boys were away at Kitty Hawk. He was a permanent feature in their shop, just as "faithful Carrie," their housekeeper, was in their home. The engine had four horizontal cylinders of four-inch bore and four-inch stroke. It was supposed to develop only about twelve horsepower. (It has been said that the Wright brothers flew in spite of their engine.) Next, they had to design propellers.

Sister Katharine, who was now teaching at high school, came home one day to find them shouting at each other about angles, sines, and tangents. She became hysterical and threatened to leave home if they didn't stop arguing. They did, for a while at least, and decided to design a propeller according to the formula of their air tables . . . and also to have two propellers whirling in opposite directions. The twin blades were eight and a half feet long and six inches in width at the tip. And finally they had to find some way to connect the motor with the shaft. A sprocket chain furnished by an Indianapolis firm solved that problem—they used it ever afterward.

Their motor turned out to have more than its expected power, so they increased the airplane's weight with its operator from 600 to 750 pounds.

The weight allowed for the operator, incidentally, was 145 pounds —and fortunately both brothers weighed about that. Wilbur was now thirty-six and Orville thirty-two. Both were now in fine physical trim; Wilbur stood 5′10¼″ and Orville, 5′8½″. They were both smooth-shaven; the elder had a prominent aquiline nose, firm thin lips with slight upward lines at the corners, a little baldness at the forehead; the younger's hair was thick and curly, brown with a hint of red. Both had grayish-blue eyes, keen, quick, and frank. Both had soft voices, Wilbur's more inclined to staccato speech. Both were swift in physical action, deft and nimble.

They were simple, dedicated men. Neither of them ever married. In the words of the late writer Mitchell Wilson: "They fell in love with the idea of human flight and married it." Wilbur once said that they didn't have the means to support "a wife and a flying-machine too."

Their plane was a huge bird of 510 square feet, its cream-colored wings spanning forty feet. There was a twin vertical rudder behind, a twin horizontal rudder in front. The scene again was Kitty Hawk. The spectators were few, five in all. The actors were ready for the climax of the drama. The birth of the Age of Aviation was at hand.

They had left Dayton on September 23, 1903, arriving two days later at their old camp at Kill Devil Hill. Orville's letter to Katharine began, as usual, "Dear Swes," and told of the 107-mile-per-hour wind that had torn away the anemometer cups, of the lightning that flashed at night, and the hordes of mosquitoes. They were putting up a new camp building, to be a shed forty-four feet by sixteen by nine; were practicing with the old glider; and in rainy or windless weather they worked on the new machine. In a later letter to his father, Wilbur told of a forty-three-second glide which broke their world record of the year before. Then came a dreadful gale which almost wrecked their camp building. At 4 A.M. one morning they had to apply interior braces to their structure; Orville went out in the storm to climb a ladder to the roof—the tar-paper roofing was flying off. Wilbur came out to hold the ladder while Orville hammered in the nails. The building was saved.

Dr. George Spratt joined them on October 23; the year before he had given the Wrights a useful hint on a technicality which later they had verified with their wind tunnel. Octave Chanute came on November 6 but the wretched cold and windy weather was too much for the aging engineer; he departed after a week of misery.

During the first test of the airplane on the ground, the steel tubing shafts of the propellers twisted out of shape. Doctor Spratt took the shafts to Dayton for Charley Taylor to fix, but didn't return. Both Chanute and Spratt missed the real fireworks in December.

The new shafts were delivered on November 21. But the sprockets for the chain drive broke loose, and the Wrights applied the standard remedy for loosened bicycle tires—Arnstein's bicycle cement. Thus the sprockets were frozen in place.

November 28 saw a bad accident which required that Orville return to Dayton to repair one of the new shafts, from which a piece of metal had broken off. He returned to camp on December 11. On December 14, a launching rail was laid down on the slope of Kill Devil Hill. Wilbur won the toss for the first test of the flier. They'd take turns thereafter. He climbed in and lay on his stomach. There was trouble with the releasing device. They fixed it. Then the plane shot forward prematurely, Orville clinging to the right wing struts and running alongside the plane. The machine had lifted only six or eight feet from the end of the track. Now at a distance of some sixty feet from the track it was only fifteen feet from the ground. Shortly it lost headway and crashed on its left wing. The flight lasted three and a half seconds and covered 105 feet.

It was truly a flight, but so abortive that the Wrights were not satisfied to claim it as man's first flight. At least it had proven the efficiency of their propellers.

Thursday, December 17, was sunless and wintry. The long strip of white sand between ocean and sound was spotted with gray pools of water. At ten thirty-five in the morning, there was a wind of twenty-seven miles an hour. The first flight, with Orville taking his turn aboard, took only twelve seconds, reaching an altitude of about fourteen feet and coming to earth about a hundred feet from the end of the track. It was this flight which Orville later described this way: "The course . . . was exceedingly erratic, partly due to the irregularity of the air, and partly to lack of experience in handling this machine. The control of the front rudder was difficult on account of its being balanced too near the center . . . it turned too far on one side and then too far on the other. As a result the machine would rise suddenly to about 10 feet, and then as suddenly dart for the ground." While this flight in a machine carrying a man only lasted twelve seconds and spanned only a hundred feet, Orville called it "the first in the history of the world." So did the history books.

Three more flights were made that day. The second and third spanned about 175 feet, but the fourth, against a 21-mph wind, lasted 59 seconds and covered 852 feet. Then the plane was parked and took a somersault in the wind, smashing it beyond immediate use.

This was the plane—the Kitty Hawk "Flyer"—about which this historic telegram was sent to his father by Orville: "Success four flights Thursday morning all against twenty-one mile wind started from level with engine power alone average speed through air thirty one miles longest 57 seconds inform press home Christmas Orevelle Wright." The misprints in the telegram included the speed of the wind, the number of seconds of the final flight (59, not 57), and the spelling of Orville's name. Other than that, it was accurate . . .

Before they had left home that year, their father had given them a dollar, saying, "Now let's hear from you when there is news." The bishop got his dollar's worth!

(His real reward came on May 25, 1910, when at the age of eighty-two he had his first ride in his sons' vehicle. Orville as pilot held the craft down to a conservative altitude but his enthusiastic father shouted, "Higher! Higher!")

In the March 1904 issue of *Popular Science* there appeared a piece by Octave Chanute based on his speech to the American Association for the Advancement of Science on December 30, 1903. Titled "Aerial Navigation," it hailed the fact that "an initial success has been achieved with a flying machine." He told how the Wrights had experimented for three years with gliding machines—"and it was only after they had obtained thorough command of their movements in the air that they ventured to add a motor . . . too much praise can not be awarded to these gentlemen [for] applying . . . a new and effective mode of control of their own." He described the plane in detail and praised them for planning and building their own motor, adding: "They evolved a novel and superior form of propeller; and all this was done with their own hands, without financial help from anybody."

In an earlier issue, published the very month that the Wrights made

Wilbur in 1909.

Orville in 1909.

Early in June 1909 President William Howard Taft received the Wrights (Wilbur at his right; Orville and Katharine at his left). There were medals for the boys and an autographed copy of this photograph for Katharine.

One of the Wrights' demonstrations was a flight over water. Here is Wilbur ready to start from Governors Island. It was the first such flight.

The second airplane accepted by the Army, the Model "B," is shown here in a flight over College Park, Maryland. It had a four-cylinder 30-hp engine. Wing span: 39 feet.

the first successful flight, the magazine stated: "The flying machine is no longer problematical; it is simply a question of the time necessary to put things together."

In today's context these timely reports seem hardly noteworthy. But they were—the press acidulously ridiculed and neglected the Wrights' achievement. Fred Kelly tells that as late as 1907 a Dayton paper called them "inventors of the airship" (a term reserved for lighter-than-air machines) and called Orville "Oliver." He points out also that at the time of the first flights no press association sent a man to Dayton to get the facts. The *Scientific American* received a marked copy of a January 1, 1905, issue of *Gleanings in Bee Culture,* which carried a report by A. I. Root of a later flight by the Wrights. Said the venerable magazine: ". . . the only successful 'flying' that has been done this year must be credited to the balloon type." Kelly remarks that by then the Wrights had totaled 160 miles in their various flights. By December 15, 1906, *Scientific American* relented and carried an acknowledgment of the achievement, commenting also on "the unostentatious manner in which the Wright Brothers of Dayton, Ohio, ushered into the world their epoch-making invention of the first successful aeroplane flying machine."

"The world's first regular flying field," said *Popular Science* in 1929, "was an eighty-acre cow pasture eight miles from Dayton. Here [at Huffman field], in 1904–5, the brothers developed the airplane, making hundreds of flights when no other human beings flew at all. They learned to steer and to circle, steadily increased their own records of distance and duration."

The 1905 plane, tested at Kitty Hawk, was now fitted to carry two persons, and the controls changed so that the pilot would sit upright instead of lying prone. There were many improvements: a new engine, a new method of launching, and subtle changes in the front elevators to improve stability and avoid tailspins.

At first it had been a sport, then it had become an obsession to get a motorized glider with a pilot into the air, but now the Wright brothers began to ruminate about the *uses* of their invention. Certainly it must have value for their country, perhaps just for scouting in time of war or for carrying messages speedily. Other countries were more interested than ours in the news of a practical flying machine—the British War Department sent a representative from the Royal Aircraft Factory and the French sent a scout, followed by a military commission —but the Wrights were determined that the United States Government must have priority on the control of their invention.

The U. S. Army was not interested. The military authorities who were told about the plane, either through letters from the Wrights or through communications forwarded to them, one from no lower a personage than the Secretary of War, brushed off the queries. The brass simply didn't believe there was such a machine and were not interested in looking into it. A possible explanation of this ineptitude is the disaster of Langley's aerodrome, into which project $50,000 had been poured down the drain. After all, it was only about a year after that disaster, and the press had so carelessly missed the big Kitty Hawk story that the successful flights were reduced to unbelievable rumor. Also, the Board of Ordnance and Fortification assumed that the letters were actually bids for financial support.

Under the goading of their friend Chanute, the Wrights tried again, later in 1905, assuring the Board that they didn't want money but wanted merely to know the requirements for submitting details of their machine.

Result: another brush-off letter, which said that no further action would be taken until an actual machine that could carry an operator and could fly was produced.

At that very time the Wrights had begun negotiations with the British for a plane carrying two operators. Those negotiations, however, were halted at the end of 1906, when word came from the British that they did not wish to buy a plane. A further effort with the U. S. Army by Henry Cabot Lodge, U. S. Senator from Massachusetts, got nowhere even though a report of Wilbur's twenty-four-mile flight in thirty-nine minutes in 1905 was shown the general in charge of the Ordnance Board. The general (Crozier) promised to send a representative to see the Wrights but never did.

It was not until 1907 that the War Department deigned to express interest, and that was because it had learned that the Wrights were negotiating successfully with foreign governments. As reported in the Dictionary of American Biography: "At the very end of the year 1907, after an interview between Wilbur Wright and the chief signal officer, General James Allen, specifications were issued and bids asked for a "gasless flying machine" to carry two men weighing [a total of] 350 pounds, with sufficient fuel for 125 miles."

Previously the Wrights had offered to build a plane for $100,000 but had been told that such an amount would have to be approved by Congress at its next session. Now, to be sure that money wouldn't stand in the way of their bid, they changed their bid to $25,000. There were twenty-two bids in all but only the Wrights received a final contract. And now they had to produce the machine.

That effort was to lead to the most disastrous flight in their history. While Wilbur went abroad to pursue the hot negotiations with the French, Orville stayed home to handle the deal with Uncle Sam. A hazardous test course was laid out at Fort Myer, Virginia, a suburb of the national capital. It was not ideal, since there were barracks, car

Left, a view from Kill Devil Hill, at Kitty Hawk, North Carolina, during the twenty-fifth anniversary celebration of the Wright brothers' first powered flights there on December 17, 1903. Although those flights had begun the Age of Aviation, there was no celebration of them at the Smithsonian Institution.

Below, Orville Wright, center, receives the Distinguished Flying Cross from former Secretary of War Davis in February 1928, twenty-five years after the 1903 flights at Kitty Hawk. It is America's highest aviation award and a duplicate was also presented, posthumously, to Wilbur Wright.

This picture of Orville Wright in his aviator's helmet was taken around the time, in 1928, when he sent the Kitty Hawk Flyer to the Kensington Museum near London, England. His reason: although it was the first powered plane to fly, the Smithsonian Institution had given credit to the Langley Aerodrome.

lines, telephone poles, ravines, and wooded hills, with no level spots for emergency landing. But as always Orville managed. His first public flight there was made on September 4, 1908. It was brief. But the next day he stayed up for four mintues. A contemporary report stated: "The crowd went crazy." On September 10, Orville astounded the onlookers even more by flying nearly an hour in the morning, and in the afternoon an hour and five minutes, circling the parade grounds at an altitude of 120 feet. It was a world record. Everything looked bright, especially when Orville was congratulated by the Secretary of War and other officials.

Then came the flight a week later. Lieutenant T. Selfridge had requested that the War Department assign him as passenger in the tests. Orville and Selfridge were laughing as their craft rose late in the afternoon of September 17—so goes the *Popular Science* report. They began to circle the field; laughter froze on their lips within a few seconds. Orville heard an ominous tap-tapping. He glanced back and found that control of the vertical rudder was gone. A cracked propeller blade had snapped the rudder wire. The machine wobbled for a crash on the bank of its fourth circle, 150 feet up. He tried to balance by warping alone. He leveled the craft for a down glide, but had only seventy-five feet left. Now the *front* rudder was out of control! All he needed was twenty feet more. But it was too late. The last dive of the plunging machine ended fatally.

Selfridge died within a few hours. Orville suffered broken ribs and a fractured left leg. As he lay on the ground after the crash his first words were: "Tell my sister I'm all right."

For four days and nights in the military hospital to which he was carried, Orville was unable to sleep but was comforted by the continual presence of Katharine. The death of Selfridge and the apparent end of their efforts for the Army were almost more than he could bear. Then came the news that Wilbur, at Le Mans, France, had set a new world's duration record of one hour and thirty-one minutes.

Orville had his first sleep in days. Wilbur's flight proved that the Fort Myer disaster did not spell the end of airplane flight. Besides, it had fulfilled the Wrights' contract with the French, and Wilbur now was able to cable much-needed money to his brother.

They had mortgaged their home, their father had retired from the ministry, and their savings were gone. The disaster had cooled off the Army and money from that source seemed indefinitely postponed. Success with the French saved the Wrights at this crucial time.

After seven weeks in the hospital, Orville sailed with Katharine for Europe. It was January 1909.

What happened to the Wrights abroad is a chapter in itself, a much-deserved triumph which made up for their own country's slothful recognition of their accomplishment.

Above, the Kitty Hawk Flyer as it was displayed in the Kensington Museum near London. The Smithsonian Institution had labeled the Langley Aerodrome as the first airplane "capable" of flight.

On October 7 and December 9, 1903, the Langley Aerodrome fell into the Potomac. Right, report of the December failure in the Washington *Star*. The Wrights took a dim view of letting the Smithsonian exhibit their plane next to one that bore a label that was patently untrue.

COLLAPSE OF THE AIRSHIP.

AIRSHIP FAILS TO FLY

Prof. Langley's Machine Goes to River Bottom.

PROF. MANLY ABOARD

THE LATTER RESCUED FROM PERILOUS POSITION.

Test of the ... Off the Arsenal

Right, Glenn Curtiss poured fuel on the Wrights-Smithsonian controversy by flying the rebuilt but altered Aerodrome in 1914. The changes were based on the Wright brothers' patent.

After Secretary Abbot of the Smithsonian admitted the facts about the Curtiss claim and gave rightful credit to the Wrights, the Flyer was displayed there, forty-five years after the 1903 flights.

When Orville was in the United States to work on the tests for the Army, Wilbur became his own chief mechanic and cook at Le Mans, France. His bedroom was a largish packing case within his shed hangar. He had a cot, a washstand, and a camp stool. He made his own breakfast on an oil stove. A piece of hose attached to a water pipe comprised the bathing facilities.

The French took to the air-riding Yankee immediately. He was an austere personality from their point of view, which might have accounted for some of their admiration. He didn't smoke or drink, had no time for women, and he kept the Sabbath religiously—no tests were ever allowed on the Lord's day. He became an object of awe and Le Mans was visited by peasants as though it were a shrine. Pictures and statuettes of the American were hawked in Paris streets.

At Le Mans, on the last day of 1908, Wilbur surpassed his previous record with a flight of two hours and twenty minutes which won him the Michelin prize, worth $4,000.

After the arrival of Katharine and Orville, now recovered from his accident, they moved to a winter resort in southern France, known as Pau. Here they were given a field, a hangar, and free quarters in a hotel. They were even given a French chef to cook for them, but the brothers soon left Katharine to his ministrations and the comforts of the hotel while they moved to their accustomed quarters and home cooking at the flying field.

The French Wright Company now arranged for Wilbur to give a course in piloting to selected pupils. Meanwhile, European royalty began arriving at Pau to see exhibitions and perhaps fly with the daring innovators. First came King Alfonso XIII of Spain. He requested an exhibition flight on Sunday, but despite the mandatory royal request the Americans politely replied they'd be glad to entertain His Majesty on any day but Sunday. That turned out to be the next Saturday. The king was greeted by Katharine, who had taken on the job of her brothers' "social manager." She'd been taught by Lady Northcliffe how to curtsy to a king but her true nature came to the fore as she simply shook the monarch's hand. His Majesty smiled and complimented her in perfect English, then mourned that his Queen and Cabinet had vetoed his desire to take a flight.

He did sit in the machine with Wilbur, asking innumerable questions and showing his knowledge of the problems of aviation. Later he lunched with the Wrights at the hotel and the next day shook hands cordially with Orville and Katharine as his entourage was leaving, also saluting the American lady by tipping his hat.

Katharine was taken by Wilbur on her first flight. The occasion was a launching during which VIPs such as the former Prime Minister Arthur Balfour, Lord Northcliffe, the publisher, and the Duke of

Manchester vied for the honor of pulling on the rope which raised a weight to the top of a small tower. When it was allowed to drop, the weight provided the motive power for a catapult that launched the plane. It was probably the first manual labor that the titled VIPs ever performed in their lives.

Then it was learned that Kind Edward VII of England was coming to Pau. He arrived on March 17, and the inventors and their sister were presented to him at the field. Again, Katharine skipped the curtsy and shook hands. The King listened courteously to the explanations about the airplane but seemed uninterested in the mechanical details.

After Wilbur had landed from the later demonstration flight in the presence of Edward VII he said again to his sister: "Sterchens, don't you want to climb in?"

She said she couldn't because of her big hat, but, as prearranged, Orville came up with a cap and veil and handed them to Katharine.

Of all his happy moments, this may have pleased Wilbur the most —taking his beloved sister for a spectacular ride in his and Orville's invention—in the presence of a crowned head and cheering onlookers who hailed the first woman to fly.

Wilbur was invited to be guest of honor at a dinner in Paris given by the French Air Club. It was on this occasion that he gave his classic explanation of why he didn't like to make speeches: "I know of only one bird, the parrot, that talks," he said, "and it can't fly very high."

On Good Friday of that year the Wrights were in Rome to make demonstration flights and deliver a plane to the Italian Government. Wilbur arrived earlier and had an audience with King Victor Emmanuel III. The King spoke English and asked many informed questions. He was not as effervescent as the King of Spain had been or as indifferent as the King of England.

There was also a visit by Orville and Katharine to the Crown Prince of Germany but that was to be the following year, while Wilbur stayed in the States to give New York its first sight of an airplane. The visit to Tempelhofer Field near Berlin to meet the prince was another triumph, with the young prince begging Orville to take him up. But Orville hesitated to risk the life of an heir to the throne. The Crown Prince persisted, and later, after Orville had interviewed the Empress and gained her consent, Wright took her eldest son for a short ride, whereupon the prince presented the aviator with a diamond-studded stickpin. The diamonds formed the letter *W*. According to the knowledgeable Fred Kelly it stood not for Wright but for Wilhelm! (*Deutschland über Alles.*)

The climax of the Wrights' negotiations with the United States

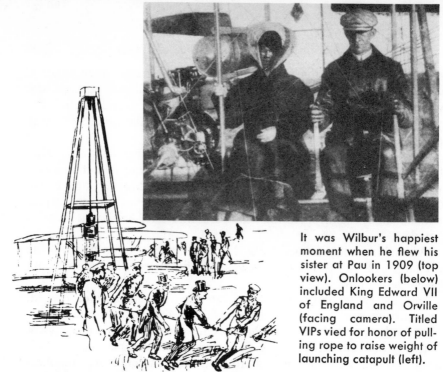

It was Wilbur's happiest moment when he flew his sister at Pau in 1909 (top view). Onlookers (below) included King Edward VII of England and Orville (facing camera). Titled VIPs vied for honor of pulling rope to raise weight of launching catapult (left).

The Empress of Germany looked on from the back of the royal car as Orville flew at Tempelhofer Field, later to become Berlin's great airport.

The French took to the air-riding Yankee, Wilbur Wright. They admired his austere personality; he didn't smoke or drink, had no time for women, kept the Sabbath religiously. No tests were allowed on Sunday at their many flights.

The Crown Prince of Germany pleaded with Orville for a ride at Tempelhofer Field. He got it.

On Good Friday, 1909, the brothers met King Victor Emmanuel in Rome. He asked many informed questions.

King Alfonso XIII of Spain, left, sat with Wilbur, asked innumerable questions, and showed knowledge of aviation problems. He wanted to take a flight with Wilbur, but his queen and cabinet vetoed the idea.

King Edward VII of England, in derby, visited at Pau with Wilbur (foreground) and Orville (left).

Army occurred the year before the experience in Germany. The account of the events of June and July 1909, as later published in *Popular Science,* cannot be improved upon. It read (with some condensation):

When the Wright brothers, with their sister Katharine, returned to New York in 1909, after hobnobbing with European royalty, they were greeted as heroes. The Aero Club of America, lukewarm to the inventors two years before, honored them at a luncheon. And at their home city of Dayton, Ohio, there was a great reception. An open carriage decked with flowers and drawn by white horses met the inventors who, when they had returned from Kitty Hawk six years before, had ridden in an old surrey drawn by a single nag, ignored as eccentric bicycle men who "thought they could fly." This time the simple dwelling on Hawthorn Street was smothered with flags and paper lanterns for night illumination.

President Taft received the boys and Katharine at the White House in early June to present a pair of heavy gold medals . . .

On the afternoon of July 30, 1909, at Fort Myer, the younger brother and his passenger, Lieutenant Benjamin D. Foulois, stepped aboard a newly completed airplane (in place of the one wrecked with Orville the year before) for a cross-country flight of unprecedented hazard. Foulois had been assigned as the government observer for the test, which was to determine whether Uncle Sam should buy the plane and establish the nucleus of an Army air service. Wilbur and Katharine, who were present, were afraid. The pilot and his passenger well knew the peril . . . Orville was yet lame from the crash on that very spot last year when his companion, Lt. Selfridge, had been killed.

The brothers had scouted the ten-mile course over hill and dale, rocks and woods, seeking a possible landing place in case of trouble, and had found absolutely none . . .

President Taft stood watching the takeoff. So did a great crowd on the military field, buzzing with excitement, whispering about the previous accident . . .

Orville and his passenger were not laughing this time . . . The plane became a dot over hills and ravines, then faded out of sight in the distance.

Wilbur stood like a statue, field glasses to his eyes, a watch in hand. His agitated sister was beside him . . . He had closely figured the time the plane should reappear . . . "He is overdue!"

Charley Taylor, trusty mechanic of the Wrights, could not stand the strain as the minutes accumulated, and wailed: "He's down! He's down!"

Katharine turned on him with a sharp reprimand . . . A cousin of the Wrights, Professor David W. Dennis, stood beside them.

At last, Professor Dennis yelled: "There he is! There he is!"

. . . A mighty cheer and tumult of motor horns arose from the parade grounds as Orville and his companion came gliding home . . . The delay had been due to wind and a strayed balloon marker. But the plane made a record for passenger transport, fourteen minutes at forty-two miles an hour, and earned a bonus of $5,000 for its speed. President Taft congratulated the brothers on the spot.

"The final tests . . . in July 1909," declared Paul E. Garber in the Smithsonian Institution booklet *The National Aeronautical Collections* (1965) . . . "were completed to the satisfaction of the War Department and the machine was purchased the next month for the contract price of $25,000 plus a bonus of $5,000 for exceeding the stipulated speed by attaining an average of 42.583 miles per hour."

He tells that this plane—"at that time the outstanding aircraft in the world"—was chosen for permanent preservation in the National Museum, "where it was placed in 1911 and where it hangs today."

Mr. Garber omits the embarrassing fact that the truly outstanding aircraft in the world—the first to fly, in 1903—did not receive its rightful accolade for over three decades after the 1911 date.

But, at last, the War Department was "satisfied." What if its cold disdain and contemptuous treatment of the Wrights had broken their spirit, and they had given up their efforts to persuade a reluctant establishment?

Other complications beset the inventors. Neither had much enthusiasm for business but they organized a million-dollar company with an ornate office in New York. They still kept the office above the old bicycle shop in Dayton.

In addition to the problems of contracts abroad and at home, they had to deal with numerous infringements on their 1906 patent. Probably the most important suit was the one they brought against the Aerial Experiment Association, which had been formed by Alexander Graham Bell and his associates. The dispute involved Glenn Curtiss, one of its executives, who had previously asked the Wrights' advice about details of wing construction. Innocently they answered his queries only to find later that their innovations were being used without credit and for commercial purpose. Their protests were brushed off, with the claim that AEA did not intend to use the innovations commercially. Curtiss formed the Herring-Curtiss Company. His plane, the "June Bug," contained movable surfaces (ailerons) at the tips of the wings. The Wrights brought suit. In his book, Fred Kelly notes that Judge John R. Hazel issued a restraining order on January 3, 1910, but that it was not until January 13, 1914, that the U. S. Circuit Court of Appeals issued their decision in favor of the Wrights. Once and for all it was decided that movable surfaces on the wings infringed the patent.

It was this court decision which led to Glenn Curtiss' remarkable

At Fort Myer, Virginia, on July 30, 1909, Orville Wright demonstrated their new biplane to enable the U. S. Army to decide whether Uncle Sam would buy it and thus establish an Army air service. The first military plane made a flight lasting fourteen minutes.

In the crowd that watched the test of the plane flown by Orville were Wilbur, Katharine, their trusty mechanic Charley Taylor, and the President of the United States, William Howard Taft.

In place of a plane wrecked the year before, the Wrights built this one in accordance with their contract with the Army. The Army's requirement was a speed of 40 mph and Orville attained an average of 42.583 mph, thereby earning the Wrights not only the price of $25,000 for the plane but also a $5,000 bonus for exceeding the stipulated speed. The craft was launched from a track.

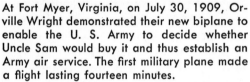

Picture above again shows the historic first military plane with Orville, left, and his passenger, Lieutenant Colonel Benjamin D. Foulois, whose photograph is also shown at right. Foulois was assigned as the government observer for the test and became America's one-man air force in 1910. The picture below shows Orville circling Fort Myer in 1908, the year before the successful test flight. In the course of these earlier tests Orville achieved the first flight of longer than one hour. Panorama of Fort Myer can be seen at bottom of this historic picture.

contract with the Smithsonian Institution to rebuild the Langley plane, recounted later in this chapter.

All in all there were at least a dozen suits, including some in France (against Blériot and Santos-Dumont) as well as in Germany.

The Wright brothers won every patent suit that was ever decided in court.

In 1911 Wilbur had to go abroad to testify at one of the trials. The brothers were now planning to build a new home in the spring of 1912. "All I want," wrote Wilbur from abroad, "is a bathroom for myself."

But he never got it. Nor did he see the new house. On May 30, back from his trying experience abroad, Wilbur died in their little house on Hawthorn Street.

"The doctors called it typhoid fever," reported *Popular Science,* June 1929, "but his friends believed that Wilbur was worn down to his grave by lawsuits. In his delirium he labored to tell the court all about the airplane, just how he and his brother created it, explaining a thousand intricate details. In a lucid period he said that when he recovered he wanted to spend the rest of his life helping other inventors."

Orville became president of the company but by 1915 he had sold it at a good profit. With Wilbur gone, he had little heart for the business side of his and Wilbur's invention. When John R. McMahon visited him in Dayton in the late 1920s (for the series in *Popular Science*), Orville was working alone in his office workshop on an automatic stabilizer for aircraft, and on a later visit McMahon found him interested in a scheme to drive a boat with an air propeller; he had also rigged up a furnace regulator—chains through the floor of his living room—to save walks to the cellar.

The final irony is that the Wright Company was eventually merged with Curtiss and is today the thriving Curtiss-Wright Corporation.

Ultimately the Wright brothers' "Kitty Hawk Flyer" was placed on exhibit, suspended from the ceiling, in the North Hall of the Arts and Industries Building of the Smithsonian Institution's National Air Museum. But it was not placed there until forty-five years after the flights on December 17, 1903. The story behind the delay (a small part of which was caused by World War II) shocks any biographer of the Wrights, who can only conclude that their treatment by certain secretaries of the Smithsonian Institution was a national disgrace, although belatedly rectified.

The unwitting originator of the little-known cause célèbre was the same Professor Samuel P. Langley, secretary of the Smithsonian Institution, who had written to them (and Chanute) in 1902. Langley was given $50,000 in 1898 by the Board of Ordnance and Fortification of the War Department to experiment with his man-carrying plane, the aerodrome. He worked with his assistant, Charles M. Manly, who by 1901 had constructed an engine of fifty horsepower, weighing about two hundred pounds; the huge plane was launched from a houseboat on the Potomac on October 7, 1903—but it failed, and Manly, entangled in the wrecked machine, almost drowned. They tried again on December 8 but once more the aerodrome literally flopped into the Potomac. Altogether $70,000 had been spent on the project. The Army board canceled the contract and, early in 1906, Langley died a disappointed and defeated man.

On December 9, 1903, when Orville Wright was returning from Dayton to Kitty Hawk by train, he bought a newspaper and read a dispatch from Washington, D.C., describing the crash of the aerodrome. In the midst of their crucial experiments, the failure of Langley deeply disturbed the brothers.

However, their four successful flights took place only eight days later. Of the first, which lasted only a few seconds (twelve to be exact), Orville wrote: ". . . it was nevertheless the first [flight] in the history of the world in which a machine carrying a man had raised itself by its own power into the air in full flight, had sailed forward without the reduction of speed, and had finally landed at a point as high as that from which it started."

And, as has been previously noted, the fourth flight that day, by Wilbur, lasted fifty-nine seconds and covered 852 feet.

Anxious to honor its late secretary, Langley, the Institution labeled his plane on exhibit at the Smithsonian the first machine "capable" of flight, neglecting to state that it hadn't flown. Langley's successor as secretary and adamant champion was Charles D. Walcott. When Wilbur gave Langley credit in a private letter for encouraging human flight, Walcott used it, in his Annual Report of 1910, to give the impression that the Wrights acknowledged their indebtedness to Langley's scientific work and that therefore he, not they, deserved the credit for the airplane. In addition, in his presentation of the Langley Medal to the Wrights, Walcott made no reference to the fact that they were the first to fly.

Despite Wilbur's offer in 1910 to reconstruct their plane that had made the 1903 flights, Walcott continued to make clear that the Institution didn't want it. No further communications between him and the Wrights took place for six years.

In 1914, two years after Wilbur's death, the Wright interests won their patent suit against Glenn H. Curtiss. Thereupon Curtiss poured fuel on the controversy by "restoring" the aerodrome (with the approval of the Smithsonian plus $2,000). *Popular Science* reported that Curtiss had been given two honors. One was the award in May

1914 of the Langley Medal "for aerodromics," a pound of pure gold, for his service in the development of artificial flight, presented to him by his associate, Professor Alexander Graham Bell. "The other," the report continued, "was his selection by the Smithsonian Institution to prove that Prof. Samuel P. Langley, the Institution's famous secretary, had actually built a flying machine that could fly."

After Curtiss' alterations of the aerodrome—which it turned out were largely based on the Wright brothers' patented innovations—the plane flew several times but only for a few seconds each time at Hammondsport, New York, in May and June 1914.

The Smithsonian's report of the Curtiss flights stated no modifications had been made and when the aerodrome was restored to its original form and put back on display it still was hailed, on its label, as "The first man-carrying aeroplane capable of sustained free flight . . ."

To which Orville Wright replied again and again that it was not "capable"—it dived into the Potomac. He claimed that Curtiss had altered Langley's original design, which, he said, could never have flown.

After Wilbur's death in 1912, Orville was too grieved to pursue the subject with the Smithsonian.

However, when the original Wright plane was exhibited at MIT in 1916, Dr. Alexander Graham Bell, a regent of the Institution, wrote to Walcott, asking him to contact Orville. This resulted in a meeting between Orville and Walcott but nothing came of it. In fact, Orville Wright finally gave up on Secretary Walcott. A lecture in London in 1921 by Griffith Brewer, revealing the true nature of Curtiss' changes in the aerodrome tests of 1914 was dismissed by Walcott with the usual denials. Orville's effort in May 1925 to get help from Chief Justice William Howard Taft, chancellor of the Institution, also failed.

In an effort to explain though not justify Dr. Walcott's behavior, *Popular Science* published this comment (January 1929): "Doubtless he was sincere in the belief that an eminent scientist, his friend and colleague, had to be right against a pair of young 'bicycle men' of Dayton, Ohio, who never looked inside a college door."

When Walcott died in 1927 he was succeeded by Dr. Charles G. Abbot. In 1928 Orville sent the "Kitty Hawk Flyer" to the South Kensington Museum near London, to be exhibited there for at least five years (it actually stayed twenty years!). Secretary Abbot began to attempt a reconciliation which would lead to the return to America of the famous plane. Said *Popular Science* in July 1928: "Formal credit (to the Wrights) from the Smithsonian Institution for having made the first man-carrying flight in air history marks the latest step in the controversy . . . Prominent aviation officials hope the Smithsonian

Institution's latest action will induce Orville Wright to bring his plane back."

Orville's wish was simple: for the Smithsonian to publish, in parallel columns, a comparison of the features of the original Langley aerodrome of 1903 with those of Curtiss' remodeled 1914 plane. He felt that such a comparison would clearly demonstrate to the world that the changes were based largely on the Wright brothers' patented inventions.

Alternate proposals by Abbot continued until 1942. At last, on October 8 of that year, Orville approved a Smithsonian draft of the apology and comparisons. It was thereupon included in the Smithsonian Institution Annual Report for 1942 with the title: "The 1914 Tests of the Langley 'Aerodrome.'" The by-line was C. G. Abbot, Secretary, Smithsonian Institution.

"It is everywhere acknowledged," Abbot wrote, "that the Wright brothers were the first to make sustained flights in a heavier-than-air machine at Kitty Hawk, North Carolina, on December 17, 1903."

He went on to cite "acts and statements of former officers of the Smithsonian Institution" in connection with the Hammondsport tests of 1914 which had caused Orville to send the plane to England in 1928. He called Secretary Walcott's contract with Curtiss "ill considered and open to criticism" in the light of the Court having pronounced him an infringer of the Wrights' patent. He included details of the reconstruction of the Langley plane and the admission: "the longest time off the water with the Langley motor was approximately five seconds."

"It is to be regretted," Abbot went on, "that the Institution published statements repeatedly (1914, 1915, 1917, 1918) to the effect that these experiments of 1914 demonstrated the Langley plane of 1903 *without essential modification* was the first heavier-than-air machine capable of maintaining sustained flight."

He then presented the detailed comparison Orville had requested of the Langley machine of 1903 with the Hammondsport machine of May–June 1914. The list included thirty-five items comparing the wings, rudder, system of control, power plant, launching equipment and floats, and weight.

Abbot then closed the confession on behalf of the Smithsonian with the sincere regret that the Institution employed, to make the tests of 1914, an agent who had been an unsuccessful defendant in patent litigation brought against him by the Wrights. He regretted also the false statements made by his predecessor, especially the unqualified credit to the late Secretary Langley for a success which only the Wrights had achieved. He hoped that the publication of his paper would clear the way for Wright to bring back his plane to America and promised that "it would be given the highest pace of honor, which is its due" in the U. S. National Museum—if only Wright would bring the Kitty Hawk machine back to America!

The following year, 1943, President Franklin D. Roosevelt wrote to "Dear Orville," asking him to reserve December 17 for a dinner in Washington to celebrate the fortieth anniversary of the first flight of the Kitty Hawk craft. Orville not only accepted the invitation but also agreed in a later letter to FDR to announce at that dinner the return of the "Kitty Hawk Flyer" to the U.S.A.

World War II delayed the return of the plane until 1948.

The Smithsonian Institution booklet, "The National Aeronautical Collections," reported the denouement:

> On December 17, 1948, the forty-fifth anniversary of the first flight, this famous aeroplane popularly known as the "Kitty Hawk Flyer" which had been lent to the South Kensington Museum in London, England, was returned to America and deposited in the United States National Museum (a part of the Smithsonian Institution)* by the heirs and executors of Orville Wright. He had died on January 30 of that year: the presentation was in accordance with his expressed intention. The ceremonies were attended by nearly a thousand prominent officials of the government and the air industry, noted fliers, and admirers of the Wright brothers.

Absent: the late Orville Wright, who had died at the age of seventy-seven.

* On July 1, 1976, the new Air and Space Museum of the Smithsonian Institution opened its doors to visitors. There the "Kitty Hawk Flyer" has finally found a resting place worthy of its reputation.

CHAPTER 8

Charles M. Hall—
Alchemist of Aluminum

CHARLES MARTIN HALL was not a protean genius, like Bell and Edison. The list of his inventive triumphs is brief, indeed singular. But his one real contribution to technology fully met those three golden goals that every striving inventor seeks: he solved a problem that had baffled great minds for decades; he transformed the world around him; and he became very, very rich.

His master stroke was the discovery in 1886, when he was just twenty-two years old, of a practical way to produce aluminum, thereby changing it from a rare and costly curiosity to a key metal in our industrial society.

Aluminum is the most abundant metal in the earth's crust, amounting to some 8 per cent of the stuff beneath our feet, notably in clay. Yet until 1825 no one had ever seen the silvery-white element. For, unlike copper, silver, and gold, aluminum is never found in its pure, elemental form. It occurs naturally in compounds such as aluminum oxide, or alumina, found in high concentration in the ore bauxite (named after the French village of Les Baux, where it was discovered).

Until the 1820s the isolation of aluminum from any of its compounds by any means proved impossible. Sir Humphry Davy, the great British scientist, had isolated sodium and potassium by using electrolysis. Essentially, this involves passing an electric current through a chemical compound in solution to break it into its components. With a metallic compound, the metal collects at the negative electrode (a result capitalized on now as in Davy's time in electroplating). Davy tried the same method with aluminum, but failed, although he was so sure of the eventual outcome that he named the element in advance. In 1825 the Danish pioneer in magnetism, Hans Christian Oersted, converted aluminum hydroxide to chloride, and extracted the metal chemically with potassium, a process later

Treasure chest holds first silvery buttons of aluminum—once so costly it was used for jewelry—that Hall made in 1866, opening the way to aluminum pots and pans (below) and myriad other applications.

Charles Martin Hall (above) at twenty-two invented a way to extract aluminum from ore that cut the price of the formerly precious metal to pennies a pound, and made it a familiar sight in every home's kitchen.

repeated with better results by the German chemist Friedrich Wöhler. By 1845, Wöhler was able to achieve only a "grayish dust, with a few globules, the largest of which was not bigger than a pinhead," according to an early *Popular Science* account. In 1854 a French chemist, Henri Sainte-Claire Deville perfected this chemical approach, substituting sodium, which he extracted from sea salt, for the "rare, expensive, difficult, and somewhat dangerous potassium." He also prepared the aluminum chloride by treating bauxite with chlorine. In this way he managed to collect enough of the metal to cast the first aluminum ingot, which astounded the world when it appeared at the Paris Universal Exposition in 1855, where it occupied a place of honor next to the crown jewels.

Immediately, a vogue for the light, lustrous, and precious metal swept the fashionable world. Because the Deville process was slow and costly, and yielded small quantities, the price of aluminum was prohibitive, although it had come down substantially from $500 a pound, so one of its favored uses was in jewelry. A *Popular Science* author writes: "Napoleon III [who had helped subsidize Deville] entertained guests at a table set with aluminum forks. The King of Siam wore an aluminum watch fob. And when the Prince Imperial of France was one year old, a minister of state bought him the rarest thing he could find, an aluminum rattle."

With improvements in the basic extraction process, the price slowly fell, and utensils of aluminum began to appear next to the jewelry at the Paris Exposition of 1867. Still, in 1884, when a 100-ounce aluminum cap was cast for the Washington Monument (the largest object ever made of the metal up to that time) it was displayed in the Fifth Avenue window of a New York jeweler—Tiffany. The price of aluminum was then eight dollars a pound.

What Charles Martin Hall did can perhaps be best understood in terms of price. His new process, put to the commercial test in 1888, quickly dropped the price to one dollar a pound. By 1914 it was eighteen cents a pound, low enough to create a revolution and bring aluminum into every kitchen.

Here is an excerpt from a prophetic article that appeared in *Popular Science* in 1894, while the revolution was in full flood: "New uses are constantly found for the pure metal; less employed in jewelry, it is more used in the modest ranks of plated ware and kitchen vessels. In Germany it has been introduced experimentally into the equipment of soldiers . . . the Russian army tried horseshoes of aluminum, and the horses of the Finnish dragoons, on which the experiment was made, are said to have gained perceptibly in speed by it. It has been introduced into machines, to reduce the dead weight—a gain of special value for aerial navigation and for cyclers. Its application to aerostats [airships] is talked of."

The origins of this revolutionary discovery—the Hall process—were in the best tradition of American enterprise. They were recorded by Professor F. F. Jewett, the man who was the key catalyst in Hall's invention. Jewett was head of the chemistry department at Oberlin College, where Hall was a student, and had made of him a kind of protégé. Jewett writes of Hall:

"My great discovery has been the discovery of a man. When I went to Oberlin in 1880, on my return from four years' teaching in Japan, there was a little boy about sixteen years old who used to come to the chemical laboratory frequently to buy a few cents worth of glass tubing or test tubes or something of that sort and go off with them." (Hall was at this time a few months shy of seventeen and had attained his full height of five feet eight inches. He continued to look like "a little boy" for virtually the rest of his life.) "I made up my mind that he would make a mark for himself some day because he didn't spend all his time playing but was already investigating. That boy was Charles M. Hall . . . Hall was an all-round student, but he did have a special liking for science."

Jewett continues: "After he had entered college and was part way through the regular course I took him into my private laboratory and gave him a place by my side—discussing his problems with him from day to day.

"Possibly a remark of mine in the laboratory one day led him to turn his special attention to aluminum. Speaking to my students, I said that if anyone should invent a process by which aluminum could be made on a commercial scale, not only would he be a benefactor to the world, but would also be able to lay up for himself a great fortune. Turning to a classmate, Charles Hall said, 'I'm going for that metal.' And he went for it. . . .

"I loaned him what apparatus I had to spare, what batteries we could develop . . . we finally got the current that was needed. Soon after this he was graduated and took the apparatus to his own home; apparatus which he himself made and which I had loaned him. . . .

"About six months later he came over to my office one morning, and holding out his hollowed hand said: 'Professor, I've got it!' There in the palm of his hand lay a dozen little globules of aluminum, the first ever made by the electrolytic process. This was the 23rd of February, 1886." Those original, silvery buttons have been preserved as a souvenir of the feat.

Like that of many another inventor, Hall's achievement resulted mainly from persistence. After experimenting for a while with chemical methods of extracting aluminum, he decided to concentrate on an electrolytic approach. He reasoned that water solutions containing aluminum compounds did not work because the aluminum that was freed instantly reacted with the water. So he resolved to find a substance that would dissolve alumina when it was molten (in such a bath, any trace of water must evaporate). He set up his laboratory in the family woodshed. He built a crude clay crucible and heated it with the single burner of a secondhand gasoline stove. Then began a series of attempts to find the right solvent. He started with fluorspar—calcium fluoride—but it refused to melt. (Hall did not know that fluorspar's melting point is 2,500° F, far beyond the heating capacity of his primitive furnace.) Magnesium fluoride and aluminum fluoride also declined to melt. Sodium fluoride and potassium fluoride did melt but would not dissolve even a pinch of alumina. Finally, on February 19, 1886, he tried the mineral called cryolite—sodium aluminum fluoride. It melted, and it dissolved the alumina.

But would the long sought solvent yield up aluminum when electrolyzed? Hall borrowed a battery from the ever obliging Professor Jewett, rigged up carbon rods as electrodes. When he turned on the current, he saw gas bubbles rising at one of the copper rods, indicating that a reaction of some kind was occurring. But no aluminum formed in the molten cryolite. Now Hall made a crucial intuitive leap. He guessed that the electric current might be decomposing the silica in his clay crucible, freeing silicon to combine with, and imprison the aluminum. To test his idea, Hall made a crucible lined with unreactive carbon.

On February 23, 1886, he repeated the experiment with his carbon-lined crucible. After several hours, he poured the molten contents into one of his mother's old kitchen skillets. When the cryolite had solidified, and while it was still hot, Hall shattered the mass into bits with a hammer. And there, in the bottom of the pan, were the silvery buttons of metal that Hall whisked to the campus to show Professor Jewett.

In one of those startling coincidences that spatter the pages of the history of invention, a young Frenchman named Paul L. T. Héroult independently discovered exactly the same process, using instead of a battery a small dynamo in a tannery he had inherited in Gentilly, France; and was granted a French patent for it on April 23, 1886. Fortunately for Hall, the rules of the U. S. Patent Office regarding foreign inventors held that an American with a conflicting claim need only prove that his invention had been reduced to practice before the date of the foreign patent. And this Hall was able to demonstrate, by a scant two months. Hall eventually received his patent for the electrolytic process on April 2, 1889. He wrote to his sister Julia: "Our patents were issued Tuesday. I saw them one day last week all done up in gold lettering, blue ribbon, etc., as pretty as a new bank note." For the further titillation of coincidence gatherers, Héroult was born the same year as Hall, and died the same year.

Born December 6, 1863, in Thompson, Ohio, Hall grew up a minister's son in Oberlin, Ohio—a religious community. Here he is at age twenty-seven, five years after graduating from Oberlin College and inventing a practical electrolytic process for producing aluminum. He retained a remarkably youthful look all his life.

Hall's parents, Heman Bassett Hall and Sophronia Brooks Hall, were married in 1849 and spent ten years as missionaries in Jamaica. Reverend Hall, a graduate of Oberlin College and Oberlin Theological Seminary, was the son of a trustee of the college, and his uncle was its first president-elect. Charles had three older sisters and two younger ones, and an older brother, George.

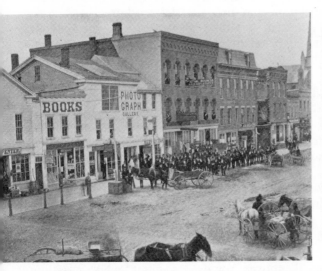

The campus of Oberlin College, which Hall attended until 1885, faced this street, West College Street. The third of the three frame buildings from the left was originally Oberlin Hall, the first college building. Hall's great inspiration came from a remark by his chemistry teacher, Professor F. F. Jewett (right), that a commercial aluminum process would make its inventor rich.

At first glance, Hall—callow and relatively untrained in chemistry, compared to some of the scientists who failed in the quest for aluminum—seems an unlikely candidate for his role. But a search of his background turns up the key ingredients: high intelligence, passionate interest, and an overwhelming drive toward success and riches.

Charles Martin Hall was born on December 6, 1863, in Thompson, Ohio, about thirty-five miles east of Cleveland, into a family of clerics and educators. They were tightly linked to Oberlin, a religious colony that was founded in 1833 and consecrated to the loftiest ideals of Christian living, combining high-mindedness and a lack of luxury, and focusing intellectual activity in Oberlin College. Hall's father, Heman Bassett Hall, was a poor minister who was an alumnus of both the college and Oberlin Theological Seminary. *His* father had been a trustee of Oberlin College, and his uncle was its first president-elect. Heman married Sophronia Brooks, whom he met at Oberlin, in 1849, and shortly thereafter the two joined the American Missionary Association, a Christian anti-slavery society with strong bonds to Oberlin. For ten years they served in the West Indies, and then returned to Thompson in 1860 with their five children—three girls and two boys, one of whom died a year later. There, Reverend Hall served as pastor of the Congregational church, and there Charles was born.

He seemed to be an unusual child from the first. Under his mother's tutelage, he became a precocious reader. Apparently around age six, he was using one of his father's old chemistry textbooks as a primer. (Hall later said, "My first knowledge of chemistry was gained from a book on chemistry which my father had studied in the forties. I still have the book, published in 1841. It is minus the cover and title page, so I do not know the author.") He became a voracious reader and developed an early interest in mathematical problems. When Charles was ten, his father moved the whole family (now including two more girls) to Oberlin. This was to be the seminal period in Charles's life.

Charles had breezed through an elementary school education in a remarkably short time, and his parents decided to wait a year before starting him in high school in Oberlin. During this year he studied music and the piano, acquiring what was the beginning of a considerable mastery of the instrument. (Like Bell, Hall would spend many hours thundering out Beethoven sonatas at night, while wrestling with stubborn problems of invention.) During three years at Oberlin High School and a year at Oberlin Academy he also studied part time at the Oberlin Conservatory of Music, so that his consuming passion for chemistry, invention, and music grew together. Hall was constantly experimenting with crude, homemade equipment and such chemicals as his mother's kitchen and the village pharmacy could provide. In one early experiment he tried to make some fireworks, and the resulting fire ruined a good tablecloth. His father's stern reproaches centered as much on the frivolity and indeed the moral iniquity of fireworks as on the loss of a valuable object in a home where money was in very short supply. Charles apparently smarted from frugality imposed by a minister's meager income. (In a letter to his sister Julia early in college he said, "Yes, I really think I shall be a rich inventor some day.") With his wealth, he would give his family, and especially his mother, the ease they had never possessed. But shortly before he was graduated from Oberlin College, Sophronia succumbed to a stroke.

The day she died, Charles pledged that some day he would build a monument to her memory in the form of a great building on the Oberlin campus, with her name carved on it in granite.

Growing up in the puritanically Calvinist atmosphere at Oberlin, immersed in books from early childhood on, perhaps dominated by an overwhelmingly female household, single-mindedly striving for success as an inventor, Hall was shaped for the rest of his life. At Oberlin, tobacco and alcohol were regarded as tools of the devil, and even tea drinking and novel reading were not suffered blithely. When Ohioan James A. Garfield won the presidency in 1880, a delegation of 600 jubilant Oberlin students took a special train to Mentor, to congratulate their hero. Charles went with them. When they arrived, General Garfield was sitting on his porch smoking a big black cigar. For Charles, the occasion was spoiled. And even as a mature, successful, and somewhat more cosmopolitan man, he would permit no one, with a few rare exceptions, to smoke in his home. In fact, his involvement with art collecting later in life led him to formulate the theory that the introduction of tobacco had snuffed out the creative impulse in artists for the previous 300 years.

Perhaps it was an attribute of what can only be called priggishness that led Hall never to marry. He had one recorded romance, which may be one of the least ardent courtships in history. It was directed toward Josephine Lucretia Cody, who had attended some of his classes at the conservatory while he was going to high school, but whom he seemed not really to notice until they were both seniors in Oberlin's class of '85. They shared a mutual love for music, and their first formal outing was to a concert.

Josephine was from a noted Cleveland family (one of her relatives was Colonel W. F. "Buffalo Bill" Cody). Although there was apparently no formal engagement, Charles assumed that she would some day become his wife, after he had made a fortune from inventing, and Josie seems to have agreed to this vague arrangement, the idea being that after graduation she would teach music in Cleveland

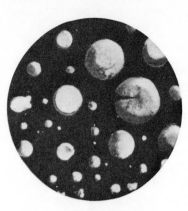

These aluminum buttons, retrieved from a mass of molten cryolite allowed to cool in his mother's skillet, are the first Hall made by his new electrolytic process in 1886.

Captain Alfred E. Hunt, a leading metallurgist of the 1880s, foresaw a mighty industry based on Hall's process. He formed the Pittsburgh Reduction Co., which became today's Aluminum Company of America.

Arthur Vining Davis and Hall poured the first commercial aluminum ingot at the Smallman Street works, of which Davis was superintendent.

C. M. HALL.
MANUFACTURE OF ALUMINIUM.
No. 400,665.   Patented Apr. 2, 1889.

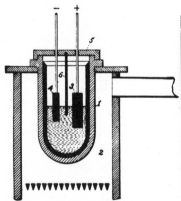

This priceless patent laid the foundation for a great fortune. A French inventor—Héroult—had made an independent discovery of the process at almost the same time, but Hall was eventually awarded priority.

The reduction pots at the Smallman Street works of the Pittsburgh Reduction Co. (1889) were a far cry from Hall's original, tiny crucible. Each carbon-lined pot could hold some 250 pounds. Molten aluminum collected at the bottom of the pots.

Powerful new electrical sources, like these steam-powered 1,200-ampere dynamos at the Smallman Street works of the Pittsburgh Reduction Co. opened the way to industrialization of Hall's electrolytic process. It takes large amounts of current to make a pound of aluminum.

Made a trustee of Oberlin College in 1905, Hall here visits his home town the following year. His legacy to the school was worth many millions. Financial success came in part from widespread use of aluminum cookware, after qualms about its safety were refuted, as *Popular Science* noted in September 1892, above.

Large aluminum reduction pots were photographed in 1914 at a plant in Massena, New York, built in 1903 near the St. Lawrence River, the third installation of the Pittsburgh Reduction Co. By this time the company's fortunes were thriving. Hall was becoming wealthy.

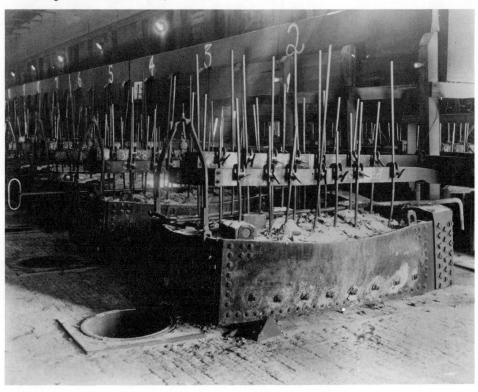

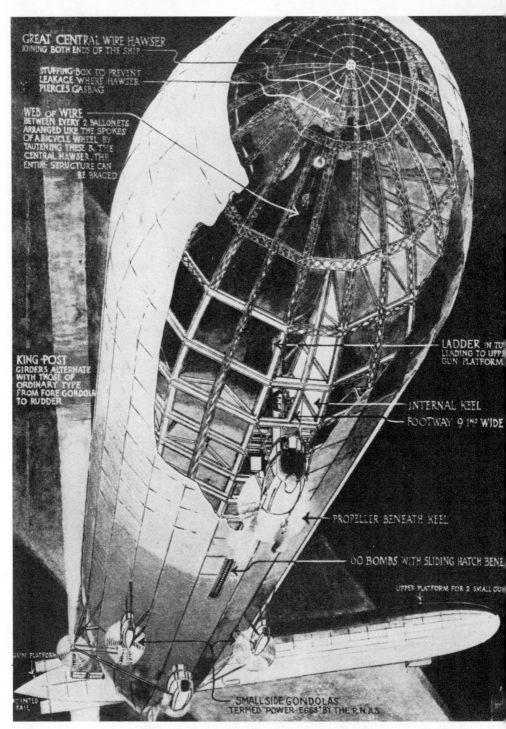

GREAT CENTRAL WIRE HAWSER
JOINING BOTH ENDS OF THE SHIP

STUFFING BOX TO PREVENT
LEAKAGE WHERE HAWSER
PIERCES GASBAG

WEB OF WIRE
BETWEEN EVERY 2 BALLONETS
ARRANGED LIKE THE SPOKES
OF A BICYCLE WHEEL. BY
TAUTENING THESE & THE
CENTRAL HAWSER. THE
ENTIRE STRUCTURE CAN
BE BRACED

KING-POST
GIRDERS ALTERNATE
WITH THOSE OF
ORDINARY TYPE
FROM FORE GONDOLA
TO RUDDER

LADDER IN TU
LEADING TO UPPE
GUN PLATFORM

INTERNAL KEEL
FOOTWAY 9 INS WIDE

PROPELLER BENEATH KEEL

00 BOMBS WITH SLIDING HATCH BENE

UPPER PLATFORM FOR 2 SMALL GUN

GUN PLATFORM

POINTED
TAIL

SMALL SIDE GONDOLAS
TERMED "POWER-EGGS" BY THE R.N.A.S.

The use of aluminum in "aerostats" was forecast in an 1894
Popular Science article on the "past and future" of the
metal. The prediction materialized in the lightweight frames
of Count von Zeppelin's dirigibles. This cutaway drawing is
from a *Popular Science* account of 1917.

Without light yet strong aluminum, the aircraft industry would never have gotten off the ground. By the 1920s aluminum wings and bodies were being used in passenger airliners, like Ford's 1925 "Tin Goose" trimotor.

Aluminum proved its worth in deep-diving submersibles like the 51-foot-long *Aluminaut* (left), capable of diving almost three miles and of lifting 3 tons, and the two-man sub *Alvin* in 1968. The Johnson-Sea-Link submarine (right) used a plastic bubble in an aluminum skeleton for maximum visibility. These subs are made of aluminum to resist corrosion.

while Charles pursued his projects. For the next several years, while Charles was helping develop the infant aluminum industry, he wrote sporadically to Josie, and paid an occasional visit to her family home in Cleveland. By the spring of 1889, his fortunes had progressed to the point where he actually proposed to the girl. But he then became so engrossed in aluminum that the engagement languished, then collapsed. After he had gone on a trip abroad without even letting her know, and after he let a full year go by without paying her even one single visit, the long-suffering Josie had enough. In 1892, she brought their seven-year "courtship" to an unsentimental end, telling Charles she was going to Germany for a year's study. Soon after her return, in 1893, she married a lawyer and settled in Chicago. Characteristically, Charles could not really fathom why Josie had ruptured their romance. Perhaps the most significant part of his reaction was pleasure that the engagement had been kept virtually a secret, so that he would not have the embarrassment of having to tell too many people what had happened. The idea of marrying anyone else never seems to have occurred to him.

One of Charles's excuses was that he was waiting for the money to give Josie the fine things he had promised: a big house, with two grand pianos and beautiful Persian carpets. But for some time it had been very clear that he was soon destined to achieve this goal.

Like most inventors, Hall had some initial difficulties in developing his discovery.

First, there were two abortive experiences with small-scale financial backers, whose money was needed to secure the necessary patents and to demonstrate the commercial feasibility of Hall's process. The first set were aquaintances of his older brother George, who was a minister in Boston. But Judge Henry Baldwin and a Mr. Brown were timid men and quickly dropped out when they saw no dazzling results for their $1,500 investment. Next, in 1887, Hall's uncle, a Cleveland physician named Dr. Brooks, enlisted the help of two gentlemen engaged in the chemical business, but they proved so avaricious that Hall would not conclude an agreement with them.

In July 1887 Hall began a year with the Cowles Electric Smelting Company of Lockport, New York, during which he was to demonstrate his process, receiving $75 a month, and an extra $750 after ninety days if the company chose to continue with the project. The company also received an option to purchase the Hall patents for a one-eighth interest in the stock of the company. Hall encountered mechanical difficulties, never got his $750, and Cowles never took up their option. Hall left in disgust. But one of the friends he had made in Lockport promised to put him in touch with a brilliant young metallurgist, Captain Alfred Hunt, who was a partner in the Pittsburgh

Testing Laboratory, which had been trying to produce aluminum.

The meeting of Hunt and Hall in the summer of 1888 gave birth to a new industry and a giant company, eventually to be known as the Aluminum Company of America—Alcoa. Hunt was a man of considerable vision and no less audacity in business. Hall told him that he could produce aluminum at fifty cents a pound instead of the going rate of eight dollars a pound, whereupon Hunt decided to form a company to exploit Hall's process, first called the Pittsburgh Aluminium Company, and two weeks later renamed the Pittsburgh Reduction Company, and capitalized at $20,000. A small plant was built at Smallman Street in Pittsburgh, with reduction pots designed by Hall to contain the molten cryolite and alumina. Two large Westinghouse dynamos supplied about 2,400 amperes of current.

In the fall, Hunt secured an assistant to help Hall run the plant. He was Arthur Vining Davis—another minister's son just out of college. He lived in the room across from Hall's and the two young men soon became fast friends—a friendship that was to endure for all of Hall's life. Davis, the company's first employee, later became Alcoa's president and chairman of the board. On Thanksgiving Day, 1888, Hall and Davis poured the first commercial aluminum ingot, and stored it in the office safe. As the technical problems were overcome, production went up. By summer of 1889, the little plant was turning out 1,300 pounds of the once-precious metal a month.

The company expanded, with new investors bringing the capitalization up to a million dollars. Hall became a major stockholder, receiving 3,525 of the 10,000 shares and was made vice-president in charge of technical operations. Soon he valued his holding at about three hundred thousand dollars. In January 1890 his salary was raised to $125 per month, and in the same month he sold sixty shares of stock to Andrew W. Mellon, the industrialist, for $6,000. Another young man might perhaps have felt secure enough to marry, but Hall did not.

Despite litigation over conflicting patents, and competition from the Cowles plant, the company prospered. By 1893 (the year Josie married) it had built a new plant in New Kensington, Pennsylvania, established foreign operations, and was planning another plant at Niagara Falls, New York, the first industrial facility to use Niagara's hydroelectric power. For years, Hall lived in rented rooms in Niagara Falls. In 1902 he finally decided he could manage a house of his own, and leased a large one there. Now he started acquiring Oriental rugs, and apparently got stuck with some "eight and nine dollar Bokhara rugs" that he shortly regretted buying.

By 1907, even Hall could not have denied that he was a rich and successful inventor. His company, its name now changed to the Alu-

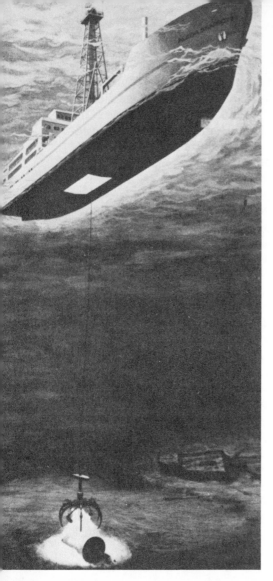

All-aluminum beer barrels revolutionized the handling of draft beer. They
do not need to be lined.

Aluminum foil, useful in cooking and
food storage, fostered the spread of
the ubiquitous charcoal grill.

Built entirely of a new aluminum alloy with
high resistance to sea-water corrosion, the
Alcoa Seaprobe (above and below) can recover 200-ton objects from 6,000 feet deep.

All-aluminum cars are attractive for
rapid-transit lines; these cars are for
San Francisco's BART system.

Incredibly, this boyish-looking photograph of Charles Martin Hall was taken when he was forty-two, a wealthy bachelor living in Niagara Falls, New York, near an aluminum processing plant. His hobby: collecting Oriental rugs. He died nine years later.

minum Company of America, was turning out fifteen million pounds
of aluminum a year. It owned bauxite mines, an alumina refinery, and
three aluminum plants in New York and Canada. Hall was a bachelor
of forty-two, with the look of a boy of twenty, indulging his hobbies
of music and collecting. He got rid of his old bicycle, which he used to
pedal between his house in Niagara Falls and the plant, and bought a
new Packard touring car. In 1905 he had been elected a trustee of
Oberlin College, and in 1908 he was elected president of the alumni
association. He drove the whole way from Niagara to Oberlin in his
new Packard to attend the reunion of his class, celebrate the seventy-
fifth anniversary of the school, and hear for the first time a splendid
pipe organ he had jointly given to the chapel with another benefactor. In 1910, when his old chum Arthur Vining Davis was elected
president of Alcoa, Hall's dividend income on his stock, worth
millions, rose to $170,000 a year. In 1911, he was awarded the pres-
tigious Perkin Medal for chemistry, and at the presentation ceremony
heard his French rival Héroult speak graciously of his achievements.

But this serene existence was interrupted by serious illness. Already
in 1908 he had complained to his physician, Dr. William H. Hodge,
of feeling tired and run down. Hodge had found that Hall's spleen was
enlarged, thought he was simply overworked, and told him to take
the winter in Florida. Feeling better, Hall sailed for Europe the following June, but suffered a painful attack that the ship's doctor diagnosed as a kidney infection. Arriving in England, he quickly summoned Hodge, who brought with him the famous Sir William Osler.
They found Hall anemic, diagnosed the problem as Banti's disease,
and recommended surgical removal of the spleen, which was done by
the Mayo brothers in Rochester, Minnesota. Nevertheless, in 1912 he
had a painful attack of what seemed to be appendicitis. Instead, emergency surgery disclosed a massive hemorrhage.

Today, medical specialists would probably diagnose Hall's disease
as one of the leukemias. At any rate, he lived on another couple of
years, knowing he would probably die soon, without displaying any
great emotion at the prospect. Here is an excerpt from a letter he
wrote in June 1913 to the class reunion he was too tired to attend:

Dear Classmates:
   The last two years I have spent principally in being ill. I have had
some unusual experiences. Several times the doctors expected me to
die, and once I was about to die. One sometimes wonders how he
would feel in the face of such an announcement and how the future
would appear to him. Bacon says, "Men fear death as children fear
to go in the dark, and as that natural fear in children is increased
with tales, so is the other." In my case there was no fear.

Hall made use of some of the time remaining to him to read his favorite magazines (including *Popular Science Monthly*) and make suggestions to his colleagues about refinements in aluminum processing. He also made out a complex will, quite in keeping with the very large sums of money he had to bestow. When he died, on December 27, 1914, aged fifty-one, he left one third of his residuary estate to Oberlin College, an amount that was worth at least twenty million dollars in 1951. And in a special bequest, he set aside 600 thousand dollars for a large auditorium to be built on the Oberlin College campus. He instructed that the following inscription be carved on the building's wall:

In loving memory of
SOPHRONIA BROOKS HALL
This building was
erected by her son
CHARLES M. HALL

The promise was fulfilled a little belatedly. Although the bequest was received by the school a few years after Hall died, construction of the auditorium did not begin until 1951.

CHAPTER 9

Marconi, Mr. Wireless—
De Forest, Mr. Radio

AROUND the turn of the twentieth century two wholly unknown young men entered the lists of the world's hopeful inventors. Neither was a true scientist; one pointedly avoided saying he was. Each worked independently on the selfsame, weird—and, for then, cockeyed—idea. Both were destined to exert a profound influence on the lives of everyone on their planet for all time to come. Their names were Guglielmo Marconi and Lee De Forest, and the subject of their tinkering was communication without wires, despite the fact that more than two generations of learned men had explored the possibilities of the idea with unsatisfactory results.

There were other striking, peculiar parallels between the lives of Marconi and De Forest. Both were born at about the same time. Each was brought up in an environment that had a far-reaching influence on their attitudes and behavior in later life. Both made, and lost, a lot of money. Both were brilliant. Each became famous at an early age. Both dreamed dreams that were not big enough. Both had a penchant for falling in love willy-nilly, and each had problems in marriage.

The contrasts between the two men were more apparent, as we shall see.

From the minds of Marconi and De Forest came inventions that helped make possible thousands of wondrous accomplishments in the decades that followed, among them accurately controlled space flights of many millions of miles and the photographing of other planets in the solar system, manned landings on the moon and television pictures therefrom, artificial earth satellites that relay television and telephone signals between continents and provide data for amazingly accurate weather forecasts, new systems of navigation for surface ships and aircraft alike, electronic eyes that pierce veils that the human eye cannot, and radiotherapy for the human body.

Marconi made wireless work. De Forest gave it a voice—it became "radio."

Let's take a look at these men as major contributors to an age of scientific miracles.

MARCONI, FATHER OF WIRELESS

Guglielmo Marconi had the soul of a poet and the inner strength of an ox. The sky could fall in, and imperturbably he would set about to discover what caused it. His single-mindedness on his chosen subject of research, wireless, and complete detachment from the workaday world, including attendance at meals, so incensed his father Giuseppe that his mother and he had to hide his experimental devices to save them from destruction. Of the relationship between mother and son, Degna, the eldest of Marconi's daughters, wrote, "He was her heart's child." Annie Marconi, an Irish lass whom Giuseppe had pursued and won, indulged her boy. When Marconi was twenty-seven his mother was still writing him about dressing warmly in cold weather. To save his energies, she performed for him such petty duties as writing family social letters. It was Annie who, recognizing Guglielmo's singular gifts of concentration and persistence, made his first business contacts for him in London. It was Annie who saw to it that he was privately tutored and taught him flawless English, with the result that he spoke flawless Italian with a British accent. All his life Marconi displayed such self-assurance that most people he encountered considered him cold. There is some support for the conclusion that his austere manner was rooted in a basic shyness. In the English countryside where he erected his first great wireless mast he would stop to chat with children as he bicycled along the roads, and by invitation of ordinarily reserved Cornishmen joined a local cricket team. On one occasion, in New York, Marconi fended off an interview by clamoring reporters because he was too busy mending a doll for a little girl. Perhaps his warmth was reserved for simple people he trusted.

He could be puckish. On one of his many visits to America, he grew annoyed by reporters' questions, and to one—what was he working on now?—he replied, "I have invented a machine that sees through walls." A lot of his subsequent mail was from fluttery women protesting his invasion of their privacy. On another day, on a transocean steamer, members of his staff were having trouble launching kites for amusement. Marconi appeared. He launched a kite with ease. Later his frustrated audience discovered he had prevailed on the captain to alter course and provide a better launching wind.

Yet a New York newspaper reporter, getting his first look at Marconi—blond and blue-eyed, looking for all the world like something from Trafalgar Square, not the Via Veneto—described him as "a serious, somewhat self-centered young man who spoke but little and then always to the point."

As a personality, Guglielmo Marconi was an extremely complex man, with a glacial, almost forbidding exterior. Yet he was a soft touch for anyone with a hard-luck story. One biographer characterized Marconi as "the last survivor of a romantic age in science."

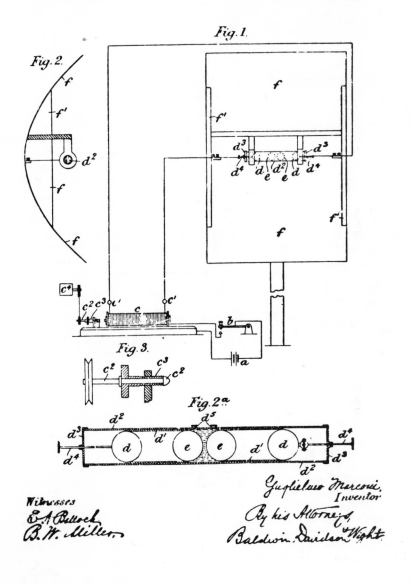

G. MARCONI.
TRANSMITTING ELECTRICAL SIGNALS.

No. 586,193.

Patented July 13. 1897.

Fig. 1.

Fig. 2.

Fig. 3.

Fig. 2ª.

Witnesses
E. A. Bullock
B. W. Miller

Guglielmo Marconi,
Inventor

By his Attorneys,
Baldwin Davidson & Wight

Marconi's original U.S. wireless patent, No. 586,193, issued in 1897, included drawings showing the transmitter's
front elevation (fig. 1) and a vertical section of it (fig. 2),
as well as other views. A loyal Italian, he let Italy use his
inventions without charge.

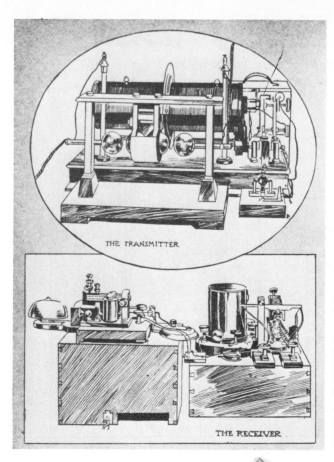

THE TRANSMITTER

THE RECEIVER

Here are drawings of other vintage Marconi equipment used as the inventor experimented with longer and longer wavelength (which ultimately would prove a mistake) to extend the range of his signals. While England was the site of his main research work, it had not been his first choice. He preferred Italy. But the Italian Government turned down a request by his father Giuseppe for a subsidy. Later, when he was successful, Rome ordered its navy into an active collaboration with him.

Shown here is an exact reproduction of the apparatus used by Marconi to send his first distant signals—before his attempt at transatlantic wireless. Original apparatus was burned. Many inventions he simply bought—such as the carbon-arc frequency generator of England's William Duddell and the direction finders of Italy's brilliant workers, Bellini and Tossi.

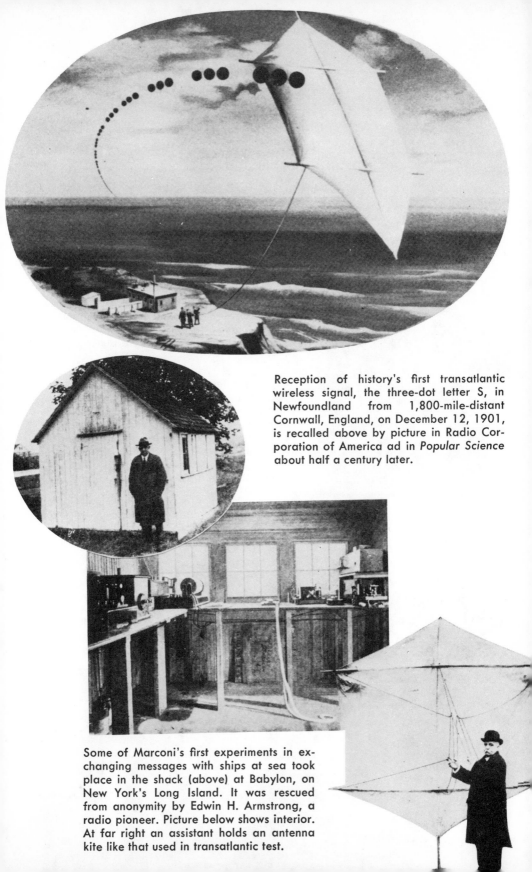

Reception of history's first transatlantic wireless signal, the three-dot letter S, in Newfoundland from 1,800-mile-distant Cornwall, England, on December 12, 1901, is recalled above by picture in Radio Corporation of America ad in *Popular Science* about half a century later.

Some of Marconi's first experiments in exchanging messages with ships at sea took place in the shack (above) at Babylon, on New York's Long Island. It was rescued from anonymity by Edwin H. Armstrong, a radio pioneer. Picture below shows interior. At far right an assistant holds an antenna kite like that used in transatlantic test.

Radio, television, and radar towers are integral parts of the landscape today, but at the turn of the century these four wood structures in Cornwall, England, supporting the Marconi transatlantic "aerial," were a local oddity when they were built.

In photo at left two assistants join the inventor outside the lab for picture of themselves at the Glace Bay, Nova Scotia, station in 1903. Below them is the station which received first complete transatlantic messages. In 1901 Marconi forecast commercial transatlantic service. It was initiated in 1907 at 10 cents a word and 5 for press dispatches.

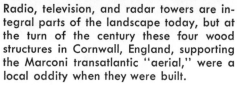

To preserve the moment for history, the picture of Marconi below was taken in his Newfoundland work shack when the wireless first spanned the Atlantic. He cabled England: "Confirm that signals were received here Thursday and Friday direct from Cornwall." His message added, "Receiving wire suspended by a kite."

He could be tart-tongued, even to royalty. When Marconi wireless systems were being installed on scores of ships, including many of German registry, by his British-incorporated firm before the First World War, Marconi was invited to a court dinner at which Kaiser Wilhelm II was present as a guest of the Italian King and Queen. Marconi had been having a row with the Germans over his patent rights.

"Signor Marconi," said the Kaiser icily on introduction, "you must not think that I have any animosity against yourself. It is the policy of your company I object to."

Responded Marconi with an equal lack of warmth, "Your Imperial Majesty, I should be overwhelmed if I thought you had any personal animosity against me. However, it is I who decides the policy of my company."

Queen Victoria didn't fare much better at Marconi's hands. Early in the inventor's career the Queen's son, Edward, Prince of Wales, was convalescing from a knee injury aboard the royal yacht off the Isle of Wight when she decided she wanted daily reports on his progress delivered to her island residence, Osborne House. Marconi, "that Italian electrician," as the Queen called him, was summoned to set up sending and receiving stations afloat and ashore. Examining his workmen's installation at Osborne House, he crossed a garden reserved to Her Majesty.

This was reported to the Queen. "Get another electrician," commanded she.

"Alas, Your Majesty," she was told, "England has no Marconi."

Conscious of the rebuke, the inventor sat stonily in his hotel until the Queen dispatched a carriage for him and granted him an audience. Later King George V knighted him.

Marconi did not recognize defeat. In preparation for an attempt to span the Atlantic with a wireless signal, he erected tall masts at Poldhu, Cornwall, and on Cape Cod. Storms wrecked both installations. Marconi simply rebuilt the one in Cornwall, redesigned for more strength, and decided the one in New England should be relocated in Newfoundland to shorten the distance he must bridge.

His faith in himself was never clearer than in the days preceding and following his receipt of a signal, the Morse code letter *S,* from Poldhu on a gale-tossed kite aerial—used to save installation work—at St. John's, Newfoundland, on December 12, 1901. Prior to that, the greatest distance he had bridged was 225 miles. Those few miles had proved that the curvature of the earth was no bar to wireless telegraphy, but 1,800 transatlantic miles was something else again. Through hours of listening with no result, Marconi never lost hope. Then it came, the signal of three dots. Marconi knew nothing about reflections from the sky. It was not until a year later that two physicists, Oliver Heaviside and Arthur Kennelly, established that the transmission of electromagnetic signals was possible despite the curvature of the earth because an ionized layer of atmospheric particles many miles high reflected them.

Immediately, voices were heard questioning Marconi's statement that he had succeeded. Only three men had been present in the storm-buffeted shack when the signal arrived, Marconi and two companions. One of the two helpers was too deaf to hear it. Was this sufficient confirmation? "Proof is, of course, still absent . . ." said the eminent British scientist Sir Oliver Lodge. London's *Daily Telegraph* added, "Despite the detailed, signed statement by Signor Marconi . . . there was an indisposition . . . to accept as conclusive his evidence that the problems of wireless telegraphy across the Atlantic had been solved by the young inventor." (Marconi was twenty-six.) As related by Degna Marconi in a witty, detailed portrait of her father, even Sir William Preece, engineer-in-charge of the British Post Office, who had been an ardent partisan of Marconi's for five years, was not convinced.

Three months after the event *Popular Science Monthly*, while accepting the fact of transatlantic wireless communication, cautiously commented that "there seem to be decided limitations to the utilization of wireless telegraphy . . . A map of the world showing all cable connections is a very complicated affair, and the supplanting of these cables by wireless apparatus is out of the question, at least until the Marconi system is evolved into something very different . . ."

When, shortly after the event at St. John's, the American Institute of Electrical Engineers decided to honor Marconi with a banquet, many reputable members did not want to risk attending. What if this young upstart had been wrong? If Marconi noticed, he gave no sign. In the end the holdouts were shamed into appearing.

Marconi was innately snobbish, and this is why: He was well born, the son of a wealthy landowner in Bologna. His mother came from a rich family and had been brought up in a castle, the real thing. Sheltered throughout his youth, he was nonetheless no dilettante. He was physically courageous, never asking his workmen, climbing monkey-like over his huge aerial apparatus, to do what he would not do himself. After an automobile accident that so injured his right eye it had to be removed, he insisted on walking to the operating room unaided. Nothing stimulated him more than a storm at sea pummeling the yacht he acquired after the World War; he stayed on the bridge until it subsided. Seasickness he called "a thing of the mind."

In dress he was, in the language of the day, a dandy. Always impeccably attired in white flannel trousers, navy jacket, and captain's cap while afloat, with a monocle dangling from a black silk ribbon around his neck, he ruled his domain with a soft but imperious voice. He was punctilious about time. He had several watches disposed around his vessel, and never tired of telling his guests what time it was in New York, Melbourne, or Montevideo. If lunch was fixed for 1 P.M., woe betide the latecomer, and letters to him were returned if they did not bear the date and address at the top.

His ability to concentrate was enormous, and it made him absent-minded. Once he forgot one of his small daughters, left behind on a beach, and the child almost drowned trying to swim back to the yacht. When he had a problem on his mind he would sit for long hours at the piano, playing the same theme, sometimes the same phrase, until suddenly he rushed to his laboratory as though struck by lightning. "There is no such thing as genius," he was wont to say, "only hard work."

He was a creature of habit. Promptly at 8 A.M. each day he sat down to a breakfast of tea, two soft-boiled eggs, bread, butter, and marmalade. He chose that menu because he could get it regardless of where in the world he might be. He smoked cigarettes, especially when under pressure, and now and then drank wine in small quantities. His first wife, who took over the duties of his solicitous, indulgent mother Annie, caught him early in her marriage tossing soiled socks out a steamship porthole because it was simpler to buy new ones than to have them laundered. He was openhanded with money and a soft touch for anyone with a hard-luck story. He enjoyed hobnobbing with royalty and with glamorous figures of the theater and movies, including the world-famous tenor Enrico Caruso, Constance Bennett, Douglas Fairbanks, and Mary Pickford. He was on friendly terms with Cardinal Pacelli, later Pope Pius XII. At the apogee of his career he was considered for the post of Italian ambassador to the United States.

For all his seeming impassiveness, Marconi in his private life carried on with many an attractive woman besides the two he married, his daughter Degna recalled. His uninhibited affairs shocked both his first wife, Beatrice, and his second wife, Christina, after he had had his first marriage annulled in order to wed her. It showed the wisdom of Italy's Queen Elena when she had once remarked to Beatrice, "A man like Marconi should never marry."

During the last two years of his life, amid signs all was not going well with his second marriage, he battled successive illnesses. He died in 1937.

What really, in the end, had Guglielmo Marconi contributed to man's knowledge of wireless communication? In a review of the state of the art in 1927, *Popular Science Monthly* pointed out that in

1867, seven years before Marconi was born, Professor James Clerk Maxwell, a British physicist, enunciated a theory of transmitting electromagnetic waves that was based on experiments of Michael Faraday as early as 1832. In the 1880s Heinrich Hertz, in Germany, generated waves that could be measured, from an electric spark gap. In 1891 Nikola Tesla invented a tuning device to separate different wavelengths from each other.

"My chief trouble," Marconi said later in life, describing how he stumbled on to the subject of "Hertzian waves" at the age of twenty, "was that the idea [of wireless] was so elementary, so simple in logic, that it seemed difficult to believe no one else had thought of putting it into practice . . . The idea was so real to me that I did not realize that to others the theory might appear quite fantastic." Historian Orrin E. Dunlap wrote, "Marconi's simplicity of thought enabled him to accomplish what skilled mathematicians and theorists had failed to do because they became entangled in deep technical approaches."

Decades after Marconi had devised a radio direction finder as a by-product of his successful search for a directional wireless aerial, Sir John Ambrose Fleming, a close associate in the early days who built the special transmitter for the Poldhu–St. John's transatlantic test, said: "Marconi was able to locate very closely the direction of a ship sixteen miles away . . . This discovery illustrates very well Marconi's power of intuitive invention. He did not arrive at any of his results by mathematical prediction. In fact, I think his mathematical knowledge was not very great." To the end, Marconi never claimed to be a scientist.

The hidden ingredient in Marconi's nature, that only history exposed, was a will of prodigious proportion.

Four years before he spanned the Atlantic, Marconi, already referred to by the popular press as "the boy wizard," was quoted by the New York *World* as saying, "I am uncertain as to the final results of my system. My discovery was not the result of long hours and logical thought, but of experiments with machines invented by other men to which I applied certain improvements."

The modesty may have rung true, but the import of the statement was a masterpiece of omission. By then he had blocked out his future. Two years earlier his father, Giuseppe, by now a convert to Guglielmo's cause, had asked the Italian Government to help his son financially. The government refused. When Marconi's mother, Annie, promptly arranged for help in London, he spent the first four months there scrupulously protecting his patent position. He was secretive about his experiments. His public pronouncements usually were as vague as the one quoted by the New York newspaper. Only when he filed for patents did he disclose what he had been working on. In

1900 he applied for what proved to be his key patent, a "tuned or syntonic and multiplex telegraphy on a single aerial."

His goal was to take over the rich business of the cable companies. Almost 200,000 miles of submarine cables, carrying dot-and-dash code signals, had been laid on the beds of the world's seas. Morse had invented telegraphy in 1837, and two decades later the first transatlantic cable (which promptly parted) had been paid out over the stern of a steamship. Vast fortunes were invested in the cables. British capitalists alone held 100 million dollars in cable stocks. Each Atlantic cable cost three million. That would pay for a dozen or more wireless circuits—if, indeed, wireless could be made to work—and, more important, slash the cost of sending intercontinental messages.

Marconi founded a wireless telegraph company, sold stock, demanded and got control, and proceeded to improve on the gold lode that he had recognized—an acceptable receiving apparatus for electromagnetic waves, wireless's missing link. With his patent, he tried to blanket a tuning device patented by Sir Oliver Lodge in 1897, was balked by a court decision, and later bought out the Lodge system for a large sum. When Fleming invented a diode "valve" for wireless in 1904, Marconi claimed ownership of it under the terms of a contract. He bought out an Edison patent proposing telegraphy without wires. He sued anyone for patent infringement at the drop of a hat. He even had De Forest in court for setting up a wireless telegraph company using Marconi ideas, and won. In 1914 he won his most important patent-infringement suit, against the National Electric Signaling Company of Pittsburgh. This put him in control of all wireless transmission in and from the United States. His profits snowballed.

From 1904 on it was, for the most part, a downhill pull for Marconi. Fame and fortune came unbidden. He would have been the dream client of any latter-day press agent. In 1898 he wirelessed the progress of yacht races off the Irish coast for London newspapers. That put the daily press in his pocket. In 1899 he wirelessed the minute-by-minute progress of the yacht race, off New York, between the *Shamrock* and *Columbia* for the America's Cup. Was it shrewdness or coincidence that he was under contract for this to James Gordon Bennett, publisher of the New York *Herald?* Nor was it mere chance that *McClure's Magazine,* one of the most widely circulated of American periodicals, ran a wholly uncritical series of articles on Marconi —leading a professor at Clark University, in Worcester, Massachusetts, to write Samuel McClure, the publisher, in 1898, urging that he forswear publishing things on such absurdities as wireless. Marconi actively cultivated friendships with writers and reporters, and especially with their bosses. (The U. S. Navy was a little more impressed

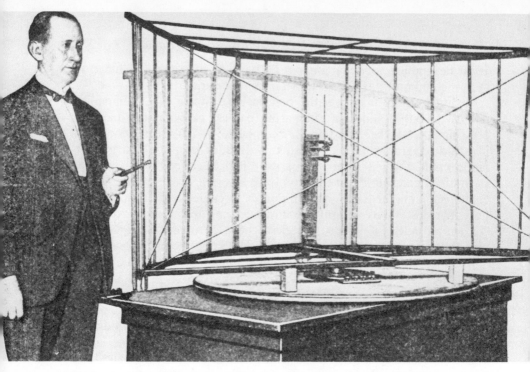

Times change, and so do names that men apply to their inventions. In the photo above, inventor Marconi, to quote from the March 1924 issue of *Popular Science*, is showing off a "radio searchlight," a directional antenna.

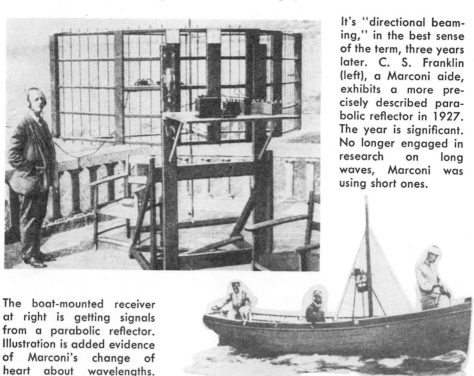

It's "directional beaming," in the best sense of the term, three years later. C. S. Franklin (left), a Marconi aide, exhibits a more precisely described parabolic reflector in 1927. The year is significant. No longer engaged in research on long waves, Marconi was using short ones.

The boat-mounted receiver at right is getting signals from a parabolic reflector. Illustration is added evidence of Marconi's change of heart about wavelengths. Here Franklin tests receiver for picking up short-wave signals in the late 1920s.

In 1919 Marconi's widespread business interests had led him into merchandising wireless components. As this advertisement in *Popular Science* states, the Marconi Wireless Telegraph Co. of America was the sole distributor for De Forest vacuum tubes.

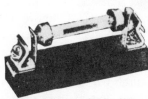

A parabolic reflector at Hendon, England (left), was used in the inventor's experiments with directed short waves. After World War I Marconi bought a yacht that had belonged to Austria's Archduke Stefan and converted it into an elaborate lab.

than the professor. In 1901 John D. Long, its civilian secretary, reported after Marconi had conducted a series of tests for it with indifferent results, "The Chief of Equipment appointed a board to consider the advisability of discontinuing the homing-pigeon service and substitute for it some system of wireless.")

But it was current events themselves that burnished the bright image of the Father of Wireless. No sooner had Marconi announced in 1901, two days after the event, that he had spanned the Atlantic than the Anglo-American Telegraph Company served notice that he was infringing on its exclusive rights—its submarine cables to Europe emerged from the ocean right at the scene of his triumph, St. John's, Newfoundland. Nobody in his right mind attacks a hero. A storm of public resentment ensued. A New York *Times* editorial sharply criticized the cable company. The great Alexander Graham Bell of telephone fame offered the use of his estate at Cape Breton for a station. Thomas Edison came to Marconi's defense.

In 1899 the ocean liner *St. Paul* published *The Transatlantic Times,* containing Marconi news messages. On an Atlantic crossing in 1903 Marconi himself inaugurated the *Cunard Daily Bulletin,* containing news. For days this landed him on page one of European and American newspapers.

By early 1902 more than seventy ships were equipped with wireless, forty-nine of them naval vessels, the rest oceangoing freight and passenger liners. Twenty wireless stations were operating in Great Britain alone. Stations were "Marconi wireless stations" and operators "Marconi operators." Only four years had elapsed since Marconi emerged from obscurity to become a world figure. In Italy he was a national hero.

Then within a half-dozen years began a series of rescues at sea, effected through wirelessed messages for help—the stuff of raw drama —and Marconi was assured of immortality. In 1909 the luxury liner *Republic,* Mediterranean-bound, was mortally damaged in a collision with the S.S. *Florida* off Nantucket Lightship. Vessels responding to the *Republic's* call saved 1,650 persons. Only four seamen and two passengers were lost. John R. Binns, the Marconi operator aboard the *Republic,* was presented with a watch for his bravery by no less than Guglielmo Marconi himself on behalf of the board of directors of Marconi's Wireless Telegraph Company. For a time in the 1920s Binns wrote for *Popular Science,* billed as "America's first wireless hero and most famous writer on radio."

In the next few months four more potential sea disasters were averted by the wirelessed call "CQD"—Come Quick Danger. In 1913 fire swept the *Volturno,* en route from New York to Rotterdam. Of the 657 aboard, passengers and crew, 421 were saved.

But the greatest tribute to the validity of Marconi's constant preachments on safety via wireless, and the biggest and most senseless loss of life, occurred in April 1912. A new, swift, and "unsinkable" greyhound of the sea, the *Titanic,* was on her maiden voyage from Southampton to New York. Marconi and his wife, Beatrice, had been invited by the White Star Line to be its guests on this trip. The *Titanic* carried Marconi wireless. But the press of business forced Marconi to leave on the *Lusitania,* which sailed three days earlier (and in 1915 was sunk by German submarines with a loss of 1,198 lives). Beatrice was to follow him on the *Titanic.* Marconi had booked passage for both of them on the *Titanic's* return trip. Then their son Giulio, not yet two years old, contracted a fever. Beatrice had to wireless her husband she would be delayed. Daughter Degna and she stood on a headland on the morning of April 10 and watched the *Titanic* as the ship stood out to sea. A bit less than 1,300 miles from New Jersey's Sandy Hook the *Titanic's* vitals were ripped out by an iceberg. She carried lifeboats for only a third of her passengers and crew.

As she slid under, in less than three hours, into 2,760 fathoms of icy water, only a few miles away steamed the *California,* her wireless silent because the operator had shut down for the night. By the time rescue vessels arrived in response to the CQD signal (replaced soon after by today's SOS), 1,517 persons had perished. They saved only 721. After that disaster, Marconi—who was one of the first aboard the *Carpathia,* the principal rescue ship, to interview the wireless men when she docked in New York—experimented with and campaigned for a bell alarm system for ships with only one wireless operator aboard, and for wireless sending and receiving apparatus for lifeboats.

So great was Marconi's fame that his wife Beatrice, anxious to contact him on a trip, broadcast a message addressed only to "Marconi Atlantic," and it was passed around from ship to ship on the sea-lanes until the inventor was located.

Once, though, he sought anonymity. In New York when the First World War erupted, and apprehensive that as a citizen of a nation aligned with those against the Central Powers he might be taken prisoner, he sailed for Southampton incognito, prepared at any moment to hide at the keel level if the ship were stopped by a German submarine.

An anxiety to succeed, clouding his judgment, plus a lack of expertise in business, gave Marconi some bad times. One of his early associates commented that he had little administrative and organizing ability. He did not inspire friendships among his staff. Out of 700 persons on his payroll, probably not more than a half-dozen knew him well enough to speak to him. Prematurely, after he spanned the Atlantic in 1901, he announced: "If my system of wireless telegraphy can be commercially established between different parts of the earth, in regard to which I may state I have not the slightest doubt, it would bring about an enormous cheapening in the methods of communication at present existing." He thought wireless transmission could be reduced to a cost of a cent a word, as compared with cable's twenty-five cents. So pervasive was his influence that the quotations on cable stocks tumbled. But now he began running into technical problems.

In 1904 he remarked as his business affairs grew more and more troublesome, "A man cannot live on glory alone." To keep his business going and meet his payrolls, he invested the last of his own funds in his company. Until it became imperative, he did not tell Beatrice of his precarious financial position. It was not until six years after receipt of the S message from Poldhu at St. John's that he was able to announce the inauguration of unlimited transatlantic wireless service. In celebration, the flags of Italy, Nova Scotia, Great Britain, and Canada flew at Glace Bay, Nova Scotia, where he had built his transmitting-receiving station.

In 1912 a trumped-up "scandal" broke, involving speculation in the American Marconi company's stock. Some of it had been acquired by British cabinet members, including Lloyd George, Chancellor of the Exchequer. Marconi was negotiating a contract with the British Government for a network of wireless stations. A select committee of Parliament was appointed to investigate. Out of his depth in the rough game of politics, Marconi testified indignantly, denying any wrongdoing. Everyone named was absolved. The investigation fizzled.

He suffered other money problems. The collapse of a bank he headed after the war taxed his resources, as did the financial settlement in his divorce. The Great Depression was hard on his funds, and before he died the company that he no longer controlled denied him the services of even a secretary.

But nothing clouded his vision of the future, with its poetic overtones. To a *Popular Science* reporter in 1928 he predicted radar (achieved), the facsimile transmission of messages and pictures (achieved), the radio beacon (achieved), developments that would render navigation's solar observations and the magnetic compass obsolete (achieved), and the control of machinery at great distances by wireless (achieved). He looked for refinements in television, then in the experimental stage, "where the action in a whole race course or football field can be shown at a distance." And: "I cannot foresee as a commercial possibility television in the home, but it is a possibility for theaters." Almost three decades before that interview he had forecast international wireless telephony.

He dreamed, but not big enough. On one postwar day he whooped with laughter while scanning the headlines of a Seville, Spain, newspaper. It said he was communicating with Mars. If he had lived thirty-four years longer, he would have seen pictures of the planet taken by a spacecraft guided to its vicinity and operated by wireless.

If Marconi was no great shakes as a business man, he was even less politically perceptive. Benito Mussolini, the Fascist dictator, was quick to pander to the inventor—he was a national asset. Marconi became a member of his party, and headed the Italian Royal Academy and the National Council of Scientific Research. By now he was a marchese and a senator in what passed for Italy's legislature. In 1927, arriving in New York, Marconi told the press, ". . . Fascism is doing a fine work in Italy. Italy, under Mussolini, has turned the corner. His bold, audacious political and financial policies have transformed the country." Marconi's new wife, Christina, broadcast praise for the state of Italian women under Fascism. Neither she nor her husband mentioned that the new life-style given Italians was at the expense of human dignity and personal freedom. In 1930 Marconi became a member of the Fascist Grand Council. In 1935 he defended Mussolini's unprovoked attack on Ethiopia in defiance of the League of Nations. It was an irony when, after the Second World War, Marconi's birthplace of Bologna became a hotbed of Communism, Fascism's arch enemy.

A couple of years before his death in 1937 Marconi visited with David Sarnoff, head of the powerful Radio Corporation of America, whom he had hired as an office boy at the age of fifteen for $5.50 a week. Sarnoff remembered the *Titanic* disaster vividly—as a Marconi operator, he had manned his key for seventy-two hours straight in New York, receiving, transmitting, and relaying messages. To Marconi, radio was still a marvel. "We know it works," the inventor remarked to Sarnoff, "and how it works, but we don't know why it works."

He originally achieved wireless communication over long distances despite a fundamental error. Speaking decades later before the Institute of Radio Engineers in New York, he said, "I admit that I am responsible for the adoption of long waves for long-distance communication. Everyone followed me in building stations hundreds of times more powerful than would have been necessary had short waves been used. Now I have realized my mistakes . . ."

For the time remaining to him, he concentrated his research on short and ultrashort waves.

Near the end, ill from heart attacks and periodic bouts with malaria —contracted in the Balkans, where he had gone in a huff when Beatrice turned down his first proposal of marriage—Marconi asked, "Have I done the world good, or have I added to the mess?"

It was a sad epitaph for a man whose honors and awards from governments and societies everywhere, including the Nobel prize in physics, were numbered in the dozens.

DE FOREST, FATHER OF RADIO BROADCASTING

Lee De Forest was an incurable romantic with a gift for building self-destruct mechanisms into his undertakings. He spent his youth agonizing over what he would do with his life, and much of his maturity blundering amiably from small victories to defeats. He lacked Guglielmo Marconi's tough inner texture—indeed, ruthlessness. In compensation, he had a mind that fingered restlessly everything with his frame of vision. Marconi got into wireless because it fascinated him, yes, but determined to make money out of it; De Forest, because research and discovery brought him to the highest pinnacle of excitement. He was a born inventor. When he died he had more than 300 patents to his credit, including two of outstanding merit. One of those two brought him world renown and profit. De Forest contributed just one trail-breaking idea to the world wireless community, but that was enough to elect him to the science and invention hall of fame. I. I. Rabi, Nobel laureate, described it as ranking with the greatest of all time.

De Forest's youth told a lot about the man. Born in Council Bluffs, Iowa, where his father was a Congregational minister, he was taken at the age of six to Talladega, Alabama, where his father became the head of one of the earliest colleges for Negroes.

"It was a difficult environment for a boy," he recalled at the age of fifty-five for *Popular Science*. "I could not associate with the Negro children on terms of equality, and the children of the white families in the town were not permitted to associate with me because my father was committing the then unpardonable sin, in Southern eyes, of educating Negroes. My brother and sister and myself, and the few other children of white teachers of the college, had to build up a little social system of our own, which was too narrow and limited to be good for us. Out of such an environment a boy grows up either arrogant or diffident. He has had no opportunity to associate with his equals, and feels himself either superior or inferior to all with whom he comes in contact.

"I came through that experience shy, diffident, without knowledge of the world or of life. I had plenty of book knowledge, but none of practical affairs. My father, by the utmost frugality, managed to find enough money to send me to a preparatory school in the north, an obscure, sectarian school at Mount Hermon, Mass., where my schoolmates were farm boys, unfamiliar with the cultural standards of my parents' home but far beyond me in their ability to adjust themselves to the give-and-take of community life. The result was to drive me farther into myself, so that when I finally entered Yale I probably was the most timid, unsocial student who ever went to New Haven."

He had the benefit of a revolving scholarship available over the years to members of his family.

By now he had been in and out of love three admitted times, and probably more.

Enrolled in Yale's Sheffield Scientific School, he was graduated in 1896, took graduate work, won a doctorate, and went to work at telephone research for the Western Electric Company in Chicago, was fired for inattention to duty, and then heard of Marconi and wireless. That did it. "I knew," he said, "I had found my niche in the scheme of things." When, in 1899, Marconi set up his primitive wireless apparatus to report the America's Cup race, De Forest got to look at it. Here was a lush, almost wholly unexplored, field.

For five years, 1901 to 1906, De Forest produced prodigiously but to little effect. He took out thirty-four patents, none with any impact on the wireless communications business. He borrowed money for equipment of his own design to report the international yacht races in 1901 for the Publishers' Press Association. The equipment didn't work. In 1902 he got involved with a stock promoter who organized the American De Forest Wireless Telegraph Company. Several years later he discovered his directors were making off with the company's money by selling the assets to a dummy corporation. De Forest resigned, taking with him only his pending patents. A fortune had melted away.

In 1906 De Forest made Fleming's diode valve, or receiver, into a triode by adding a grid. To the detecting function of the diode he added amplification. Combined with other developments in the field, this also permitted "modulation"—other signals such as the human voice and musical notes could be made to ride piggyback on a carrier wave. This was what he called his "Audion" tube.

De Forest put aside his Audion for a time after he engineered it. To the end he insisted that he had not merely improved on Fleming's valve, that he had, in fact, not known of Fleming's work and had begun his own work from scratch on a detector-amplifier with the unique quality of direct–alternating current conversion. The courts did not support his claim to having arrived at a tube of Fleming's internal configuration independently. That was another De Forest failure. But the courts resoundingly affirmed his invention of the three-electrode Audion. De Forest's use of it had to be deferred because a high-vacuum pump to prevent oxidation of the metals in the electrodes did not appear until 1909.

Lee De Forest was sketched from life for *Popular Science* by B. J. Rosenmeyer in 1929, and the accompanying cut-line said: "Sole inventor of the three-element vacuum tube, by recent judgment of the highest court in the land, Dr. De Forest stands as the radio pioneer who made practical wireless communication beyond the limited field of code telegraphy and so gave the world broadcasting of speech, music and entertainment. He also was the first to record sound on a motion-picture film." He invented the Audion tube in 1906, but it took a world war to prove its value. Combat wireless was a big plus for America.

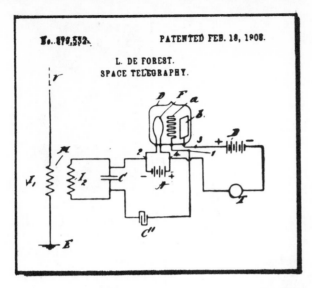

De Forest put a grid between the heated filament of Fleming's "valve" and the anode or plate to control the flow of electrons, thus obtaining a large voltage change at the plate for a small voltage at the grid—the first amplification of a signal.

At right is a typical radio vacuum tube with its three important parts—filament, grid, and plate. When assembled, the plate enclosed the other two parts. The importance of the invention lay in amplifying a wireless signal picked up by an antenna. This eliminated need for generating a high-power signal.

By 1920 the vacuum tube had assumed many configurations and uses, as the De Forest collection at the left will attest. Spanish, British, and American, they are detectors, amplifiers, and oscillators. Largest tube was a ½ kilowatt oscillator. The filament took 37 volts, the plate 1,500. The world of radio entertainment, just emerging, soon would grow to a giant.

A three-tower U. S. Navy station at Arlington, Virginia (above) in 1915 propagated voice signals on wireless that were sent first to San Francisco, 2,500 miles away, then to Paris. The latter broadcast was also heard in Honolulu, 4,900 miles away. For the times, the performance was incredible. Paris' famous Eiffel Tower (right) housed its receiving station for Arlington's radiophone broadcast.

A 1917 advertisement for De Forest's "Oscillion" (oscillating Audion) tube proclaimed its undamped oscillations of any frequency offered radio telephony of unsurpassed clarity.

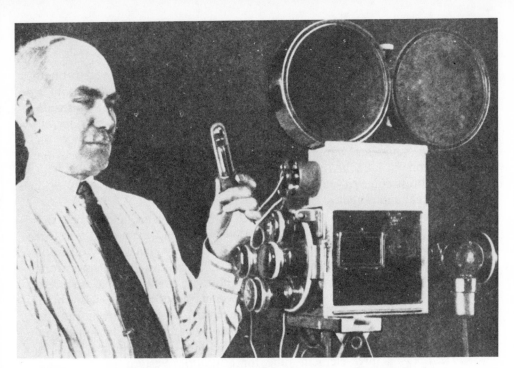

The movies could have had a voice and music years before one of Hollywood's dream factories, in a money bind and desperate for a sales gimmick, made a picture in 1927 with sound on a synchronized phonograph record starring Al Jolson. Here's De Forest in 1923 with his sound-on-film "Phonofilm" system.

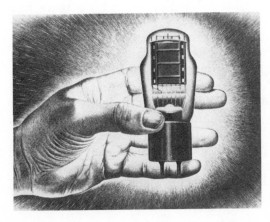

This illustration in a Bell Telephone System advertisement of 1943, in *Popular Science,* pictured the World War II descendant of De Forest's vacuum tube beneath a heading, IT OUGHT TO GET A WAR MEDAL.

After the wireless telegraph company debacle, De Forest formed the De Forest Radio Telephone Company, and was rewarded with a fairly fat U. S. Navy contract. Any American company had an inside track with potential government customers, especially the military, at that time because Washington was anxious to avoid reliance on foreign sources of supply. But this venture came a cropper when the government launched a crusade against wireless stock promoters. The De Forest concern, caught short on funds, failed. More of the inventor's real and potential funds were down the drain.

Casting about for an avenue out of his problems, De Forest the previous year turned back to his triode tube, and through it wireless began to speak. On January 13, 1910, he broadcast the voices of Enrico Caruso and a number of other Metropolitan Opera stars from New York. These were picked up both at home and at sea. He predicted that the day would come when transatlantic vessels would receive operatic masterpieces every evening, broadcast from Europe and America. The opera broadcast was just a starter. The American Telephone and Telegraph Company bought the telephone rights to De Forest's three-element tube for $50,000. Western Electric paid five times that—in those days a tidy sum of money—for the radio rights. Endlessly fiddling with amplification, De Forest saw the U. S. Navy wireless station at Arlington, Virginia, arrange 500 of his tubes in series and transmit the human voice not only to Paris but to Honolulu as well. In 1916 De Forest broadcast the results of the presidential race between Woodrow Wilson and Charles Evans Hughes. Thousands of amateur receivers within a radius of 200 miles of the De Forest radio laboratories in the Bronx, New York, were first with the news.

But it took a world war to prove the value of voice radio. The United States alone had this means of communication. In October 1918, President Wilson in plain English broadcast to Germany his suggestions for an armistice in the fighting to which his country had been contributing since the spring of 1917.

Lee De Forest's contribution, so seemingly simple, was a capstone to a long series of related events that went back to Thomas A. Edison in 1883. *Popular Science* told of it in its issue of February 1947, in an article titled, "Edison's Magnificent Fumble." Fretting over his obstinate electric lamp, Edison saw his filament burn brightly for a time, then sputter and go out. In the process the inside of the bulb blackened. Something was carrying the substance of the filament across empty space to the glass. Edison inserted a metal plate in his bulb and attached a meter to it. The needle swung, proving the filament was boiling off charged particles (later called electrons). Busy with other things, the inventor ignored the discovery. More than two decades later John Fleming awoke to the significance of what was then known as the "Edison effect." From his research came what he called a "two-element thermionic value detector." Later in life it earned him a knighthood. By heating a filament in his bulb and providing a second electrode in the form of a plate to which the electrons given off by the filament could flow, Fleming had a one-way valve converting alternating current into direct. It detected wireless waves because it suppressed half a wireless frequency wave and produced a pulsed direct current corresponding to the on-and-off Morse code signals.

De Forest interposed an open-mesh grid between the heated filament in the bulb and the plate to control the flow of electrons. That enabled him to obtain a large voltage charge at the plate for a small voltage charge at the grid electrode, and that made it possible to amplify a wireless frequency signal picked up by an aerial before its application to the detector. Much weaker incoming signals could be used.

De Forest's feat in worldwide impact was somewhat akin to that of Sir Henry Bessemer, when, simply by introducing a high-speed stream of air into steel manufacture, he completely revolutionized the process.

Meanwhile Marconi's accomplishments had been building on themselves, and on the work of others, tier on tier to explode, finally, on the consumer market. In 1901 America's Professor Reginald Fessenden applied for a patent on wireless telephony, using an "electrolytic detector." He was not the first. Among others, Tesla had experimented in this field. Fessenden's idea for a high-frequency alternator had been worked out for him by General Electric's "genius," Charles P. Steinmetz. Another American, Ernst F. S. Alexanderson, constructed a 100,000-cycle machine.

Even before World War I ended, *Popular Science* began carrying advertisments for De Forest's Audion tube, and amateur radio buffs were beginning to haunt radio shops for galena crystals, headsets, and whiskerlike "feelers" to receive broadcasts. "How much distance did you get last night?" was a standard morning greeting. Future billions in radio-receiver manufacture and broadcasting profits could be glimpsed against the skyline of transmitters.

The use to which the public and industry began putting wireless astonished both De Forest and Marconi. Neither had foreseen anything like it. For a score of years and more, they had regarded Hertzian waves simply as a means of communication, mostly of a business nature and certainly for military establishments, especially navies. Applications to commercial shipping had been a foregone conclusion.

De Forest's Audion tube and its many sophistications by successive

In 1901 a wireless signal had just managed to span the 1,800-mile-width of the Atlantic Ocean; in 1969, the voices of U.S. astronauts on the moon came across a quarter-million miles, with pictures, by radio.

And in 1973, radio signals traveled more than a half-*billion* miles, to bring the world pictures and data from an unmanned spacecraft flying past the planet Jupiter.

generations of scientists and inventors were superseded, of course, in time by solid state developments in the art. But for decades it was a staple in electronics. De Forest himself lost interest in it in the 1920s. Now it was talking movies that intrigued him. His "phonofilm" imprinted a sound track on the film itself. For several years he tried to peddle the idea to the California romance factories. Nobody paid him heed. Who wanted sound? That probably was De Forest's fault. He was the world's worst salesman.

Of his phonofilm and the projector it required, he said, "I don't expect this machine to replace the speaking stage or silent movies. But I claim it makes possible a new form of screen drama by introducing music and voice here and there to produce dramatic and artistic effects." Then, in 1927, Warner Brothers Pictures, as the last gasp of a company in deep trouble, produced a movie with sound on a phonograph record synchronized with the film. It was an instant success, and the panic in Hollywood was on. This should have been a bonanza for De Forest. But he was up against a phalanx of attorneys for a behemoth of big business, Western Electric, arguing nitty-gritty questions on processes and patents. If it had been Guglielmo Marconi who produced sound-on-film, he probably could have hacked it against any and all adversaries. De Forest couldn't. He was too kindly a man. It was his last big business failure.

Of marriage failures, he had two. A third marriage took. His honors were many. As he aged, of glory he cared not, and of money, due to a Supreme Court ruling, he had a surfeit. He lived to see the air waves saturated not only with radio but with television signals as well, carrying superb achievements in pictorial news reporting, and great theater, right into the home—along with singing commercials shilling soap, dog food, deodorants, and denture adhesives—all impinging in some measure on his own, and others', pioneering that began three quarters of a century before.

If Lee De Forest lacked the fame of his contemporary, Marconi, he was spared Marconi's debilitating nervous tensions. He outlived him by twenty-four years.

CHAPTER 10

Lest They Be Forgotten— More Fathers of Invention

LISTS of great inventions and their creators, pages long, are to be found in such standard reference books as the World Almanac and the Reader's Digest Almanac and Yearbook. When this book set out to select the leading inventors since 1872 (the year our basic source, *Popular Science Monthly,* was founded), we realized our choice would have to be more or less arbitrary. In part it depended upon availability of scientific and human-interest information, about inventors to be included, in more than 1,200 issues of the magazine. Also taken into account was our judgment of the influence of each inventor's contributions upon our way of life.

Both considerations commended to us the lives and works of Bell, Edison, Tesla, Marconi, De Forest, and the Wright brothers. Several other inventors seemed to merit prominent places—notably, Eastman and Land, for their contributions to one of America's most popular leisure activities, photography. And the lifework of Charles M. Hall, who single-mindedly pursued the production of practical and economical aluminum, was appealing for its human side as well as for the element of surprise (who ever heard of Hall?).

Originators of many relatively minor but still fascinating inventions were introduced in our chapter, "They Invented Tremendous Trifles," which covered this category from *A* to *Z*—Aerosols to Zippers.

But our book would have seemed incomplete if it still omitted the inventors of such major developments as the automobile, the self-starter, the helicopter, the outboard motor for watercraft, FM radio, the long-playing phonograph record, Kodachrome film, the laser, X-rays, the air brake, the Linotype, the diesel engine, the gyrocompass, and the atomic-power reactor.

Therefore, the present chapter turns to the accomplishments of Daimler, Diesel, Roentgen, Mergenthaler, Fermi and Szilard, Sikorsky, Kettering, Armstrong, Goldmark, Townes, Evinrude,

Godowsky and Mannes, Sperry, and Westinghouse. So if you love a parade of fascinating men, in the story of their lives and ingenious inventions, read on.

Probably no two people would agree on just whom to include, and to leave out, in a book like this. In reply to any critics of our choice, we have to take recourse to the familiar words of prize-contest announcements: "The decision of the judges shall be final."

WESTINGHOUSE

The year was 1868 and young George Westinghouse, who had invented a really effective train brake, was ready to demonstrate his invention. He had gone to one railroad after another without success. But finally one, the Panhandle Railroad, had agreed to a demonstration. Westinghouse equipped a four-car train with his new air brake system, and, one morning got ready to prove its effectiveness. In the last car rode officials of the railroad. An engineer named Tate was at the controls; he opened the throttle and brought the train up to a speed of thirty miles an hour.

A 1927 report in *Popular Science* describes what happened next. "Arrangements had been made to keep the crossings clear until the trial train had passed; so Tate turned to the mechanism for another inspection. In the instant that his eyes left the road a truckman, thinking that he could beat the engine to the crossing ahead, made a wild dash for the tracks. Tate's eyes returned to the road just as the frightened horses plunged madly and the driver was hurled in the path of the speeding train.

"Tate grasped the brake control and twisted desperately. With a mighty lurch the train stopped dead.

"Picking themselves up from the floor, the passengers in the rear car scrambled to the platforms and sprang to the ground. They found Tate assisting the terror-stricken truckman to arise—four feet from the cowcatcher.

"So bruised and ruffled were the witnesses that the significance of the event was slow in dawning. And then they comprehended. In saving a human life, the air brake had demonstrated its own efficiency!"

Westinghouse, who was born in 1846, was mechanically inclined as a boy. At fifteen he ran away to fight in the Civil War, but was sent home. A short time later, he began college, but did not find it a happy experience and dropped out after a year.

In 1866, Westinghouse was on a train that was delayed because two other trains on the same track had collided. It seemed to him that the problem was lack of an adequate braking system. In those days, brakemen were stationed between each pair of cars. On a whistle signal from the engineer, the brakemen began turning wheels which gradually applied the brakes. Young Westinghouse saw that if a braking system connected to every car had been under the engineer's direct control, he would have been able to stop the train in time.

He devised a number of systems. One had a braking system built into the coupling device. When the engineer put on the brakes in the engine, the next car would tend to ride into the engine and its brake would be applied. The next car would then compress the coupling system between itself and the car ahead and *its* brake would be applied, and so on. But that system had been tried and didn't work. His next attempt was to string a chain the entire length of the train under the cars. But that had problems as well.

Then one day Westinghouse was reading a magazine that reported on the building of the Mount Cenis tunnel in Switzerland. The problem there had been to operate drilling machines thousands of feet into the tunnel without having engines inside. The solution: transmit energy via compressed air. Westinghouse saw the answer to his problem immediately: a compressed-air pipe, running the length of the train and connected by flexible couplers between cars, could apply all brakes simultaneously. Within a few years, the Westinghouse air brake had replaced all others, and is still used to this day on trains all over the world.

Westinghouse went on to develop one of the first practical railroad signaling systems and established the Union Switch and Signal Company. He got interested in natural gas as a fuel and invented the first practical gas meter, an automatic cutoff regulator, and a leakproof piping system. And, a short time later, he established the Westinghouse Electric Company, which became the primary organization responsible for the introduction of alternating current in this country. (Details of this part of his work are contained in the chapter on Nikola Tesla, with whom he worked on this development.)

Before he died, George Westinghouse received over 400 patents and established several giant industrial companies. After his death, his colleague, Nikola Tesla, wrote these words: "An athlete in ordinary life, he was transformed into a giant when confronted with difficulties which seemed insurmountable. He enjoyed the struggle and never lost confidence. When others would give up in despair he triumphed. Had he been transferred to another planet with everything against him he would have worked out his salvation."

MERGENTHALER

"In war and in commerce, on our farms and in our workshops, in travel and in our homes, almost every mechanical process, once

At the first demonstration of George Westing-house's newly developed air brake, a wagon driver tried to beat the train to the crossing. He was thrown, and fell to the tracks. The air brake stopped the train four feet from the unconscious man, saving his life. At right: inventor's portrait.

Ottmar Mergenthaler (left), an instrument maker, built several unsuccessful typesetting machines designed by his customers. Later, he conceived the novel idea of a typecasting machine (far left). It was the first real advance in printing since the invention of handset movable type centuries earlier.

slowly and laborously effected by manual or animal labor, has been quickened generation after generation by new appliances or inventions, except the work of typesetting," said an article in the December 1891 issue of *Popular Science*. "That is as slow now as when Coster or Gutenberg did the first European typesetting early in the fifteenth century."

The man who changed that was Ottmar Mergenthaler, born in 1854, who emigrated to this country in 1872. He was an expert scientific instrument maker who built models for other inventors. By 1876, some of his customers had asked him to build typesetting machines. But despite the fact that Mergenthaler himself occasionally suggested improvements, none was successful.

In 1893, Mergenthaler opened his own business in Baltimore and began working on a machine to eliminate the hand setting of type.

Until that time, all machines had been based on the same idea: design a device to do mechanically what a printer had done manually; that is, set individual letters into lines of type. Mergenthaler had a different idea: design a machine that did not *set* type from an available supply, but *cast* type as needed.

In the machine he designed, a relatively small number of brass matrixes or molds were dropped into place as an operator hit the typewriter-like keyboard. Then, when the entire line was completed, molten metal poured onto it and an entire line of type was cast at one time. Mergenthaler's second version of the machine even had automatic justification: when a line had been typed, a series of little wedges shoved up between the words, separating them by the right amount to make the line precisely fit the width of the column.

The new Linotype machine—so named because it cast a *line of type* at a time—was a rapid success. One man with such a machine could do the work of three to four printers using the old hand-setting technique. It went into use quickly; on August 26, 1884, Mergenthaler received his first patent. On July 3, 1886, the first twelve machines made by the company for the New York *Tribune* went into operation and were used to compose a part of that day's paper. They soon found use in scores, then in hundreds of other papers across the country.

Mergenthaler himself disagreed seriously with some of the policies set up by the company established to exploit his invention, and resigned in 1888. But so deep was his interest in the new device that he continued to work on it, eventually getting more than fifty patented improvements, even though he had no further financial interest. He died in 1899 of tuberculosis, brought on, according to contemporary accounts, "by constant application and never ending anxiety."

DAIMLER

No one man invented the automobile. It grew out of the work of a generation of inventors. But a key chapter of the story was written by a German engineer named Gottlieb Daimler, who developed the first lightweight, high-speed engine and thus cleared the way for the development of the modern automobile.

Daimler was a short, sturdy, shy man committed to the ideal of hard work. On one occasion a woman asked him to teach her son how to invent. He replied that there was no secret he could impart; if the son wanted to be an inventor he should do what Daimler did: work every day from five in the morning until eight at night, taking only a half-hour off for lunch.

The man who was to play an important role in the development of the automobile was born in Schorndorf, near Stuttgart, Germany, on March 17, 1843. His father, a master baker, wanted young Gottlieb to become a municipal employee and thus be eligible for a pension. But the boy was mechanically inclined and became an apprentice gunmaker instead. He saved his money and by 1857 at the age of twenty-three was able to spend two years studying at the Polytechnic in Stuttgart.

For the next twenty-three years he was employed as engineer and technical director by several companies working on engine development. But by 1882, at the age of forty-seven, he decided to establish his own business and put to work some of the ideas that had been growing in his mind.

The self-powered vehicle was not new in Daimler's time. The first crude steam-powered cars had been built decades earlier, and a scattering of those heavy, inefficient vehicles had been seen on the roads of Europe and America. But the attention of the workers of the time was focused on the internal-combustion engine, which also had its problems.

About 1863 a French inventor named Jean Joseph Étienne Lenoir built an engine, mounted it on wheels, and traveled from Paris to Joinville-le-Pont and back, taking an hour and a half each way. That was probably the first gasoline-driven car in the world. But Lenoir apparently pursued his work no further.

Another major step had come in the 1870s when a German engineer named N. A. Otto built the first four-cycle engine and thus established the basic design used to this day. But the Otto engine had its troubles. It ran on illuminating gas and was a crude, clumsy affair. It was enormously heavy—about a thousand pounds per horsepower—and slow. It achieved a speed of no more than about 180 rpm.

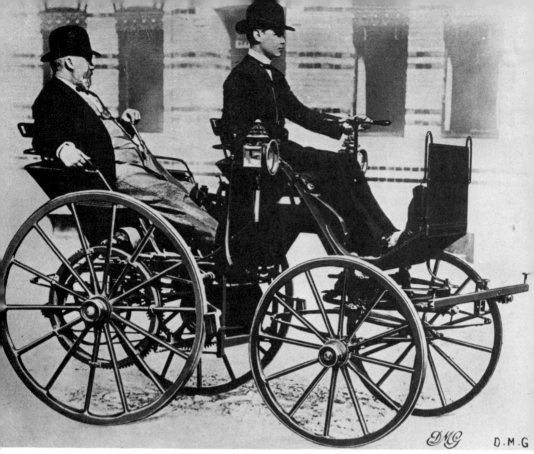

Gottlieb Daimler rides regally in the rear seat, as befits
a man credited with one of the major advances in the development of the automobile. In this 1885 model, he is
driven by his son. Daimler invented a lightweight, high-
speed engine that helped make the automobile practical.
Also making progress independently at the same time
was another inventor, Carl Benz. Ultimately, their companies became today's Mercedes-Benz Company.

Wilhelm Roentgen (right) made the startling discovery
of X-rays and the astonishing pictures he obtained as
a result. At lower right is the X-ray of a hand that was
sensational when it was reproduced in newspapers
throughout the world. Many people refused to have
X-rays made, because of the widespread belief that
seeing one's own skeleton was a premonition of death.
At lower left is an 1897 model X-ray machine.

Daimler's principal contribution was the invention of the "hot tube" system. Up to that time, the explosive mixture in the cylinder was usually ignited by a flame burning in the end of a pipe threaded to the cylinder. In 1883 it occurred to Daimler that he did not have to introduce flame into the cylinder but instead could keep the flame burning under the end of a porcelain tube that protruded into the cylinder. The tube was red-hot and ignited the charge. By regulating the temperature of the tube, Daimler found, he could explode the charge at any point in the compression stroke. Throttle valves had not yet been invented, so Daimler worked out an ingenious method of regulating the speed of his engine by regulating the exhaust valves.

This combination of improvements was enormously successful. They dropped engine weight from a thousand pounds per horsepower to ninety, and increased engine speed from 180 to 800 rpm. Daimler mounted the new engine on a two-wheeled vehicle and, on November 10, 1885, as one biographer put it, "threw the lever which tightened the belt connecting engine to wheel, and was off on a journey which was to lead him to renown and riches."

At the same time that Daimler was developing his engine, another engineer, named Karl Benz, had been working along a similar line. He had developed yet another way to set off the charge in the cylinder. He led two insulated electric wires through the cylinder wall, leaving a tiny gap between them. Then, with a battery, coil, and switch, he made a spark jump between them at the proper moment, igniting the charge. This, of course, was the ancestor of the spark plug. Benz also introduced two other major improvements that have lasted to this day: he cooled the cylinders with a jacket of water, and he smoothed out the pulses of energy from the cylinder with a flywheel. Benz's engine achieved a speed of only about 300 rpm, but it was also a great advance over the Otto engine, and in 1885, earlier in the year than Daimler's demonstration of his first vehicle (a motorcycle), Benz was rolling along the streets of Mannheim in his three-wheel auto.

As work on automobiles proceeded, racing became a primary concern of most inventors. Competition quickly showed which cars were better than which, and thus pointed engineers in the right direction. Daimler's first big success in the field came on July 1, 1894, when the first international motor race was held on the Paris–Rouen road. Of 102 starters, only fifteen finished. Daimler, achieving the unheard speed of almost sixteen miles an hour, took the 80,000-franc purse.

Four years earlier, on November 28, 1890, Daimler had formed the Daimler Motor Company, and the racing triumph gave the young firm a tremendous boost. By 1900, Daimler had designed and built a new car whose external appearance was less like the motorized carriages that had preceded it and more like the modern car that followed. He named this vehicle the Mercedes.

The first Mercedes appeared on the market in 1901, and was a striking success. But Daimler did not live to see it. He died on March 6, 1900, at the age of sixty-six.

Daimler and Karl Benz apparently never met and probably did not even know about each other's work at the time their developments were proceeding along parallel lines. And, as Daimler's company prospered in the years following the turn of the century, so did the one established by Benz, and they became fierce competitors. In 1926, the two companies merged and became Daimler-Benz, ancestor of the present-day Mercedes-Benz Company.

ROENTGEN

Roentgen was the archetypal nineteenth-century German professor: tall, bearded, aristocratic, reserved, with a haughtiness befitting one of his high rank. He was also hard-working, determined, careful, methodical. Undoubtedly many investigators had seen the effects that led Roentgen to his epochal discovery. But it was his prepared mind that recognized it for what it was.

Roentgen was born in the German Rhineland on March 27, 1845, and was originally expected to follow in his father's footsteps and become a cloth merchant. But he turned instead to science, attending Utrecht Technical School, the University of Utrecht, and the Zurich Polytechnical School.

Until he was fifty, Roentgen led the life of a professor, teaching and performing esoteric physics experiments. Physicists at that time were fascinated by the effect of electron beams on various substances. Many years earlier, a glassblower named Heinrich Geissler had found that if he pumped air out of a glass tube, filled it with certain gasses, and then applied a high voltage to two wires protruding through the tube, the gas would glow—as it does in a modern neon tube. An Englishman named William Crookes put metal plates in the ends of the tube to increase the effect, and a German physicist, Philipp Lenard, cut a window in the glass, covered it with aluminum foil, and showed that the electrons, though trapped by the glass, would penetrate the foil. When crystals of certain fluorescent chemicals were brought near the aluminum window, they glowed in beautiful colors, excited by the electron beam.

On November 8, 1895, Roentgen was experimenting with a Crookes tube in his darkened laboratory at the University of Würzburg when he noticed a strange thing. As he turned the tube on, a soft glow on the bench a yard away caught his eye. He turned off the power to the tube and the glow faded away. Power on, and it came back.

Roentgen turned on the light and found that the glow was coming from a small fluorescent screen coated with barium platinocyanide that he had been using in another experiment and had set aside the day before. Yet it was much too far from the tube for the weak electron beam to reach; the electrons penetrated only a fraction of an inch of air. Roentgen moved the screen still farther down the bench, but the glow when the tube was on persisted.

The physicist suspected that he had found something important, but he was typically cautious. "I have discovered something interesting, but I do not know whether my observations are correct," he told a colleague. Then he disappeared into his laboratory to find out what it was.

Over the next seven weeks Roentgen rarely emerged and must have stopped his work only briefly to sleep and eat. A few days after Christmas, he turned over a carefully prepared paper entitled "On a New Kind of Rays" to the secretary of the Würzburg Physical Medicine Society for publication, and sent copies and selected X-ray pictures to physicians he knew in several European cities.

What Roentgen discovered in those seven weeks of seclusion was the existence of a hitherto unsuspected form of energy, which he called X-rays. He did not know it at the time, but it was a form of electromagnetic radiation, similar to radio or light, but at a shorter wavelength. And this wavelength gave it the apparently magical ability to penetrate all kinds of light opaque substances as though they were not there.

During his weeks of seclusion, Roentgen investigated the extent of this penetrating power. "We soon discovered that all bodies are transparent to this agent, though in very different degrees," he wrote. "I proceed to give a few examples: Paper is very transparent; behind a bound book of about one thousand pages I saw the fluorescent screen light up brightly, the printer's ink offering scarcely a noticeable hindrance." He went on to describe how the rays easily penetrated tinfoil, pine boards, aluminum, and many other substances, with only lead and gold being so opaque that a relatively thin sheet of either stopped the rays entirely.

Roentgen also discovered that flesh was reasonably transparent to X-rays; bone, less so. And he discovered that X-rays darkened photographic emulsions. Thus during his experiments he had produced an X-ray picture of his hand. And it was this picture, which was shortly thereafter picked up and reproduced by newspapers all over the world, that caused a sensation. "Popular interest was focused upon the fact that X-rays would reveal a bony skeleton within its case of fleshy tissue," wrote Dr. D. W. Hering, a professor of physics at

New York University in *Popular Science* in 1897, "and the famous picture of a hand in which the bones thus stood revealed was soon to be found in every city of Europe and America. The realism of this weird picture simply fascinated all who beheld it."

Physics laboratories everywhere were equipped with Crookes tubes and high-voltage sources. So "the incredulity which greeted the first reports of Prof. Röentgen's famous discovery," continued Professor Hering, "gave place upon their confirmation to a delirium of enthusiasm, experimentation, and expectation." Within a few weeks, doctors around the world were taking their patients to physics labs to have a look inside. In fact, on January 17, 1896, a Dr. Exner, a friend of Roentgen's, used X-rays to examine a crookedly healed finger that had been injured by a bullet. Thus the discovery was put to work in practical medicine less than twenty days after it was announced—perhaps a record in the application of a new scientific discovery to human problems.

The public at large was at once astonished, intrigued, and alarmed. Many refused to be X-rayed, because they considered seeing one's own skeleton a premonition of death. Others objected on various grounds. A London journal, apparently missing the point, commented: "We cannot agree with the newspapers in regarding this discovery as a revolution in photography; there are very few persons who would care to sit for a portrait which would show only the bones and the rings on the fingers." Others had different worries. "The process has its threatening aspect," commented one writer. "If one can photograph through wood and black walls, and in the dark, too, then privacy is impossible." Assemblyman Reed of New Jersey introduced a bill prohibiting the use of X-rays in opera glasses in theaters. And a London firm advertised X-ray-proof underclothing.

When the Nobel prizes were established in 1901, Roentgen received the first award in physics. He was heaped with medals, awards, honorary degrees. But his privacy, though not destroyed by X-rays, was gone. He was a celebrity, and no longer able to remain an aloof, remote German professor who spoke only to his peers. He became bitter and frequently lapsed into melancholia. He went to Stockholm to receive the Nobel prize, but refused to make a speech or take any part in the ceremonies.

In 1923, at the age of seventy-eight, he died of intestinal cancer, perhaps induced by his years of experiments with X-rays, since the danger of prolonged exposure to them was unknown in early days. His will was followed precisely. His body was cremated, and all of his scientific and personal letters, papers, and correspondence were burned.

DIESEL

Ask any technically knowledgeable individual for an explanation of what makes a diesel engine different. He'll tell you it's lack of an ignition system. The piston compresses the gases in the cylinder to a very high pressure, the compressed gases get hot, and the heat thus generated sets off the charge of oil sprayed into the cylinder at the proper moment.

Yet Rudolf Diesel, the French-born German engineer who invented the engine that transformed his name into a lower-case household word, saw compression ignition as an incidental feature of his engine. Its principal distinguishing characteristic, he said, was a phenomenon scientists call isothermal combustion.

The distinction is important not only in understanding the principle of the diesel engine, but also because it tells something about the man. Rudolf Diesel, unlike Edison, Bell, and many other late nineteenth-century experimenters, was one of the first of a new breed of technologist: the scientific inventor. His contribution was not the result of experimentation. It grew instead from a painstaking analysis of the fundamental laws of nature. Diesel was an expert in thermodynamics, the science of heat flow, and knew how to calculate how much of the potential energy locked in fuel could be converted into mechanical energy. The diesel engine was born in an attempt to build the world's most efficient machine by designing it to conform to the basic laws of thermodynamics.

Diesel's training was ideal for this task. He was an honor student at the Munich Technical Institute, graduating in 1880 at the head of his class. Shortly thereafter, he went to work in Paris for a refrigeration company founded by his thermodynamics professor, the celebrated Carl Linde. Refrigeration in those days was an exciting field on the forefront of technological innovation. And it involved thermodynamics, the subject in which the young Diesel was absorbed.

As they do today, engineering students during Diesel's school days studied a slim volume called *Reflections on the Motive Power of Heat and on Machines Fitted to Develop That Power* written by the French physicist Nicolas Carnot in 1824. In those days, heat was not generally understood to be a form of energy as it is now conceived. Carnot had so defined it, and showed that heat in an engine causes the basic working gas in its cylinders—usually air or steam—to expand and push against a piston. In the process, the heat disappears, having been converted into mechanical work. Further, his mathematical analysis proved that the efficiency of an engine was not, as commonly thought, dependent on the working fluid used, but was determined by the

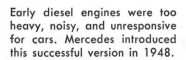

DIESELS THAT GO TO SEA

The size of Diesel engines that power ocean liners can be gauged by the dwarfed figure of the man in foreground

The world's first "Carnot engine" was what Rudolf Diesel (left) set out to make. It would conform to the ideal thermodynamic cycle that had been described by the French physicist Carnot years before. Diesel never accomplished that goal. But his engine is still noted for its efficiency and now powers everything from ocean liners (above) to cars.

Early diesel engines were too heavy, noisy, and unresponsive for cars. Mercedes introduced this successful version in 1948.

range of temperatures through which the working fluid passed. The theoretical maximum efficiency of an engine, he said, could be calculated by subtracting the lowest temperature reached by the working fluid from the highest, then dividing that figure by the highest (all temperatures on an absolute scale such as degrees Kelvin). He also developed a series of curves relating pressure and volume in an engine, describing the operation of a theoretically perfect heat engine. These curves were called the Carnot cycle.

In 1876, Nikolaus Otto had invented the machine that still bears his name, the four-cycle Otto engine. This is the internal-combustion engine that to this day drives most automobiles. By the 1880s, fueled by illuminating gas, it was applied to many jobs. But the Otto engine, Diesel realized, had a very low Carnot efficiency. Even the steam engines then widely in use averaged no more than 7 per cent efficiency —they turned only 7 per cent of the energy in the fuel into useful work.

The reason for such low efficiency was that the pressure–volume curves showing what went on inside these two engines were far from the Carnot ideal. Diesel's dream was to build what he called a Carnot engine, designed to reproduce the theoretical Carnot curves as closely as possible in an actual machine.

His early plans called for an engine that would compress the working fluid—air—to a pressure of 250 atmospheres—almost 4,000 pounds per square inch. This would produce a temperature of 800° C. Then, if the gas were allowed to expand to a pressure of one atmosphere and twenty degrees, he calculated, his engine would have an astonishing efficiency of 73 per cent and use one sixth to one tenth the fuel of any other engine.

The key to this startling efficiency, and the principal claim that Diesel made in his 1892 patent application, was isothermal combustion. In the Otto engine, for example, temperature and pressure rise suddenly when the inflammable mixture in the cylinder burns explosively. This is a violent departure from the smooth Carnot pressure–volume curves. Diesel planned an entirely different sequence. In his engine, the air in the cylinder would reach its maximum temperature as the piston compressed the working fluid to its minimum volume. Then, the fuel would be injected and, because of the high temperature of the air, would burn spontaneously. But as it burned, the expanding air would press against the piston, doing work. As a gas expands, it cools. The rate of fuel injection—and thus the rate of burning and expansion—would be precisely regulated so that the heating effect of combustion and the cooling effect of expansion would be exactly balanced. Thus work would be done without raising the temperature of the working fluid. No excess heat would have to be removed—and wasted—as in an Otto or steam engine. All heat would be converted into mechanical energy. The only losses—aside from friction—would grow out of the fact that some of the energy generated (and stored in a spinning flywheel) would have to be used to recompress the working fluid for the next cycle.

Diesel was not a modest man. In 1892 he patented his basic idea; in 1893 he published a highly promotional volume with the sweeping title *Theory and Construction of a Rational Heat Engine to Take the Place of the Steam Engine and of All Presently Known Combustion Engines*. Despite its highly detailed drawings and flawless mathematical analyses, his work to this time was totally theoretical; he had made no attempt to build an actual engine. The purpose of the book was to raise money to do it.

It was a success. Two major German firms, Krupp in Essen and the Maschinenfabrik in Augsburg, agreed to put up money. Diesel expected to turn his theory into hardware overnight. But it did not happen. In fact, he was never able to build an engine that translated his elegant theory into machinery very accurately. There were many difficulties. The extreme compression ratios he sought were far beyond the technology of the day. And there were even more fundamental barriers: experimental work proved to Diesel that true isothermal expansion in an internal-combustion engine is impossible; it calls for more air than is necessary for combustion. And the work of handling and compressing that extra air takes more energy than can be supplied by the fuel needed to keep the combustion isothermal. Thus he was forced to leave the ideal Carnot cycle further and further behind. In fact, before 1900, Diesel himself gave up any serious attempt to achieve the Carnot cycle in his working hardware. Yet, committed to it by his patent and his fierce pride, he continued to refer to his engines as Carnot cycle machines—at least on ceremonial occasions.

Still, despite this retreat from theory, the engines he built were far more efficient than any others then in existence. Today's diesels—whose operation is fairly remote from the Carnot cycle—achieve a respectable 40 per cent efficiency or so, as good as the biggest, highest-temperature steam turbines and twice as efficient as the gasoline engine.

By the turn of the century, development of the diesel was well underway—though not at the pace Diesel had predicted—and Diesel himself had profited significantly. The two German companies with whom he had signed licensing agreements were paying him royalties of 50,000 marks a year. The American beer magnate from St. Louis, Adolphus Busch, gave him a million gold marks for exclusive manufacturing rights in America, and several other deals produced lesser amounts.

The till then modestly fixed Diesel understandably considered himself wealthy. He moved into an elaborate apartment in Munich, set up luxurious offices next door, and began construction of what he considered a suitable mansion.

Diesel never doubted that his engine would fulfill his original sweeping predictions and replace all other power sources quickly. But engineering development of any genuinely new device almost always takes ten to thirty years, and the diesel engine was no exception. The inventor, convinced that his income would expand endlessly, invested large amounts of money in oil wells and speculative real estate ventures. But he was a better engineer than a businessman. His investments declined in value, his income did not soar as he expected, and he soon found himself unable to meet his expenses.

On September 29, 1913, in the company of two friends, he boarded the ship *Dresden,* a steamer bound from Antwerp to Harwich, England. That night, the fifty-five-year-old inventor had dinner with his traveling companions and at ten o'clock, after a stroll on deck, bade them a cheerful good night and went to his stateroom. He was never seen again, and the next morning it was discovered that his bed had never been slept in.

No one will ever know for sure what happened to Rudolf Diesel. For a time, baseless rumors circulated that he had been murdered by the Germans in those pre-World-War-I days to keep him from giving technical secrets to the English. Finally, in 1940, his son, Eugen, wrote a biography of the inventor in which two facts were disclosed. First, after his death it was found that Diesel was some $375,000 in debt, his property was heavily mortgaged, and he would soon have been forced into bankruptcy—no doubt an intolerable prospect for the proud engineer. And, second, shortly before his death he had talked of various methods of suicide with his younger son, Rudolf, Jr. It was not a grim discussion, Rudolf remembered later, and he had thought nothing of it at the time. But, he recalled, his father had concluded that the best way of taking one's own life would be jumping off a fast ship.

EVINRUDE

The tale may even be true. Ole Evinrude and Bessie Emily Cary were on a picnic on a hot August day in 1904 or 1905. The picnic was held on an island in Lake Michigan two and a half miles from shore. Bessie sighed that she would give anything for a dish of ice cream. Ole, gallant despite the temperature, hopped into a rowboat, rowed the two and a half miles to shore, got the ice cream, and rowed back.

The ice cream was melted, but the trip was not wasted. Ole

The idea for the world's first outboard engine (above) was born in 1904 when Ole Evinrude's girl friend wanted a dish of ice cream, and Ole (right) rowed two and a half miles to get it for her.

Charles Kettering (left) invented the self-starter. The 1913 80-pound version (bottom) shrank in three years to 14 pounds (top). Kettering also invented the Delco generator system and battery-powered ignition.

resolved on the spot that he would invent a better way to propel a boat than with oars.

Ole Evinrude had been born in Norway in 1877; his family came to America when he was five and settled near Cambridge, Wisconsin. He was interested in mechanics as a boy, and at the age of sixteen went to Madison to become an apprentice machinist and gradually became a master patternmaker. He also became fascinated by engines during the early years of the century and constructed several.

Ole eventually set up a firm to produce small internal-combustion engines. But he was interested only in the mechanical side of the business. The bookkeeping was handled by a neighborhood girl named Bessie Cary. In 1906 they were married. A short time later Ole began to work seriously on his idea for an outboard engine.

The result was an instant success. Shortly after Ole developed his first outboard, he lent it to a friend to try out one Sunday. The next day the friend returned with an order for ten, and the cash to pay for them. More orders came in from others who saw the new device. Mrs. Evinrude, who quickly became business manager of the new company the two of them established to make motors, wrote an ad for the Milwaukee paper. "Don't row!" it shouted. "Throw the oars away! Use an Evinrude Motor!"

The business grew steadily, with Ole attending to design and manufacture of the outboard motors and Bessie finding financing to expand the enterprise and generally running the commercial end. By 1913, though, Bessie's health was failing, so they sold the then thriving company and retired, and the two of them spent the next few years in travel.

When the company was sold, Ole had to agree not to go back in the business for at least five years. But a few years later he dreamed up a new two-cylinder engine design—the original Evinrude was a one-lunger—that could develop 50 per cent more power for the same weight. So in 1921, eight years after the sale of the original company, he and Bessie founded the Elto Outboard Motor Company, the name coming from the first letters of *E*vinrude's *L*ight *T*win *O*utboard. This business was a success, too, and in 1929 the Evinrudes merged Elto with the Lockwood Motor Company and the original Evinrude Company that they had sold sixteen years before. Ole became president of this company, which eventually became today's Evinrude Motors.

Bessie, who had retired in 1928 due to recurring health problems, died in 1933. Ole died the following year.

KETTERING

"Basically, I am a screwdriver-and-plier inventor and I think that all inventors should be at home at a workbench." And that's where Charlie Kettering spent a lot of his long life, inventing or developing an incredible list of items from the self-starter to the high-compression automobile engine. And in the process, he and the many associates he directed at General Motors' famed research laboratories transformed the automobile from the balky, cantankerous contraption it was at the turn of the century into the sleek, well-mannered, responsive machine it is today.

Charles Franklin Kettering—the famed "Boss Ket" of General Motors—was an engineer by training and a highly qualified authority in a wide range of disciplines from chemistry to electronics. Yet he was always scornful of the "experts" who, he said, always knew all the reasons why a thing couldn't be done. Kettering believed that most worthwhile advances were made by a single, determined individual. "If you want to iron a thing down to mediocrity," he said, "get a committee to pick flaws in it. Why? Because only one man in a thousand has imagination." When Charles Lindbergh made his famous solo flight across the Atlantic, Kettering's wife commented that it was wonderful that he had done it alone. "It would have been still more wonderful if he had done it with a committee," replied the sharp-tongued Kettering.

The man who was to have such a profound effect on the field of transportation was born in an Ohio farmhouse on August 29, 1876. He graduated from Ohio State University in 1904, and a few years later took a job at the National Cash Register Company. While at NCR he was responsible for the electrically operated cash register, the first simple, low-cost printing register, and one of the first accounting machines designed for banks, among other things.

Kettering was never one to be pushed around. And he loved in later years to talk about how he dealt with sticky situations. "My boss was going to Europe," he recalled in an article he wrote for the *Saturday Evening Post* in 1958, "and he wanted the job [the development of the electric cash register] finished before he took off. 'Give Kettering twice as many men so he can finish it up in half the time,' he said. When I objected to this idea he asked, 'Why can't you? If ten men can dig ten rods of ditch in a day, then surely twenty men can dig twenty rods.'

"I replied, 'Do you think that if one hen can hatch a setting of eggs in three weeks two hens can hatch a setting in a week and a half? This is more a job of hatching eggs than digging ditches.'"

In 1909 Kettering left NCR and formed the Dayton Engineering

Laboratories Company—Delco—and went into business in a hayloft. But from that hayloft came a stream of mighty developments. He invented the first electrical ignition system for automobile engines, which soon replaced the magnetos then in use. It first appeared on the 1910 Cadillac, and it so impressed Cadillac president Henry Leland that he was soon back with another assignment. Leland's friend, a man named Byron T. Carter, had offered to crank the engine of a stalled car for a lady. The engine backfired—a common occurrence—and the flying crank broke Carter's jaw. He later died of complications growing out of the accident. Leland asked Kettering if he could invent a way to start cars without cranking them.

The experts "looked at their formulas and said it was impossible," recalled Kettering, "that we would need batteries and an electric motor larger than the engine itself and wires five times as heavy as we used." But, Ket reasoned, they were thinking of a continuously running motor. If only a few seconds of cranking was needed, you might get by with a much smaller motor. So he abandoned theory, went to his workbench, and tried it. It worked, and it still works in every car today, exactly according to the principles Ket laid out.

Kettering's parents lived on a farm in the early days of the century and had no electricity. So he developed the first practical engine-driven generator to furnish electric light. This became the famous "Delco" that was used on millions of farms.

In 1916, Kettering sold his company to General Motors for nine million dollars, and a few years later accepted an offer to set up a central research laboratory for the company and become its director. The list of accomplishments that he and his associates achieved over the next thirty-one years until his retirement in 1947 chronicle the development of the automobile into its present advanced state, and touch on several other fields as well. They developed leaded gas, which ended the plague of destructive engine knock in what would become modern high-compression designs. Kettering worked with an associate named Thomas Midgley on this problem, and, characteristically, in describing it took his usual shots at the establishment. "Happily neither Tom nor I was an orthodox chemist or thermal engineer, so we were wholesomely ignorant of the obstacles."

The new anti-knock fuel was hailed in 1924 by *Popular Science* and others as the key to high-compression auto engines, with their advantages in efficiency and mileage. (It was not until 1973, almost a half-century later, that the nation's Environmental Protection Agency publicly accused leaded gasoline of threatening people with lead poisoning, by spewing more than 200,000 tons of lead yearly into the air they breathed—as well as disabling the catalytic converters just being developed for smog-free car exhausts. The agency forthwith began issuing regulations designed ultimately to reduce the amount of lead in all gasoline to an insignificant figure by public health standards—and to assure a supply of totally leadless "gas" for users of coming catalytic-converter cars.)

Kettering was convinced that the heavy, sluggish diesels of the 1920s, then used mostly in ships and as stationary engines, could be improved. "He set out to develop a lightweight, two-cycle diesel engine that would do twice the work at half the cost," says his former associate Richard Terrell. He did it, and the General Motors diesel locomotive soon ran the old steam locomotive off the rails.

Under his direction, and often with his direct participation, the lab developed: methods of painting a car in one hour (it had taken thirty days until then); Freon, the universally used refrigerant; winter oils; four-wheel brakes; two-way shock absorbers; chromium plating; fixed-focus headlights; safety glass; variable-speed transmissions; and many, many other items.

Kettering believed that the big thing wrong with our educational system was that it taught students to be afraid of making mistakes. That was obviously not one of his problems, and he was frequently far off target himself. In a 1929 *Popular Science* article, for example, written by someone obviously infected with a bad case of hero worship, Kettering is quoted as predicting that "within ten years we'll have automobiles safely traveling 100 miles an hour, weighing less than a thousand pounds, costing less than a thousand dollars, and covering eighty miles on a gallon of gas. Maybe we won't be using gas at all," he continued, and pointed out how much unharvested energy was contained in sunlight.

Kettering was a man of many odd talents. He could write with both hands simultaneously, for example, writing something different with each. In later years he wrote and spoke extensively, giving vent to his strongly held beliefs. Some examples of the Kettering mind:

"Pure research is pure bunk."

"A 'good break' occurs when you hacksaw your way through ninety-nine strands in the cable of difficulty, and then circumstances step in and break the final strand for you."

"A problem is not solved in the laboratory. It is solved in some fellow's head. He only needs the laboratory apparatus to get his head turned around so he can see the thing right."

"When a project is set up for experimental evaluation, often there is not a chance in a thousand it will work the way you want it to, but it won't fail the way you expect it to, either. That is the way you learn."

Kettering thought that traditional thinking was the greatest bar to innovation. "Now suppose you want to invent an airplane and no airplane has ever been invented before. There is no textbook on airplanes and there are no formulas. This ought to be an advantage, but the average man is always tempted to lean on something in the past. The early inventors leaned on what they knew, the bird. The Darius Greens made wings that flapped and covered them with feathers. But it happens that a bird is built for more than flying. It is made to lay eggs, digest worms, and build nests. A man who wants to fly doesn't want to digest worms, too."

In 1947, at the age of seventy-one, Boss Ket officially retired from General Motors. But it would have been difficult for anyone watching his daily activities to tell. He continued to work in his shops and laboratories, continued to press toward even higher-compression engines and a flock of other projects. He visited Antioch College often, where he had set up a foundation to study photosynthesis. Kettering had become convinced in the 1920s that man should learn to harness the sun and became one of the first solar-power advocates. "If we could catch only two tenths of one percent of the energy in sunshine," he said, "we would double our food supply and everything else. If we can learn to convert sunshine without growing plants, we may be able to make the vital step toward abundance and peace. There will then be nothing to fight about."

He took an active interest in the work of the world-famous Sloan-Kettering Institute for Cancer Research, which he established with GM chairman Alfred Sloan. He spent much time working with the Thomas Alva Edison Foundation (of which he was president), strengthening methods of education. And he continued to shuttle to General Motors research installations around the country, flying his own plane into his eighties.

To the day of his death on November 25, 1958, at eighty-two, he never lost faith in the future. "I can conceive of nothing more foolish," he said, "than to say the world is finished. We are not at the end of our progress, but at the beginning. We have but reached the shores of a great unexplored continent. We cannot turn back . . . It is man's destiny to ponder the riddle of existence and, as a by-product of his wonderment, to create a new life on this earth."

SPERRY

When he was six, he invented a horseradish grater for his aunt. There is no record that he patented it, which may be the only time in his sixty-nine productive years that he did not protect an invention. His name was Elmer Ambrose Sperry, and he is best known for his invention of the gyrocompass, which has guided virtually all ships, planes, and spacecraft ever since. But that was merely the climax of an amazing career. By age twenty, Sperry was running a company set up to manufacture products he had invented and patented, and before he died he had established eight major industrial concerns to exploit his more than 350 patents.

Sperry was born in upstate New York in the town of Cortland on October 12, 1860. He was interested in machinery as a boy and took every opportunity to study it in machine shops and workshops of the area and at Cornell University. In 1876, a local YMCA, impressed by the boy's obvious talent, led a community drive and collected money to send him to the Centennial Exposition in Philadelphia. (He did not forget; in his will he left the YMCA a million dollars.) He was astonished and delighted by the scientific marvels of the age he saw there, and always said in later life that the Centennial set the course of his life.

Sperry attended Cornell for one year, was particularly interested in an early dynamo under construction there, and almost immediately devised several ways to improve its efficiency. A Cortland manufacturer, impressed with his ideas, financed the building of a new dynamo under his direction and also the construction of a new kind of arc light. These were so successful that he was sent to Syracuse to build a large dynamo to operate a series of arc lamps, and early in 1880 he went to Chicago and founded the Sperry Electric Company to manufacture dynamos, arc lights, and other electrical equipment.

The factory opened on his twentieth birthday and prospered from the beginning. He installed lighting systems in a number of cities, including Omaha, Kansas City, and St. Louis. He built and installed a 40,000-candlepower beacon on the 350-foot Board of Trade Tower in Chicago (the highest beacon in the world at the time) and got much publicity as a result.

By the middle eighties, Sperry had visited a coal mine and seen the laborious, inefficient hand labor required in that operation. So in 1888 he organized the Sperry Electric Mining Machine Company to manufacture electrically driven mining equipment. He designed and built electric chain cutters, electric generators, and electric locomotives for use in mines. That led naturally to the design of electric streetcars, and in 1890 he founded the Sperry Electric Railway Company and built a plant for the manufacture of streetcars in Cleveland. Over the next several decades he patented and built new electric automobiles and devised a different kind of heavy-duty battery that could propel a car for the unheard-of distance of 100 miles. He developed chemical processes for manufacturing caustic soda, hydrogen, and chlorine compounds from salt and started a company to do it; he built an electric fuse wire company, and much else.

But the crowning achievement of his life was the development of the gyrocompass. So long as wooden sailing ships had ruled the seas,

Elmer Sperry is best known for the invention of the gyrocompass and other navigational instruments growing out of it, including the world's first automatic ship pilot, "Metal Mike" (below, right). But his more than four hundred other inventions include a new type of generator, the world's most powerful searchlight, electrical mining machinery, and much more.

Below, "the two Leos," Godowsky (right) and Mannes, supported their research for years by playing and teaching as professional musicians. Eventually, they invented Kodachrome, the world's first successful amateur color film. It went on the market in 1935, in Kodak packages like the one pictured at left.

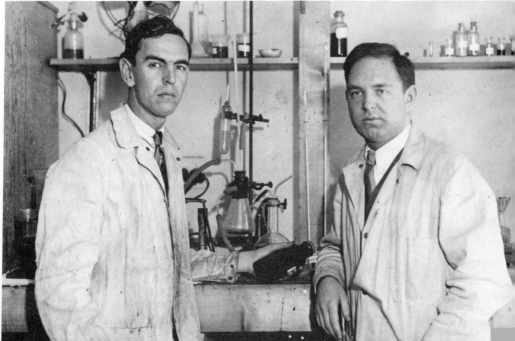

the magnetic compass had done a respectable job of navigation. Although it did not point to true north, it was close enough and navigators could compensate for the known discrepancy between true and magnetic readings.

But with the age of steel ships the picture changed. The steel hull itself introduced compass errors. And when electrical systems began appearing on ships, the magnetic fields generated by the flowing current made still more trouble. The giant fighting ships of the world's navies had still other difficulties; as their huge guns swung toward their targets, the delicately poised magnetic compass needles tended to follow.

As early as 1852 the French scientist Foucault had experimented with the gyroscope and predicted that someday it might become the basis of a compass. Many investigators had tried so to use it, but with limited success.

A gyroscope is nothing more than a weighted, balanced wheel mounted in bearings and spinning at high velocity. Its use as a compass depends on an unusual property common to any spinning body. If you push on one end of its shaft, it resists the push—that is, it tends to stay aligned with its original position. But it also pushes back—in a direction *at right angles to the direction of the original force*. Foucault had shown that a rapidly spinning gyroscope mounted in a gimbal with three degrees of freedom—that is, within three concentric rings hinged at right angles to each other so that it can assume any position in space—appears to revolve once a day. But actually it is the earth that is revolving; the gyroscope itself simply holds its position and its axis continues to point at a fixed point in space.

To make his spinning wheel into a compass, Sperry built a gyroscope in which the wheel was part of the rotor of an electric motor. Thus it could be kept spinning at high speed. He then hung a weight on one side of the innermost gimbal ring so that it hung straight down, keeping the gyro axis parallel to the surface of the earth.

It is the nature of the gyroscope to produce its counterforce at right angles to *any* force applied to it. And that includes the force of gravity on the weight on the innermost gimbal ring. To see the effect this would have, envision the gyro in such a position that its shaft points due west with its axis parallel to the earth's surface. As the earth rotates, the axis of the gyro will tend to hold its position, pointing at a particular spot in space. Thus it will no longer be parallel to the surface of the earth, and the weight, now unbalanced, will attempt to realign the shaft with the earth's surface. But the gyro responds by exerting a force at right angles to the one applied by gravity. Thus the gyro twists itself around into a more north–south position. As the earth continues to turn, the weight becomes unbalanced again, and again the twisting force is applied. The net effect is that the gyroscope continues to move until it aligns its own axis with the spin axis of the earth. In that position, gravitational attraction holds the gimbal weight in a stable position and no further twisting occurs.

The Sperry Gyroscope Company was established in Brooklyn in 1910. That same year, one of Sperry's early gyroscopes was installed on the battleship *Delaware* for evaluation by the Navy, and within a few years was on all navy ships and most merchant ships. In 1913, Sperry introduced his gyro stabilizer, which used a huge gyroscope to resist the wave forces that tended to make a ship roll. In 1914 he won first prize of 50,000 francs in a contest promoted by the French Government for the development of an airplane stabilization system.

But use of the gyroscope for navigation and stabilization in the air and on the sea was just the beginning. In a few years airplanes were getting good enough to need better means of long-distance navigation. Sperry's gyros not only gave them direction, but then became the basis for a whole cockpit full of flight instruments that allowed a pilot to control his plane even in zero visibility: the gyro turn indicator, the bank indicator, the artificial horizon, and many others. Sperry also invented the "Metal Mike," a revolutionary automatic steering device for ships. "On August 30, 1927," reported a 1928 *Popular Science* story, "the steam tanker *Pulpit Point* cleared from San Francisco for Auckland, New Zealand. Captain Owens set his great-circle course true South 38 degrees West by his gyroscopic compass and turned the wheel over to 'Metal Mike.' For twenty-one days, except for an hour in detouring the Savage Islands, no human hand touched the helm. There were cobwebs on her steering wheel when the Auckland pilot clambered aboard." Today, gyroscopes form the basis for the inertial platforms that guide all missiles, rockets, and space vehicles.

In 1918, Sperry introduced a high-intensity searchlight, five times brighter than any that went before it. It was naturally adopted for anti-aircraft work by most armies and navies of the world.

By the late 1920s, Sperry was ready to follow a familiar pattern and move on. He sold the gyroscope company in 1928—as he had sold most of his other companies—and began work on a railway car that tested the track it was passing over by shooting high-powered electric currents through it. Any cracks or imperfections in the track changed the electrical resistance. The car recognized such fluctuations and activated a paint sprayer underneath, marking the section that had to be replaced.

Sperry's inventive mind worked to the last. In June 1930, as the sixty-nine-year-old inventor lay in a hospital room dying, the weather in New York was sweltering. A large block of ice was brought into his room and a fan arranged to blow across it and cool him. "Put it in a large pan and fill the pan with water," he directed. "That will increase the surface area and thus the effectiveness." Those were his last words.

GODOWSKY AND MANNES

It may have been the strangest event in the history of science. The date was April 1935, and Eastman Kodak was ready to announce that the decades-long search for a practical color film was over. So it called a meeting of members of the staff. And in honor of the event, the two co-inventors who had achieved this marvel of esoteric chemistry showed the world's first Kodachrome slides. Then they sat down and played violin and piano sonatas for the assembled scientists.

It didn't seem strange to Leopold Godowsky and Leopold Mannes, inventors of Kodachrome. They considered themselves professional musicians first, scientists second. And never once during the nineteen years they worked to develop color film did they ever lose sight of this fact.

The strange alliance between the two Leos began when they were sixteen-year-old students at New York's Riverdale School. They were both sons of famous concert musicians, and neither ever considered any other career. But they were both interested in photography, too, and both wanted to try to develop a way to record color on film. Their first efforts began in the physics lab of Riverdale. Although they didn't know it, their early attempts simply duplicated a demonstration that the famous scientist James Clerk Maxwell, had given in 1865, in which he used three projectors to project three pictures simultaneously. One picture was red, another blue, and the third green. When the three images were superimposed, a color picture was the result.

Many scientists had tried to use the same approach to produce a practical color photograph, but none had achieved good results. Godowsky and Mannes developed such a system to the point where they got a patent on it—first of some forty they were to receive—but the color picture was dark and unsatisfactory. In 1921, the two inventors decided to give up the optical approach and turn to chemistry. The goal was to find a way to capture all the colors of the rainbow on a single piece of film.

Research teams around the world—including those at the mighty Eastman Kodak Company—had been working on the problem for years without success. But the two musicians decided to try anyhow, financing their expensive experiments with the proceeds from concerts and teaching. Eventually a Wall Street firm decided their work was worth backing to the extent of $20,000, and Dr. C. E. K. Mees, director of research at Kodak, was interested enough to supply them with chemicals, special coatings, and complex instruments at cost.

The job the two young inventors picked for themselves was a technical task of incredible complexity. The basic plan was to devise a film composed of several layers of emulsions, each sensitive to light of a certain color or wavelength. The layers would be separated by thin layers of gelatin. Different chemicals would have to be diffused into and out of the various layers, each one developing, bleaching, or dyeing the proper layer but no other, and each eventually producing at the end of a complex process colors similar to certain ones that had appeared in the original scene. When light was transmitted through the layers, the colors captured separately in each layer would blend and reproduce the original scene.

For the next nine years the inventors tried endlessly to solve the countless problems. They also continued active musical lives, with Godowsky teaching and giving concerts. Mannes even won a Pulitzer musical scholarship and a year later a Guggenheim scholarship to study composition in Rome. He accepted, and the two men continued to work separately, Godowsky in New York and Mannes in Rome, exchanging frequent letters on their progress. By 1930 they had not produced a really acceptable picture, but they were making enough progress so that Dr. Mees suggested that they come to Rochester and work at the Kodak laboratories with its matchless facilities. They accepted.

It was not a totally happy experience. The professional scientists were upset that a couple of musicians with little in the way of scientific credentials had been given the resources of the laboratory to work with. They were referred to as "those musicians" in a tone that would have done as well for "those crackpots." (The attitude today, forty-five years later, has not totally disappeared. A telephone call to Kodak for information, during research for this article, brought the response that little was available. "A lot of people here think their role in the development of Kodachrome has been exaggerated," said an informant.) It didn't help their scientific credibility that the men were always singing passages from musical classics while working in the dark. It didn't occur to them to mention that they were able to time the critical chemical processes in pitch darkness with split-second accuracy by singing passages of known length with their musicians' precise timing. Their colleagues also didn't like the fact that instead of working far into the night on their problems like serious scientists, they spent most of their evenings playing chamber music at the Eastman School of Music and giving concerts.

Early in 1933, Godowsky and Mannes developed a two-color process that produced the best color pictures to date. One of the layers was sensitive to blue-green light, the other to orange-red. The picture was fair, and Mees wanted to put the process into production. Godowsky and Mannes thought they could do better, though, and pleaded with him to wait. Highly encouraged by the two-color process, Mees threw the full power of the Kodak research organization behind them, assigning troops of scientists with doctorates in physics and chemistry to help them. But then, unable to resist pressure from elsewhere in the company during that Depression year, Mees ordered the two-color process into production despite opposition from the inventors.

But fortunately, before commercial production could get under way, Godowsky and Mannes finally produced what they had been trying for—a three-color process in which red-, blue-, and green-sensitive layers captured all of the colors of the rainbow and re-created them in a far more lifelike manner than had ever been achieved before.

The process did have one drawback. The color film had been envisioned as a product to be used by the general public. And the film fitted that requirement; it could be exposed in an ordinary camera just like any other film. But the processing was enormously complicated and difficult, consisting of twenty-eight critically timed and temperature-sensitive steps (later cut to fifteen). This was far beyond the capability of the ordinary darkroom operator or even most commercial labs. So the scheme developed was that the purchaser could shoot the film, then return it to Kodak for processing. On April 15, 1935, the world's first successful commercial color film was placed on the market.

When Godowsky and Mannes went to work as staff members at Kodak, all of their developments and patents from that time forward belonged to Kodak. But the ultimate developments made use of many patents they had taken out during the 1920s, when they were working on their own. So as Kodachrome prospered, so did the two inventors, quickly becoming affluent on the proceeds of their royalties.

The two continued at Kodak for a few more years and were instrumental in the development of Kodacolor, Ektachrome, and Ektacolor. But they had said on going to Rochester that it would be temporary; they would eventually want to go back to music. So in 1939 they returned to New York. Mannes became co-director of the Mannes School of Music, which had been founded by his famous father, and became its president when it was changed to the Mannes College of Music a short time later. He also toured extensively with a highly regarded chamber music group.

Godowsky enrolled in some courses in higher mathematics at Columbia University and bought a lavish sixty-seven-acre estate in

Westport, Connecticut, which, as one biographer put it later, combined "many of the elements of a successful banker's hideaway, a major recording studio, and an Eastman Kodak plant." In addition to his home, an artificial lake complete with hauled-in sand beaches, and sixty-seven acres of carefully manicured trees, lawns, and flowers, it contained an elaborate chemical laboratory, where he continued to experiment with film. Eventually he quit performing in public, finding his musical satisfaction instead in giving private chamber music concerts with his friends, many of whom were well-known professional musicians. For these performances, he used his three world-famous instruments; a centuries-old Domenico Nicolò Amati viola, and two violins, a 1728 Antonius Stradivarius and a 1734 Guarnieri del Gesù.

What would have happened to the musical careers of the two inventors had they not spent so much of their time developing Kodachrome is, of course, impossible to say. Although they achieved some success, neither was the world-renowned concert artist his father had been. In fact, recalled Mrs. Godowsky (who, incidentally, is the sister of the late famed composer George Gershwin), the elder Godowsky frequently complained that his son would never amount to much unless he quit fooling around with all those chemicals and spent more time practicing the violin. "I was glad we went to Rochester," said his wife, Frankie Godowsky, looking back over their lives. "It at last gave Leo a chance to prove to his father that he was capable of being a success in his own right."

ARMSTRONG

If a man makes one great invention in a lifetime, his place in history is assured. If he makes two, he is one of the giants. Edwin Howard Armstrong made three. They changed the world.

Armstrong's three critical inventions transformed radio from a trivial hobby into the full-fledged entertainment and communications medium that today covers the entire world. So fundamental were Armstrong's advances that to this day, every radio and television set makes use of one or more of his developments. In 1948, *Fortune* magazine called him "the greatest American inventor since Edison and the most important of all radio inventors, including Marconi."

When Armstrong burst upon the world of radio in the early years of the century, the new art of wireless communications was hampered by lack of a sensitive receiver. Most broadcasts could be picked up only over the range of a few miles. Earphone-wearing hobbyists fiddled over balky crystal detectors, trying to coax sounds out of the reluctant air. Armstrong was a student at Columbia University in 1911, when he developed a radical new kind of circuit, using the then

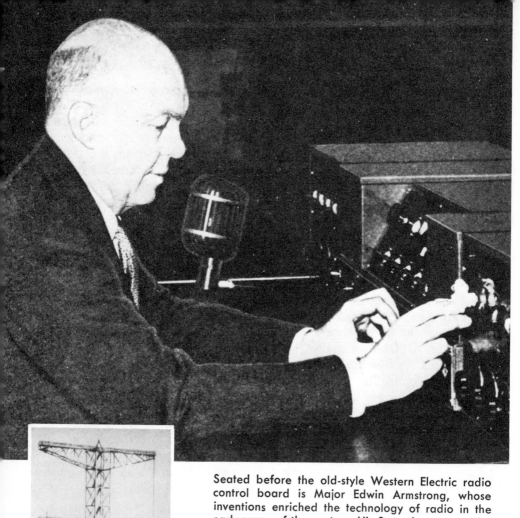

Seated before the old-style Western Electric radio control board is Major Edwin Armstrong, whose inventions enriched the technology of radio in the early years of the century. His first advance was the regenerative receiver, which took radio out of the crystal detector era. His next was the superheterodyne receiver. And his third was FM radio. At left is the still-standing transmission tower in Alpine, New Jersey, from which Armstrong transmitted his first experimental FM broadcasts.

This early superheterodyne receiver built by Armstrong in 1924 bristled with tubes and dials. But the simple principle it introduced is still the heart of every radio and television set produced today.

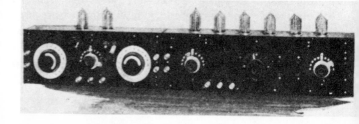

new vacuum tube. Basically, he rigged the tube so that the weak signal picked up from the air was amplified through the tube, then shunted around it and reamplified again and again until the faint whisper plucked out of the air became a roar.

Armstrong called his development a regenerative circuit. It was exactly what radio needed: a cheap, simple, reliable detector of the still novel radio waves. Observers of the day were impressed. "The keenest imagination can hardly forecast the effect of this new hookup on the radio industry in general," said a 1922 *Popular Science* story. And Jack Binns, one of the leading writers of the day on the subject of radio, wrote in the same issue: "I am convinced that the guiding hand of genius hovers over him. He is without any question the most imposing figure in the world of radio today."

When World War I broke out, radio was put to work for the first time in battlefield communications. Armstrong was commissioned a captain in the Signal Corps and sent to Europe with the assignment of finding ways to eavesdrop on the Germans. His response was to invent yet another new type of receiver, the superheterodyne, that was as big an improvement over the regenerative detector as that device was over the old crystal set it had replaced. In fact, so good was the superheterodyne that in the more than fifty years since, nobody has ever been able to come up with anything better. Every radio sold today, from the smallest transistor to the most expensive home receiver, every communications and military receiver, every television set still uses the basic superheterodyne circuit invented by Armstrong during World War I.

Home from the war, Armstrong set out to conquer radio's biggest problem in those days—static. A lot of others had tried, given up, and declared that the crackling, crashing noises induced in radio sets by lightning and other electrical phenomena would simply have to be lived with—there was no way to eliminate them. Armstrong didn't agree, and in 1933 patented an entirely new kind of radio system called FM—frequency modulation. It eliminated static entirely, by encoding the voices or music on the carrier waves in an entirely different way from traditional—amplitude modulation, or AM— radio. FM also had other advantages. The main one was that it made possible the broadcasting of true high-fidelity signals, far superior to those possible with AM.

The man who brought about these three epochal advances in the field of electronic communications combined a series of strong and not always consistent characteristics. For example, he tended to avoid publicity and seek privacy most of the time. Yet he could also be an exuberant show-off. He loved to ride motorcycles and drive cars. He courted the girl who was later to become his wife by taking her on

100-mile-an-hour dashes down Long Island parkways. And he liked to climb towers. As a boy, he had frightened his Yonkers, New York, neighbors by constantly climbing to the top of an antenna tower he had erected in his backyard for radio experimentation. Later, even after his fame spread, he always personally supervised and participated in the installation of experimental antennas on projects he was working on, swinging hundreds of feet above the ground in bosun's chairs with the construction workers.

Early in life, Armstrong began to display the disputatious nature that later became a vivid part of his character. For example, early in 1923, RCA was building its first broadcast station in New York City. The hundred-foot antenna towers were built on top of a twenty-story building on West Forty-second Street. It was Armstrong's habit to go on the roof and climb the tower from time to time, apparently to enjoy the view.

David Sarnoff, who at that time was general manager of RCA, thought it was dangerous and wrote his friend Armstrong, telling him to stop. That didn't sit well with the young inventor. So during a reception to mark the official opening of the station, while Sarnoff was in the sixth-floor studios greeting guests, Armstrong called a group of reporters together, went to the roof, climbed one of the hundred-foot towers, crawled on top of a fifteen-foot ball at its peak, and—according to eyewitnesses—did a handstand. Sarnoff, when he heard about the incident, told the guards to lock the doors and keep Armstrong off the roof.

Recognized as one of the world's foremost electronics experts, Armstrong received many honors. In the 1920s he was appointed a professor of electrical engineering at Columbia University. But, independently wealthy on royalties from his inventions, he neither drew a salary nor taught much. He did set up his laboratories at the university.

Despite his eminence, Armstrong was not, of course, the only innovative worker in the field. And in an area as complicated as radio, there must arise differences of opinion as to exactly who had done what. These squabbles eventually turned into lawsuits that were ultimately to take up most of Armstrong's time.

The first such fight involved the regenerative receiver circuit. Lee De Forest, the inventor of the Audion—the first vacuum tube amplifier—claimed that the regenerative receiver was basically his. The case eventually got to the Supreme Court, which ruled in favor of De Forest on a point of law without reviewing the evidence. Armstrong spent another $200,000, reopened the case, and again fought it up to the Supreme Court, where he lost again.

Whatever the position of the courts, there was no doubt among the professionals as to where the credit lay. The Institute of Radio Engineers, the country's most prestigious professional group, gave its highest award, the Medal of Honor, to Armstrong for his invention of the regenerative circuit. He was similarly honored by the Franklin Institute and the American Institute of Electrical Engineers.

But the fight over the regenerative receiver was to be just the warm-up for the main event. Armstrong had received the basic patent on FM radio in 1933. As always happens in a development of fundamental importance, many laboratories worked on the new advance and some made improvements and modifications. Thus in the late 1930s, as commercial FM broadcasting got under way, the industry split as to who really owned the relevant patents. General Electric, Zenith, Westinghouse, and Stromberg-Carlson lined up with Armstrong and began paying him royalties on every set they manufactured. RCA, Philco, Emerson, and several others decided that the improvements that had been made were such that Armstrong's basic patents no longer applied, and began manufacturing equipment without getting Armstrong licenses. Armstrong filed a series of lawsuits that were to occupy him for the rest of his life.

In 1940, David Sarnoff, Armstrong's old friend, made a compromise offer. He proposed to pay Armstrong a million dollars in a lump-sum settlement for the right to manufacture FM sets under Armstrong's patent. But Armstrong wanted royalties, too, and refused.

The pace of development of FM was a bitter disappointment to Armstrong. FM broadcasting started shortly before World War II. The war, with its shortages, dealt a heavy blow to the young industry. After the war, as FM was starting to expand again, the FCC shifted commercial FM broadcasting to another part of the frequency spectrum. All receiving and transmitting equipment was suddenly obsolete and the entire industry had to start over again.

And the entrenched AM broadcasting interests were not anxious to promote the new medium. Thus, instead of FM blooming in communities and neighborhoods everywhere and becoming the equivalent of a local newspaper as Armstrong had dreamed, development was slow and spotty. In many communities, FM stations simply broadcast the same program fare heard on the better-established AM stations instead of launching new community services. Armstrong felt that he and FM radio had been the victims of a conspiracy, and in 1948 brought suit against RCA and NBC, claiming that the companies had conspired to discourage FM. A few years later he filed many other suits against various manufacturing companies charging that they, too, were part of the plot.

By the summer of 1953 Armstrong was spending most of his time prosecuting his many legal actions, and at the same time trying to continue his various technical investigations. His wife, seeing the mounting strain, tried without success to get him to slow down.

Armstrong was rich; his inventions had brought in at least fifteen million dollars. He had received every honor and award his profession could bestow; he was universally recognized as the reigning genius of his field. Yet the evidence now indicates that years of court battles against people he apparently felt were trying to steal his inventions and quash his dreams had left him feeling tired, defeated. On the night of January 31, 1954, alone in his East Side Manhattan apartment, he wrote a love letter to his wife, put on his overcoat, hat, and gloves, and stepped out of the thirteenth-story window.

Mrs. Armstrong continued her husband's fight. In late 1954, she accepted a million-dollar settlement from RCA. Then, during the next thirteen years, one by one, various companies paid the inventor's widow a total of about five million dollars, bringing the long legal battle to an end. In 1967, the last suit was settled, and thirteen years after his death Armstrong won full vindication.

SIKORSKY

Igor Sikorsky learned the love of flying at his mother's knee a decade before the Wright brothers' famous triumph at Kitty Hawk. And it was also in childhood, in pre-turn-of-the-century Russia, that he determined to become one of the conquerors of the air.

It was an ambition that was to be realized in a spectacular way. At twenty-three, he had designed the world's first enclosed-cabin, multi-engine airplane, become rich and famous, and set the scene for the emergence of fleets of multi-engine planes that now circle the globe. In the 1930s, he designed and built the clipper ships that opened up transoceanic passenger flights. A decade later he launched an entirely new chapter in the conquest of the air with the invention of the world's first practical helicopter.

Sikorsky was a tall, erect man with a fringe of graying hair around his collar, a clipped, bristling mustache, a faintly accented voice, and a courtly manner—he always bowed slightly on meeting people. Life-long friends say he was never known to lose his temper or raise his voice. He wore dark suits, often with blue, rubber-soled yachting shoes, and sometimes replaced his fedora with a flying cap. In addition to aviation he was interested in astronomy (and gazed at the stars through his five-inch backyard telescope) and volcanoes; he sometimes traveled halfway around the world to see one erupt. He was often called "Uncle Igor" behind his back, but always "Mr. Sikorsky" to his face. He spent much of his time reading religious and philosophical books and believed strongly in intuition, a trait that was to figure strongly in his work.

Igor Ivanovich Sikorsky was born on May 25, 1889, in the city of Kiev in czarist Russia. His father was a doctor and professor, famous for his work in psychology. His mother was a medical school graduate. And it was she who fired the boy's imagination by reading to him about Leonardo da Vinci's helicopter designs.

In 1903, the Wright brothers made their famous flight. In the summer of 1908, the eighteen-year-old Igor first read of the feat and was fired with an irresistible urge to fly. He went to Paris—then the world center of aviation—where young daredevils were careening across empty fields in their wood, string, and fabric planes, sometimes even rising briefly off the ground. Deciding that there was little for him to learn there, he bought a twenty-five-horsepower engine and went back to Russia.

In the summer of 1909, Sikorsky put his first ungainly contraption —a helicopter—together. It had two lifting propellers rotating in opposite directions mounted on a common vertical axis. It didn't get off the ground, but Sikorsky reported enthusiastically that "It seemed to be trying to get into the air." With a scale, he demonstrated that it had developed 357 pounds of lift, just 100 pounds shy of its own weight.

Igor's father had tremendous faith in the boy and put most of the family's modest fortune into aircraft development work, even mortgaging the family's home when more money was needed. But Igor couldn't get the helicopter to work, and turned to fixed-wing aircraft.

Over the next few years he built a series of planes, several of which flew. With his fifth—the S-5—he made a series of cross-country flights, won a pilot's license, and began to earn money giving flying exhibitions. With the S-6 he flew at seventy miles an hour with two passengers, setting a new world's record. This plane so impressed the country that shortly before Sikorsky's twenty-third birthday a Petrograd firm bought exclusive rights from him and made him designer and chief engineer of its new aeronautical division. Within two years he had paid back the $25,000 his family had risked on his work and was on his way toward making his first fortune.

It was at this time that Sikorsky began to think big. He designed a huge craft with four 100-horsepower engines, a totally enclosed cabin, a washroom, a clothes closet, a sofa, a dining table, luxurious paneling, and an outdoor observation deck. It was named *The Grand*. As usual, skeptics said nothing that big would ever fly; it violated the laws of nature. (Earlier the same skeptics had pointed out that manned flight was impossible. Nature had set a limit of thirty pounds on the weight of flying creatures, or the ostrich would be able to fly.)

This flying "mechanical insect," as it was described in a *Popular Science* article in July 1941, was the world's first successful helicopter. Igor Sikorsky, left, who invented it, always flew in his business suit and turned-up-at-the-brim fedora. He developed the craft, eliminated its bugs, and taught himself to fly a helicopter simultaneously.

Father of the atomic age is Enrico Fermi (above), who achieved the world's first chain reaction in 1942. His patent for the first nuclear reactor credited the Hungarian physicist Leo Szilard (left) as co-inventor.

Sikorsky's faith in intuitive engineering helped shape *The Grand.* While the great plane was under construction, he would often go into the deserted workshop at night and brood about it. In those days, it was thought that to increase wing lift, you simply increased wing area. And since it was easier to brace short, wide wings than long, narrow ones, the plane had broad, stubby wings. But Sikorsky was not happy. "One night after everyone had gone home," he said, "I looked at the broad, short wings for *The Grand.* I did not like the 'feel' of them, and so we changed them to long and narrow.

"This horrified many people. Today we know that lift comes from the vacuum formed by air rushing over the top of the wing—and the more leading edge, the greater the lifting surface. Then we knew no such aerodynamics, but my intuition said those stubby wings would not work, and it was right."

Sikorsky himself was at the controls when it took off on its maiden flight on May 13, 1913. "I was sitting in the enclosed cabin fairly high above the ground," he recalled years later. "With no wind in my face I had the impression that the ship was accelerating very slowly yet the fact that the ailerons and elevators became active indicated that the ship was gaining speed. Finally all the shocks under the wheels ceased and I saw the Earth gradually moving away. The ship was airborne. I was flying."

In subsequent flights, Sikorsky was to take *The Grand* on some of the world's first real cross-country flights, enjoy the sensation of watching the clouds go by while standing on the outside observation deck, and receive a gold watch from an impressed Czar Nicholas II. When World War I began, he was commissioned to build seventy-five of the giant ships, which were used in bombing raids against the Germans.

During the Russian Revolution, the thirty-year-old Sikorsky escaped to New York, abandoning his half-million-dollar fortune, and went to work teaching mathematics to Russian immigrants in night school. In 1923 he got together a few Russian refugees and a few hundred dollars in capital and established the Sikorsky Aero Engineering Corporation. Although his first plane, the S-29, crashed and nearly wiped out the young company, he was soon building the famous flying boats with which Pan American Airlines established trans-oceanic passenger service. In 1929, shortly before the Depression, United Aircraft bought Sikorsky Aircraft.

Though his attention had been occupied with other things, Sikorsky had never forgotten his initial fascination with helicopters. And, in 1939, he persuaded United officials to put up development money. Other helicopters had managed to flutter briefly off the ground in Germany and France. But they had used two rotors, either on separate or concentric shafts. And there were control problems. Sikorsky was convinced that a single rotor would be more efficient, but that opened up another problem. When the rotor spins in one direction, torque tends to spin the helicopter in the other. And, since the craft is to hover and take off straight up and down with little or no forward speed, how can its flight path be controlled? Conventional controls don't become effective until some forward speed has been built up.

Sikorsky solved both of these problems by putting three small rotors near the tail of the craft. One, turning in a vertical plane, generated a force that exactly canceled out torque. Its variable-pitch blade could also guide the craft in either direction. Two more horizontal stern-mounted rotors could drive the tail up or down or make the helicopter bank. (Sikorsky eventually simplified this arrangement to use only the one vertical rotor at the rear and controlled other movements by varying the pitch of the main rotor.)

The first experimental craft was strange-looking indeed. "Sikorsky's mechanical insect is a simple open framework of welded metal tubing," reported a 1941 *Popular Science* article. "Its wings are merely the three blades of a great fan whirling horizontally above it, 28 feet in diameter. Its stabilizers, rudders, and ailerons are three 7½-foot rotors ranged across the tail."

With this rangy beast, Sikorsky had to work out two problems at one time. He had to perfect the design of the machine, and at the same time teach himself to fly it. When it would lurch off the ground at a crazy angle, for example, was there something wrong with the design, or had he simply handled the controls improperly?

Day after day over the next several years, Sikorsky would go out onto the field near the Sikorsky plant in Stratford, Connecticut, where the tethered VS-300 was undergoing tests. There, dressed in his dark suit and his slightly too small fedora with its brim tilted up fore and aft, he would climb onto the "front porch" of the strange-looking machine and crank the engine. Through nineteen major alterations over the next two years and with his constantly improving piloting skills, he developed the modern helicopter into a practical device.

In May 1942 a Sikorsky helicopter, the XR-4, flew from Connecticut to Wright Field, Ohio, for delivery to the Army Air Forces. It was the first extended flight of such a craft, and marked the beginning of a new chapter of military and aviation history. The helicopter saw brief use on the battlefield before the end of World War II. But it was in the Korean War that it became a workhorse, transporting troops and supplies into battle and evacuating the wounded. In the process, it changed the basic tactics of war.

At the same time, it was becoming a useful means of transportation in civilian life, too, with thousands of choppers soon engaged all over the world in everything from short passenger runs to crop dusting.

Sikorsky himself was always proudest of the fact that the helicopter was used primarily to save lives, rather than destroy them. He kept a huge book of clippings during the Korean War and maintained a running tabulation. "We have now saved 7,642 lives," he would announce with satisfaction.

Sikorsky died in 1972 at the age of eighty-three. Until shortly before his death, he had continued to go to the plant that bears his name every day to consult, observe, improve. And he never tired of pointing out a sign that embodied his life's work in a particularly vivid way.

"According to recognized aero-technical tests, the bumblebee cannot fly because of the shape and weight of his body in relation to the total wing area," the sign read. "The bumblebee doesn't know this, so he goes ahead and flies away."

FERMI

It was just before dawn in the desert near Alamogordo, New Mexico. For years, teams of scientists and engineers had been working feverishly to build the world's first atomic bomb. Now, on July 16, 1945, it sat on a slender steel tower as the final minutes before detonation ticked away.

Two scientists, Emilio Segrè and Enrico Fermi, were on station nine miles from Ground Zero. Then, just before the explosion that was to change the world, "Fermi got up and dropped small pieces of paper on the ground," wrote Segrè later. "He had prepared a simple experiment to measure the energy liberated by the explosion: the pieces of paper would fall at his feet in the quiet air, but when the front of the shock wave arrived (some seconds after the flash) the pieces of paper were displaced a few centimeters in the direction of the propagation of the shock wave. From the distance of the source and from the displacement of the air due to the shock wave, he could calculate the energy of the explosion. This Fermi had done in advance, having prepared himself a table of numbers, so that he could tell immediately the energy liberated by this crude but simple measurement." While readings from the elaborate network of instruments were not available for several days, Fermi had the answers within seconds. And, points out Segrè, Fermi's answer from his simple experiment was very close to the one the complex instruments eventually delivered.

The story has been told of Fermi many times because it illustrates the way his mind worked. He was one of the world's most brilliant and creative physicists, the man who achieved the first self-sustaining chain reaction, thus giving birth to the atomic age. Yet he often found simple ways to cut through tough problems. "He had an unusual grasp of physics which he kept at his fingertips always ready to use," said Herbert L. Anderson, a co-worker in the development of atomic energy. "When a problem arose, he had the knack to be able to go to the blackboard and simply work it out. The physics just flowed out of the chalk."

Fermi was small, black-haired, and gray-eyed, and had a calm, methodical manner. He spoke slowly and in a deep voice, and, a physicist in his group pointed out, after a few months many of his associates were unconsciously speaking the same way. And while most physicists tend to become either theoreticians or experimentalists, Fermi was both. "He wanted to wrestle with nature himself, with his own hands," said Anderson.

The man who was to launch the atomic age was born in Rome on September 29, 1901. He became fascinated by physics early, and by the time he entered the University of Pisa in 1918 he had little to learn; from his own reading and studying, he was more knowledgeable than most of his professors. Over the next decade, almost single-handedly, he brought a new spirit to Italian physics. In 1926, while teaching at the University of Florence, he published a paper on the mechanics of small particles that became a worldwide sensation and ultimately resulted in one class of elementary particles being named *fermions*. By the early 1930s he had published several more sensational papers and become internationally famous. In those days, physicists were just beginning to probe the atom in an attempt to discover the fundamental nature of matter. In a brilliant series of experiments, Fermi used slowed neutrons to bombard atoms, and discovered more than sixty new subatomic particles within a few months in the early days of 1934.

But in 1938 an event of great importance to Fermi's future—and to the world's—took place. Benito Mussolini, dictator of Italy, took a cue from his German allies and published a set of anti-Semitic regulations. Fermi's wife, Laura, was a Jew. At about the same time, Fermi heard that he was to be awarded the 1938 Nobel prize in physics. He and his wife worked out a plan. Several universities in the United States had previously offered him jobs. So he quietly got in touch with one of them—Columbia University—and arranged for a position. Then he, his wife, and his two children left for Stockholm, where he was to accept the prize. Afterward, they calmly got on a ship and, instead of going back to Italy, sailed for the new world.

The U.S. physics establishment was in a state of excitement when Fermi arrived on January 9, 1939. The brilliant Hungarian physicist Leo Szilard had conceived of the basic idea of a nuclear chain reaction in 1933. It had occurred to him that if he could find an element that, when split by one neutron, would release two, it would be possible to set up a self-sustaining reaction. He applied for a patent on the idea. But at that time, nobody had discovered such an element.

On December 22, 1938, just a few weeks before Fermi arrived in New York, two German physicists named Hahn and Strassman had bombarded uranium atoms with Fermi's slow-neutron technique and demonstrated nuclear fission.

Years before, Einstein had predicted in his theory of relativity that a small part of the mass of the atom would be converted in such a reaction into pure energy. And the famous equation $E=MC^2$ showed that the amount of energy derived from even a small reaction would be incredibly large. With World War II just getting under way in Europe, most physicists saw the development in terms of a weapon— and as a race. Would German physicists be able to develop an atomic bomb before the United States? Einstein's famous letter to President Roosevelt started the United States on the road to developing a nuclear bomb. The essential first step was to demonstrate a self-sustaining chain reaction.

For the next several years, Fermi and other physicists worked out the thousands of necessary details. How many of the neutrons released by each fissioning atom would hit another atom? How much uranium would be needed? How should it be spaced? In what material should the pieces of uranium be embedded? How would the reaction be turned on and off?

When the time came for the great experiment, Fermi, father of the slow-neutron process, was obviously the man to try. In 1942, under the Italian physicist's direction, a strange 500-ton structure of carefully machined graphite bricks began to grow in a squash court under the west stands of Stagg Field at the University of Chicago. Embedded in the graphite pile were pieces of uranium. Three sets of control rods were inserted into the pile to absorb neutrons and prevent a chain reaction. When they were withdrawn, according to calculations, the pile would "go critical" and the reaction become self-sustaining.

Forty-two of the world's leading atomic physicists who had worked on the project were on hand on an instrument-studded platform at one end of the room. Fermi gave the orders and inch by inch the rods were withdrawn. Each time the clicking of the radiation counters increased. Fermi constantly made calculations on a slide rule he held, checking predictions against the performance. At three twenty-five, he gave the order to pull once again. "This is going to do it," he told physicist Arthur Compton, standing next to him.

Minute after minute, the neutron count increased as Fermi manipulated his slide rule. "His face was motionless," said physicist George

Weil whose hand had moved the rod in accordance with Fermi's commands. "His eyes darted from one dial to another. His expression was so calm it was hard. But suddenly his whole face broke into a broad smile."

Fermi closed his slide rule. "The reaction is self-sustaining," he announced quietly. "The curve is exponential."

Physicist Eugene Wigner brought out a bottle of chianti he had kept hidden behind him during the experiment. Fermi uncorked it and sent out for paper cups so everyone could have a sip. Silently, without toasts, they raised their cups and drank. There was almost no conversation. "The event was not spectacular, no fuses burned, no lights flashed," said Fermi. But, recalled physicist Samuel Allison years later, "All of us in the laboratory knew that with the advent of the chain reaction the world would never be the same again." Arthur Compton went to a telephone, called Dr. James B. Conant of Harvard, and delivered a message by prearranged code. "The Italian navigator has landed in the new world," he said.

"How were the natives?" asked Conant.

"Very friendly."

For the rest of the war, Fermi worked at Los Alamos with other scientists, developing the actual bomb that his epic experiment had made possible. Afterward, he returned to the University of Chicago's Institute for Nuclear Studies, where he did important work on atomic theory and the origin of cosmic rays.

In September 1954, Fermi learned that he had cancer. In mid-November, he received the AEC's first $25,000 award for meritorious service, but was too ill to appear at the ceremony to accept it. He died on November 28, 1954, at the age of fifty-three. Said his colleague, Dr. I. I. Rabi, "We won't see his like in 100 years."

A U.S. patent for the world's first nuclear reactor, the Chicago pile, was granted in 1955 to Enrico Fermi and Leo Szilard. It was applied for in December 1944 but could not be issued until the secret information it contained was finally made public.

GOLDMARK

In 1933, a young Hungarian engineer moved to the United States and applied for a job with the then-as-now mighty RCA research organization. He was turned down, an event that must rank as one of the major mistakes in that company's history, and one which he never tired of pointing out to RCA.

The young man was Peter Goldmark, a name still relatively unknown to the American public. Yet he has been directly responsible for three of the world's major electronic advances: the LP record, color

TV, and the video cassette. And he is now working to introduce the fourth, a comprehensive nationwide system that would change the way we do practically everything from earning our living to educating our children. And in the process, Goldmark believes, the quality of life for everyone would be vastly improved.

The man who was destined to have such a profound effect on the whole area of electronic communications was born in Budapest in 1906, studied engineering in Berlin, got his Ph.D. in physics from the University of Vienna. In 1931 he went to London to work on the then new mechanical TV systems being developed. But by 1933, with the worldwide Depression having dried up research money, Goldmark decided to move to the United States to continue his work, apparently unaware that this country was having a depression, too.

So he bundled up his cello and $250 in cash, sailed for the United States, and began looking for a job. A short time after receiving the now famous RCA brush-off, he received a letter from Paul Kesten, a CBS vice-president, who had seen one of Goldmark's articles on television in a British scientific journal and been impressed. Goldmark had never heard of CBS, but as one later biographer put it, "he would have talked to the Devil about television," and shortly found himself chief television engineer at the new network, which was then beginning to get interested in the novel form of broadcasting.

Goldmark worked on early TV systems for several years. But his first major advance was sparked in 1940, when he saw *Gone With the Wind,* the first movie he had seen in color. It occurred to him that it should be possible to transmit TV in color, even though commercial TV broadcasting had not yet come into existence. In an incredible three months of frenzied work, he developed an ingeniously simple and highly successful color TV system. It used a conventional black-and-white camera, and a black-and-white receiver on the other end. But spinning in front of the camera tube was a plastic disc containing red, blue, and green sections. The disc was synchronized with the scanning sweeps of the TV tube so that the tube transmitted one complete picture while the red filter was in front of the lens, a second picture with the blue filter in place, and a third with the green filter in position. A similar-colored spinning disc at the receiver end was synchronized so that its red, blue, and green sections were in front of the picture tube in step with those back at the camera. The viewer's eye then blended the three single-color pictures into a full-color image.

The system worked beautifully, but World War II intervened before much could be done to introduce it into commercial broadcasting. Shortly after the war, CBS asked the FCC to approve its system for public broadcasting. The FCC held a hearing to decide whether Goldmark's system or the one that had been developed by RCA would be made standard. There was no comparison. Observers reported that the CBS system produced a beautiful color picture, while, according to RCA's General David Sarnoff, who described his company's results years later, "The monkeys were green and the bananas were blue and we all had a good laugh."

The FCC approved the CBS system overwhelmingly, but RCA went to court and got an order delaying its introduction. RCA's main point was that the CBS system was not compatible with the black-and-white system then in use. Thus, as stations switched over to color, the nine million black-and-white sets then in operation would become useless unless they were fitted out with expensive converters. The RCA system, while technically deficient, was compatible; the color signals it produced could be picked up in black-and-white on any standard black-and-white receiver.

RCA took its case all the way to the Supreme Court—and lost. But in the several years it gained, General Sarnoff poured $130 million into the development of the RCA system and had it working much better. He went back to the FCC, pleaded that his system now worked, and pointed out that all the sets in the country would become obsolete if the decision in favor of CBS were allowed to stand.

The tactic worked. The FCC reversed itself and approved the RCA system, which is standard today. Goldmark's system is still technically superior in some ways, though, and for this reason has been used in some highly color-critical closed-circuit applications such as the transmission of surgical procedures in medical schools. It was also the color system chosen to transmit the color pictures of the moon back to earth during the Apollo 15 mission, so that scientists interested in precise colors could see them accurately. Then the signal was converted to the RCA system for transmission over the national TV networks.

The long color TV development and battle would have been enough to occupy most men full time. But not Goldmark. "It is as natural for Peter to invent things as to eat," says Goldmark's colleague, Nobel laureate Dr. Dennis Gabor. "He is never happier than when he is beset with an idea and tinkers with circuits until 3 A.M." The idea that led to many such nights of tinkering and Goldmark's second major invention was sparked by an irritating experience one evening during World War II. "I was at a party listening to Brahms being played by the great Horowitz," recalls Goldmark, himself an accomplished pianist and cellist. "Suddenly there was a click. The most horrible sound man ever invented, right in the middle of the music. Somebody rushed to change records. The mood was broken. I knew right there and then I had to stop that sort of thing." Goldmark, who has often said that irritation is the mother of invention and tenacity its

The red, blue, and green disc held by Peter Goldmark was the heart of the world's first successful color TV system, invented in 1942. The Goldmark system was eventually replaced by one developed by RCA, which was compatible with black-and-white TV, but is still used where extreme color fidelity is required, such as in closed-circuit medical broadcasts.

The 33⅓ rpm microgroove LP record was Goldmark's second major invention. Introduced in the late 1940s, it wiped out 78 rpm records quickly, prevailed over newer entries such as the RCA-developed 45 rpm disc. It played entire symphonic movements and other long works, without interruption.

father, went to work. And three and a half years later, using the spare time left over between his television developments and the running battle with RCA over color, he invented the LP record. Using the then new material Vinylite, he devised a method of reducing the width of the groove from 2.5 thousandths to 1.0 thousandth of an inch.

The new records had two startling advantages: they could hold a half-hour or more of music on each side, and their vinyl surfaces were blissfully quiet. When they appeared in 1948 they were a sensation and quickly replaced the old 78 rpm records entirely.

Goldmark's old adversary, RCA, reacted quickly. General Sarnoff threw his technical staff into action and developed the 45 rpm record with the doughnut-sized hole in the middle. The battle was hard-fought, but the eventual outcome was inevitable: this time RCA lost, and the Goldmark-developed LP has totally dominated the field of recorded music ever since, earning uncounted millions of dollars for CBS.

Goldmark's technical triumphs undoubtedly grew out of his character: his conviction that problems can be solved and his enthusiasm in throwing himself totally into his projects. A friend once described him as "half tyrant and half child." He drove himself relentlessly and expected all those around him to do the same. One day his secretary was late and pleaded that she had had trouble starting her car. The president of CBS Laboratories spread out some newspapers, drove the car over them, crawled underneath, found and repaired the trouble. "You now have no cause to be late any more," he said.

As the years passed, Goldmark understandably achieved the reputation at CBS of being the local genius, and was pretty much left on his own to do as he pleased. No one, it is said, ever had much idea of what he was engaged in except one CBS executive named Adrian Murphy, whose unofficial title was "Vice-President in Charge of Peter."

Left to follow his own interests, Goldmark proceeded to develop his third major invention (accent on major; he has more than 160 patents to his credit), a system known as EVR—electronic video recording. He decided that the missing element in television was the ability to see what you want to see when you want it. He envisioned a briefcase-sized unit that would sit next to the TV set, into which a viewer could slip a small cartridge of pre-recorded programming.

Over the next few years he developed a system that recorded color television programs on black-and-white film—and packed an astonishing amount of information into a very small space. A reel seven inches in diameter and a half-inch thick contained a half-hour of color programming and a stereo sound track. Individual frames could be held on the screen, so the entire Encyclopaedia Britannica could also be stored on such a reel and played back a page at a time. The reel was cheap to make because it used inexpensive black-and-white film. Yet it played back in full color. Goldmark performed this trick by recording the basic picture in black and white, and encoding the color information on another part of the film. This color code, played back into the set's color circuits, restored full color to the picture.

For a while, it seemed as though EVR were about to take off. Then came a host of other video cassette systems, most based on magnetic tape. In the last few years, a variety of video discs in which both the picture and sound are pressed into a plastic disc have been demonstrated. Predictions that such video playback systems would soon become customer products have been too optimistic; the very proliferation of many non-compatible systems has made everyone uncertain and slowed development. As various systems have approached the production stage, costs have soared and none has so far been a success in home use. Yet it is clear that within the next few years such systems will become widespread. Ironically, it now seems that Goldmark's system—the one that started it all—will not be the winner.

In December 1971, Goldmark reached the age of sixty-five—mandatory retirement age at CBS. The company wanted to keep its policy, but keep Goldmark, too. It offered him a deal: a ten-year contract to serve as consultant, for which he would receive $750,000. There would be no special duties or responsibilities; he would get $75,000 a year just to tell CBS about any ideas he might have.

He turned it down. Goldmark had an idea he thought could be developed better by a non-profit organization. So he founded Goldmark Communications Corporation, and, in co-operation with Fairfield University, got a $400,000 grant from the Housing and Urban Development Department. Goldmark's goal is not modest: he wants to change the basic social and economic pattern of the world.

As he pointed out in an article he wrote for *Popular Science* in 1972, cities develop primarily because people come together for jobs, cultural events, and education. But cities have got much too big, Goldmark says, and the resultant urban overcrowding leads to slums, crime, and other evils. It also leads to the fact that most of us now live some distance from our places of work, which means we waste a lot of time—and energy—just getting back and forth from the job.

But, Goldmark points out, with modern two-way television, people across the country from each other can be in as close touch as though they were in adjoining offices. Thus, he says, there is no reason why a giant insurance company with perhaps 20,000 people on its staff should have to cram them all into a giant headquarters building. Small branch offices could be set up in scores or hundreds of small towns or even rural communities, so that people who prefer living under such conditions could do so and still have work nearby. And with the systems now available, education, entertainment, and cultural events could also be universally available instead of only at specific locations.

Paradoxically, inventor Goldmark points out that no new technical inventions are needed for his scheme to work. All it takes, he believes, is somebody to get it started. And that is what he intends to do. Preliminary work is under way in northern Connecticut, where Goldmark hopes to have a demonstration project going within the next several years. If it works, his final great invention could be a social one: a way for people to use the electronic inventions of the last half-century to lead better, fuller, and more rewarding lives.

TOWNES

The idea of an important discovery taking place on a park bench is almost too much of a cliché to be believed. Yet, says Charles Townes, inventor of the maser (and the principle of the laser), that's where it happened.

Scientists had been trying for some time to find a way to amplify very-high-frequency radio waves. For two years, a committee of scientists and engineers sponsored by the Office of Naval Research had been working on the problem with Townes as chairman. A meeting of the committee had been called, and Townes, a professor at Columbia University in New York, had gone to Washington to attend it.

"In the spring of 1951," he wrote twenty years later in an article in *Popular Science,* "after about two years of the committee's existence and the morning before an upcoming meeting, I awoke very early, possibly because of my frustration and concern over why we had not yet found any real solution to the production of such short waves.

"I slipped out of my hotel room before breakfast to sit on a bench among the azaleas of Franklin Park in Washington, and there in the early spring morning enjoyed the freshness and beauty of these gay flowers, musing over why we had so far failed.

"The moment of insight was more vivid and complete than almost any other in my experience. I was already convinced that very-high-frequency resonators must be atomic or molecular in nature, but had previously thought there was a logical reason why molecules could not provide amplification.

"Suddenly, I recognized the fallacy in my previous thinking and that of others, and furthermore how such a system could work. A three-minute calculation on the back of an envelope showed that such a system could, at least in one form, be built."

Back at Columbia, Townes joined with two associates—graduate

Charles Townes, a Columbia University professor, led the way to a truly great invention of modern years—the wonder-working laser. It was not his first claim to fame. Earlier he had invented the unique though lesser-known maser, an ultra-precise atomic clock.

Hand-held laser gun, one of smallest of a myriad of types, shoots a ruby-red signal beam that is visible four miles away. Lasers have become useful in a wide variety of jobs from geodetic measurements to the testing of commercial products.

The earth-to-moon distance has been measured to better than 6 inches with this reflector placed on the moon during the Apollo flights. A laser beam from earth hits the reflector and comes back. Precise measurement of elapsed time gives distance.

student Jim Gordon and Dr. Herb Zeigler—to build a maser. Basically, the scheme was this. From his work in a field called microwave spectroscopy, Townes knew that molecules could exist at several different energy levels. Normally, most molecules are in a low-energy state, but can be "pumped" to a higher state by bombarding them with microwave energy. Then, if microwaves of a different wavelength hit them while they are pumped up, they decay to a lower state, giving up energy, and thus amplifying the incoming wave.

Townes and his team chose to work with the ammonia molecule, since they had studied its energy transformations and knew that a relatively convenient frequency—23,870 megahertz—could be used to pump the molecule. And they also knew how to separate high-energy molecules from those of lower energy.

The first maser, which used a beam of excited ammonia molecules, worked better than their calculations had predicted. It emitted a strong microwave signal of great purity. Under certain conditions it would oscillate automatically. Not only had Townes invented the world's highest-frequency amplifier, but the oscillating maser had an extremely stable frequency. Thus it could be used as the basis for the world's most accurate clock—one that in its final form would not lose or gain more than a second in 30,000 years. And because it could amplify very-high-frequency signals while adding far less noise of its own than more conventional amplifiers, it was immediately put into use as an amplifier in such critical jobs as receiving weak transoceanic transmissions from communications satellites.

The question arose, of course, as to what to name it. Jim Gordon, one of Townes's collaborators, recalls that one day shortly after the first maser had gone into operation, about five of those who had been involved were having lunch at the cafeteria of Teacher's College in New York. Townes said the device ought to have a name. "He immediately vetoed any name ending in the suffix -tron, and before lunch was over the name *maser* had emerged." It stood for *m*icrowave *a*mplification by *s*timulated *e*mission of *r*adiation.

But the maser was just the beginning. Townes and his brother-in-law, physicist Arthur L. Schawlow of Bell Laboratories, published a paper in 1958 describing what they called an optical maser—a maser designed to operate at the frequencies of light. In 1960, a researcher at Hughes Aircraft Company named Theodore Maiman actually built the first such device—a ruby rod whose atoms were pumped to an excited state by a bright flash of blue-green light. And it quickly became known as the laser—by simply substituting "light" for "microwave" in the original term.

In 1964, Townes received the Nobel prize in physics for his work. He split it with two Russians who had pursued a similar line of investigation independently and at about the same time. Townes has since used the discovery of the maser/laser in an attempt to spread one of his favorite beliefs: that we progress faster in science if we don't try to tell scientists what to do. "What research director in the early 1950's when the field was being born, would have had the courage to think he was going to develop a powerful new light source; a higher precision clock; a new cutting, welding, and surgical tool; the world's most sensitive amplifier; three-dimensional pictures; or any one of the many other products of maser development by setting out to study microwave spectroscopy?" he wrote in *Popular Science* in 1972.

"I didn't imagine most of them myself, and continue to be amazed by offspring of the maser. Yet it is such studies, followed primarily in universities for quite different reasons, which were the key to success and to one of the most startling developments in man's potentialities."

CHAPTER 11

Making Money On Inventions

W HEN Lincoln used the phrase "the fuel of interest" in his statement that the patent system had added it to the fire of genius, he meant very simply: the chance to make money on one's invention.

In our opening chapter, we touched upon the practical side of inventing, referring to the U. S. Patent Office's innovation, several years ago, of a new program to protect ideas for inventions. Its purpose is to give the inventor ironclad proof of the day on which he *thought* of his Big Idea.

There are many other facets to successful inventing which will be covered in this final chapter, the icing on a cake which consists of slices of many inventors' methods and experiences.

Fifty years ago the following still cogent advice appeared in *Popular Science* in an article called "Why Simple Inventions Have Proved Most Profitable":

> If you want to make your inventive ability pay you big dividends, invent something that great numbers of people will want and will be able to buy—something that will do away with or lessen some petty annoyance of ordinary life, and that can be manufactured and sold cheaply.

(The illustrations for that article in 1925 included the hairpin, the bottle top, the paper clip, the safety pin and the safety-match folder—all invented before 1872, when *Popular Science* was founded.)

A very remarkable friend of ours, Marvin Small, who dreamed up many a valuable product to fill practical needs, has described his technique for finding a need to fill: he looks in the mirror—or at pictures of men and women—and ticks off the pharmaceutical products that could be developed for the whole body—the hair, the eyes, the face, the arms, and so on to the feet. By this method he developed with George Spitzer the first can of automatic lather for shaving (Rise), which Marvin calls "one of the most important developments in shaving since the invention of the safety razor." In his book *How to Attain*

Financial Security (Simon & Schuster, 1953)—published later as a paperback called *How to Make More Money*, he described his philosophy as follows: "The key to financial security, the key to self-confidence and self-satisfaction lies in just six magic words—FIND A NEED AND FILL IT." In short, invent something people need.

Marvin wrote: "My own method of finding needs is simple. Since my experience has been largely in the drug and cosmetic fields, I set before me pictures of people and study them from head to toe. Let's take a photograph of a man, and begin with his hair. The first major need we see is some specific to prevent or stop baldness. We investigate this and find it's too big a problem—there are too many indications that the cause of baldness lies in genetic factors. We move our attention to the nose. We wonder, can we sponsor the development of a better means of treating sinusitis and post-nasal drip? Here is a worthy goal. And how about the teeth? Perhaps we can find a toothpaste or a radical form of dentifrice that will really prevent tooth decay. Or . . ."

Or. Or. Or. For instance, Marvin Small tells about his own experience with an odorless depilatory; after fifteen years of search he learned of a Czechoslovakian who had solved the problem. Result: a product called Nair, largest seller in its field.

In our chapter "Tremendous Trifles" there are a host of examples (from A for Aerosol to Z for Zipper) of such practical inventions.

So it is not necessary to be an Edison, a Marconi, a Bell, or a Wright to make a lot of money on inventions.

But you must know the rules of the game to protect your ideas. Many inventors, including those in the preceding paragraph, had to go to court to protect their patents, as you have read in preceding chapters.

The government of the United States offers excellent literature at low cost to help you decide whether to apply for a patent, how to obtain that protection, and how to promote your invention. Here is a list of booklets which you can obtain at nominal price from the Superintendent of Documents, U. S. Government Printing Office, Washington, D.C. 20402:

General Information Concerning Patents Rules of Practice of the Patent Office in Patent Cases
Patent Laws
Roster of Attorneys and Agents Registered to Practice Before the U. S. Patent Office
Directory of Registered Patent Attorneys and Agents Arranged by States and Cities
How to Obtain Information from United States Patents
Patents and Inventions: An Information Aid for Inventors

Some years ago, *Popular Science* published a question-and-answer feature, "Here's Your Guide to Successful Inventing," based on a book, *The Successful Inventor's Guide,* by Norman Carlisle and K. O. Kessler (Prentice-Hall, 1965). The questions below are just as pertinent as they were then and the answers have been brought up to date. Many of them appear in the last-named government booklet, above, "Patents and Inventions: An Information Aid for Inventors."

You have an invention. Or perhaps simply an idea for an invention. What do you do with it? How do you protect it, develop it, and turn it into the money-maker you think can be?

Here, in simple question-and-answer form, are some of the most important problems you'll face, and some pointers on how you can solve them and cash in on your invention.

Q. Are there any organizations in my area that will help me develop and market my invention?

A. Yes. Inquire of such organizations as chambers of commerce, banks, and area departments of power companies and railroads. Many communities have locally financed industrial-development organizations that can help you locate manufacturers and individuals who might be interested in promoting your idea.

Q. Will the Patent Office help me in developing and marketing my patent?

A. Only to a very limited extent. The Patent Office cannot act or advise concerning the business transactions or arrangements involved in the development and marketing of an invention. However, the Patent Office will publish, at the request of a patent owner, a notice in its *Official Gazette* that the patent is available for licensing or sale. The fee for this is three dollars.

Q. Can any other U. S. Government agency assist me in developing and marketing my invention?

A. The Business and Defense Services Administration of the U. S. Department of Commerce, Washington, D.C. 20230, may be able to help you with information and advice, as its various industry divisions maintain close contact with all the branches of U.S. industry, or you may get in touch with one of the Department of Commerce field offices.

The Small Business Administration publishes a monthly products list containing brief descriptions of issued patents likely to interest prospective manufacturers; these lists are distributed to many business organizations. You may write the agency requesting that your invention be listed in this publication, and your request will usually be granted. The Small Business Administration has more than fifty offices in the country, and it offers, through its products-assistance program, information and counsel to small concerns interested in new products.

Q. Will the Patent Office advise me whether a particular patent-promotion organization is trustworthy?

A. No. The Patent Office has no control over such organizations and cannot supply information about them. You may obtain this information by inquiring of the Better Business Bureau of the city in which the organization is located, or of the Bureau of Commerce and Industry of the state in which the organization has its place of business. You may ask your own patent attorney or agent what he knows of their reliability.

Q. How do I apply for a patent?
A. By making the proper application to the Commissioner of Patents, Washington, D.C. 20231. This includes an application fee, a petition, a specification and claims describing the invention, an oath, and a drawing if the invention can be illustrated.

Q. What are the Patent Office fees for filing an application and issuance of the patent?
A. A filing fee of $65 plus certain additional charges for claims, depending on their number and the manner of their presentation, are required when the application is filed. If the patent is granted, there is a final fee of $100 plus $10 for each page of specifications as printed, and $2 for each sheet of drawing. Estimated total cost: $229.

Q. What happens when two inventors apply separately for a patent for the same invention?
A. An "interference" is declared and testimony may be submitted to the Patent Office to determine which inventor is entitled to the patent.

Q. Are models required as part of the application?
A. Only in exceptional cases.

Q. Is it necessary to go to the Patent Office in Washington to transact patent business?
A. No. Most business with the Patent Office is conducted by mail.

Q. Is there any danger that the Patent Office will give others information contained in my pending application?
A. No. All patent applications are maintained in the strictest secrecy.

Q. I have been making and selling my invention for the past thirteen months and have not filed any patent application. Is it too late to apply for a patent?
A. Yes. A valid patent may not be obtained if the invention was in public use or on sale in this country for more than one year prior to the filing of your patent application.

Q. I published an article in a magazine thirteen months ago describing my invention. Is it too late to apply for patent?
A. Yes. The law provides that the inventor is not entitled to a patent if the invention has been described in a printed publication anywhere in the world more than a year before his patent application is filed—even if you write the article yourself.

Q. Is there any restriction as to who may obtain a United States patent?

A. No. Any inventor may obtain a patent, regardless of age or sex, by complying with the provisions of the law. A foreign citizen may obtain a U.S. patent under exactly the same conditions as a U.S. citizen.

Q. If two or more persons work together on an invention, to whom will the patent be granted?

A. If each had a share in the ideas forming the invention, they are joint inventors and a patent will be issued to them jointly on the basis of a proper patent application filed by them jointly. If, on the other hand, one of these persons has provided all the ideas of the invention, and the other has only followed instructions in making it, the person who contributed the ideas is the sole inventor, and the patent application and patent should be in his name alone.

Q. Can an inventor sell or transfer his right to his patent or patent application to someone else?

A. Yes. He may sell all or any part of his interest in the patent application or patent to anyone. The application must be filed in the Patent Office as the invention of the true inventor, however, and not as the invention of the person who has purchased the invention.

Q. How can I be sure that my patent attorney or agent will not reveal to others the secrets of my invention?

A. Patent attorneys and agents earn their livelihood by the confidential services they perform for their clients, and if any attorney or agent improperly reveals an invention disclosed to him by a client, the attorney or agent is subject to disbarment from further practice before the Patent Office. Persons who withhold information about their inventions from their attorneys and agents make a serious mistake, for the attorney or agent cannot do a fully effective job unless he is informed of every detail.

Q. Does the Patent Office control the fees charged by patent attorneys and agents for their services?

A. No. This is a matter between you and your patent attorney or agent. Guesstimated fee: $500 and up.

Q. Will the Patent Office inform me whether my attorney or agent is reliable or trustworthy?

A. All patent attorneys and agents registered to practice before the Patent Office are expected to be reliable and trustworthy. The Patent Office can report only that a particular individual is, or is not, in good standing on the register at that office.

Q. If I am dissatisfied with my patent attorney or agent, may I change?

A. Yes. There are forms for appointing attorneys and revoking their powers of attorney in the pamphlet entitled "General Information Concerning Patents."

Q. Will the Patent Office help me select a patent attorney or agent?

A. No. The Patent Office cannot make this choice for you, as it would be unfair for it to select some of its practitioners for recommendation in preference to others.

Q. For how many years is a patent granted?

A. Seventeen years from the date on which it is issued; except for patents on ornamental designs, which are granted for terms of three and a half, seven, or fourteen years.

Q. Does the patentee continue to have any control over use of the invention after his patent expires?

A. No. Anyone has free right to use an invention covered in an expired patent so long as he does not use features covered in other unexpired patents in doing so.

Q. Where can I search to see if my idea is new?

A. In the Search Room of the Patent Office. Classified and numerically arranged sets of U.S. and foreign patents are kept there for public use.

Q. Will the Patent Office make searches for individuals to help them decide whether to file patent applications?

A. No. But it will assist inventors who come to Washington by helping them find the proper patent classes in which to make their searches.

Q. Does the law provide patent protection for invention of new and ornamental designs for articles of manufacture, or for new varieties of plants?

A. Yes. If you have made an invention in one of these fields, you should read the Patent Office pamphlet "General Information Concerning Patents."

Q. If I obtain a patent on my invention, will that protect me against the claims of others who assert that I am infringing on their patents when I make, use, or sell my own invention?

A. No. There may be a patent of a more basic nature on which your invention is an improvement. If your invention is a detailed refinement or feature of such a basically protected invention, you may not use it without the consent of the patentee, just as no one will have the right to use your patented improvement without your consent. You should seek competent legal advice before starting to make or sell or use your invention commercially, even though it is protected by a patent granted to you. A worthwhile improvement often can be sold to the holder of the basic patent.

Q. Will the Patent Office help me prosecute others if they infringe on my patent rights?

A. No. The Patent Office has no jurisdiction over questions relating to the infringement of patent rights. If your patent is infringed on, you may sue the infringer in the appropriate federal court. But you must pay your own legal expenses.

Besides the government booklets we have listed, several splendid books have been published to help the inventor. Among them: *The Inventor's Patent Handbook: A Practical Guide for the Amateur and the Professional,* by Stacy V. Jones (The Dial Press, 1969). Also: *How to Become a Successful Inventor,* by Eric P. McNair and James E. Schwenck (Hastings House Publishers, 1973).

The major guidelines in the available literature are these:

1. Many people think a patent gives its owner the right to make, use, or sell the item invented. Not true. Rather, it gives the owner the right to exclude others from making, using, or selling the invention.

2. Any person who invents or discovers any *new* and *useful* process, machine, manufacture, or composition of matter (such as a chemical formula) or any new and useful improvements thereof, may obtain a patent. The law specifies that the invention must not only have a useful purpose but must also have *operativeness*—in other words, a machine which will not operate to perform the intended purpose would not be called useful. (Amusing sidelight: alleged perpetual motion machines are refused patents.)

3. Mr. or Ms. Inventor: After you are sure the features of your invention are *useful* and *new,* you should seek professional advice at a very early stage. (The law gives the Patent Office the power to make rules and regulations governing the recognition of patent attorneys and agents to practice before the Patent Office, and persons who are not recognized are not permitted by law to represent inventors. Also, patent attorneys and agents are forbidden to advertise for patent business.)

4. How do you find the "professional advice?" Actually, you are allowed by the patent laws to prepare and present your own patent application to the Patent Office. However, Messrs. McNair and Schwenck say emphatically: *"But don't ever try to do it!"* They also advise you to employ a patent attorney rather than a patent agent. Both are recognized but the former is not only licensed and registered to practice before the Patent Office, as is the agent, but he is also an attorney-at-law and a member of the bar in the state in which he practices. You can send for the "Directory of Registered Patent Attorneys and Agents," which is printed by the U. S. Patent Office, is arranged by states and counties, and can be bought from your local branch of the Department of Commerce or by sending $1.50 to the Superintendent of Documents, U. S. Government Printing Office, Washington, D.C. 20402. Also, you can get a list of registered patent attorneys and agents in your own region by writing to the Commissioner of Patents, Patent Office, Department of Commerce, Washington, D.C. 20231.

5. You should get a trustworthy friend to sign his name as witness on a dated drawing or description of your invention as well as on further steps you take—and the dates—to improve or change your invention.

6. Once you have selected your patent attorney (or agent) he will handle such details as a search for related prior patents. You can get an estimate from him, in advance, on the cost of the search. Although the Patent Office will assist inventors or their representatives at the Search Room of the P.O. at Crystal Plaza, 2021 Jefferson Davis Highway, Arlington, Virginia, by helping them find the proper patent classes in which to make their searches, most inventors hire experts to make their searches.

7. Other sources of information are the microfilm lists of numbers of patents prepared by the Patent Office, its manual of classification, as well as sets of patent copies and the *Official Gazette*—a weekly publication (since 1872!) of the Patent Office that reviews all patents. Some or all of these might be involved in the search. Many libraries around the country have the data mentioned in this paragraph.

8. After the search is made you must study prior patents in your classification and then decide whether your invention is truly new and valuable so that you can notify your attorney or agent whether or not you will seek patent protection.

9. You will execute a power of attorney or authorization of agent, which must be filed in the Patent Office and is usually a part of the application papers. All correspondence is conducted by the Patent Office with the attorney or agent, not with the inventor.

10. Now, after the application is made, you must be patient. Your representative receives a filing receipt from the Patent Office and it takes some months for him to get a report. When the examiner's report is received you must answer within six months or your application will be marked as abandoned. Incidentally, the Patent Office does *not* determine whether the invention sought to be patented infringes any prior patent. An improvement upon an invention may be patentable, but it might infringe a prior unexpired patent. Your attorney or agent will guide you in all subsequent steps, including whether it is desirable for you to apply for a trademark.

11. A trademark can be registered in the Patent Office. It relates to any word, name, symbol, or device which is used in trade with goods to indicate the source or origin of the goods and to distinguish them from the goods of others.

There is a Primary Trademark Register and a Secondary Register. A trademark to be registered in the Primary Register may *not* be descriptive. A registration is good for twenty years and may be renewed again and again for periods of twenty years.

McNair and Schwenck point out that if the inventor of Polaroid had used his own name—the Land Camera—he would have been refused registration. Cost of a trademark is about $100. Many a product whose patent has expired is still widely sold because the trademark has been established with the public and also because a trademark is longer-lived than a patent.

An example is Kodak, made up by Eastman in 1888—the patents have expired but the product lives on. It is also necessary to register your trademark in foreign countries to prevent others from doing so. You can obtain a booklet, "General Information Concerning Trademarks," from the Commissioner of Patents, Washington, D.C. 20231.

12. Once you have made application for a patent and you have reached the production stage of your product it may be marked "Patent Applied For" or "Patent Pending." These phrases have no legal effect but serve notice to possible competitors. The law imposes a fine on those who use these terms falsely to deceive the public.

There are many other details and problems involved in making money on your invention, but this summary at least outlines the preliminary steps.

You're on your way. Remember what Marconi said, "There's no such thing as genius . . . only hard work."

And while we don't agree entirely (or this book would have been titled differently) we do accept the Edison dictum that genius is one per cent inspiration and 99 per cent perspiration. (He also said: "I tell you, genius is hard work, stick-to-it-iveness, and common sense.")

It's hard to make money on an invention but look what the people described in this book accomplished!

Perhaps you can do it, too.

INDEX